BAJA
CAMPING

FOGHORN OUTDOORS®

BAJA CAMPING

The Complete Guide to More Than 170 Tent and RV Campgrounds

FOURTH EDITION

Fred & Gloria Jones

AVALON
TRAVEL

FOGHORN OUTDOORS
BAJA CAMPING
The Complete Guide to More Than 170 Tent and RV Campgrounds

Fourth Edition

Fred and Gloria Jones

Text © 2003 by Fred and Gloria Jones.
All rights reserved.
Illustrations and maps © 2003 by
Avalon Travel Publishing.
All rights reserved.

Avalon Travel Publishing is a division of
Avalon Publishing Group, Inc.

Some photos and illustrations are used by permission
and are the property of the original copyright owners.

ISBN: 1-56691-425-6
ISSN: 1089-0939

Please send all feedback about this book to:

⑤OGHORN OUTDOORS®
Baja Camping
Avalon Travel Publishing
1400 65th Street, Suite 250
Emeryville, CA 94608, USA
atpfeedback@avalonpub.com
www.foghorn.com

Printing History
1st edition—1994
4th edition—November 2003
5 4 3 2 1

Editor: Amy Scott
Series Manager: Marisa Solís
Copy Editor: Donna Leverenz
Proofreader: Leslie Miller
Graphics Coordinator: Deb Dutcher
Illustrator: Bob Race
Production Coordinator: Darren Alessi
Cover Designer: Jacob Goolkasian
Interior Designer: Darren Alessi
Map Editor: Olivia Solís
Cartographers: Mike Morgenfeld, Suzanne Service, Chris Alvarez
Indexer: Amy Scott

Front cover photo: Sea of Cortéz, North of Loreto, © Kerrick James

Printed in the United States of America by Malloy Inc.

This book is dedicated to the Vagabundos del Mar Boat and Travel Club. Our involvement in the management of club affairs has given us access to thousands of Baja aficionados who fan out over the entire peninsula every year. With its sense of camaraderie and esprit de corps, the club has afforded all of us an opportunity to form lifelong and enriching relationships with great people who share a special common bond. The previously untapped body of knowledge from this group and the current information they continue to report, along with our own extensive travels, have made this book possible.

—Fred and Gloria Jones

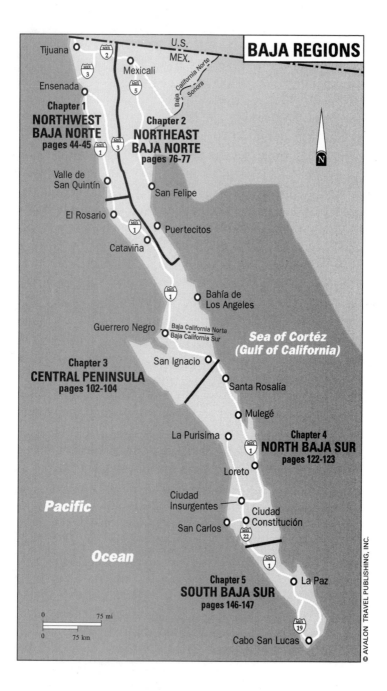

BAJA REGIONS

Tijuana

MEX 2

U.S.
MEX.

Mexicali

MEX 3

MEX 5

Baja California Norte

Sonora

Ensenada

N

Chapter 1
NORTHWEST
BAJA NORTE
pages 44-45

MEX 1

Chapter 2
NORTHEAST
BAJA NORTE
pages 76-77

MEX 3

Valle de
San Quintín

San Felipe

El Rosario

MEX 1

Puertecitos

Cataviña

MEX 1

Bahía de
Los Angeles

Guerrero Negro

Baja California Norte
Baja California Sur

Sea of Cortéz
(Gulf of California)

Chapter 3
CENTRAL PENINSULA
pages 102-104

San Ignacio

Santa Rosalía

Mulegé

La Purisima

Chapter 4
NORTH BAJA SUR
pages 122-123

MEX 1

Loreto

Pacific

Ciudad
Insurgentes

Ciudad
Constitución

San Carlos

MEX 22

Ocean

MEX 1

Chapter 5
SOUTH BAJA SUR
pages 146-147

La Paz

0   75 mi

0   75 km

MEX 19

Cabo San Lucas

© AVALON TRAVEL PUBLISHING, INC.

Contents

How to Use This Book ix
Preface xv
Introduction 1

Baja History 2
The Name • The Early Inhabitants • The Conquistadores • The Pirates • The Padres • The Mexican-American War • The Modern Era

Camping Tips 5
When to Go • Water • Ice • Sustenance • Conserving Provisions • Viewing Wildlife • Primitive Camping • Getting Stuck in the Sand • Backpacking • Boat Camping • Protection Against Insects, Sea Life, and Cactus • Problems with Sun, Heat, and Cold • Medical Care

Travel Tips 28
Licenses and Permits • Insurance • Toll Roads • Customs • Firearms and Drugs • Vehicle Preparation • Driving Safely • Fuel • Ferries • Money • Telephones • Email • Time Zones

SPECIAL TOPICS

Indian Populations 2 • Carnicería *Talk 9* • *What to Bring 16* • *Safety on the Road 34* • *Baja Ferry Rates 39*

Chapter 1—Northwest Baja Norte 43

Campgrounds 53
10 Best Beaches 71
Including:
• Camalu
• Colonet
• Colonia Vicente Guerrero
• El Sauzal
• Ensenada
• La Misión
• Maneadero
• Parque Nacional Sierra San Pedro Mártir

• Puerto San Ysidro
• Punta Banda
• Rosarito
• San Antonio
• San Quintín
• Santo Tomás
• Tecate

Chapter 2—Northeast Baja Norte 75

Campgrounds 81
10 Best Beaches 97
Including:
• Mexicali
• Puertecitos
• San Felipe

Chapter 3—Central Peninsula 101

Campgrounds 109
10 Best Beaches 118
Including:
- Bahía de Los Angeles
- Bahía de Sebastian Vizcaíno
- Cataviña
- El Rosario
- Guerrero Negro
- Laguna Ojo de Liebre
- Punta Abreojos
- San Ignacio
- Vizcaíno

Chapter 4—North Baja Sur 121

Campgrounds 129
10 Best Beaches 142
Including:
- Bahía Concepción
- Bahía Magdalena
- Ciudad Constitución
- Loreto
- Mulegé
- Puerto Escondido
- Puerto López Mateos
- San Carlos
- San Juanico
- Santa Rosalía

Chapter 5—South Baja Sur 145

Campgrounds 155
10 Best Beaches 168
Including:
- Bahía Magdalena
- Cabo San Lucas
- La Paz
- La Ribera
- Los Barriles
- San Bartolo
- San José del Cabo
- Todos Santos

Resources 171

Spanish Phrasebook 172
Glossary 182
Information Sources 183
Tourist Assistance, Embassies, and Consulates 188
Road Signs 191
Special Days in Mexico 195
Metric Conversions 196

Index 197

How to Use This Book

The Baja California Peninsula consists of two states. The northern state is officially known as Baja California, but since that is easily confused with the entire peninsula, it is commonly referred to by visitors and locals alike as Baja Norte. The southern state is Baja California Sur, a name shortened to Baja Sur by one and all. For greater detail we have divided *Foghorn Outdoors Baja Camping* into five chapters: Northwest Baja Norte, Northeast Baja Norte, Central Peninsula, North Baja Sur, and South Baja Sur. A map showing the five divisions is on page vi. A detailed map of each region appears at the beginning of the corresponding chapter.

The chapters are further divided into areas that constitute natural clusters of campgrounds. At the beginning of each chapter a general description of these areas is followed by the activities and points of historic and cultural interest that can be enjoyed there.

How to Find an Ideal Camping Spot

1. If you know the name of the specific campsite where you'd like to stay or the name of the surrounding geographical area or nearby feature—town, beach, *bahía* (bay or harbor), *punta* (point), river, national park, etc.—look it up in the index and turn to the corresponding page.

2. To find a campground in a particular region of the peninsula, first turn to the Baja Regions map on page vi and decide in which region your destination lies. Then you have two choices: You may turn to the corresponding chapter to read further on the area and its campgrounds. Or, you may turn to the detailed maps at the beginning of each chapter to locate individual campgrounds or beaches. Campgrounds are listed numerically on each map, indicated by a white number enclosed by a black square. To read further about the campground, match its number to the one in the corresponding chapter.

10 Best Beaches

At the end of each chapter, we have highlighted the 10 best beaches in the region. Some of these overlap with the general campground listings, while others are open solely for day use or are accessible only to hardy adventurers driving ATVs or motorcycles. You can easily locate these beaches on the map and within the chapter by looking for the numbered sun symbol icons (🌞).

Distance Markers

In the directions to campgrounds and beaches, we often mention "Km such and such," referring to the numbered markers located along most stretches of highway in Baja. All have black numbers painted vertically on them, with "Km" appearing at the top of most. Some are missing or difficult to see, but don't worry—you will spot another before long. These kilometer posts run sequentially between certain cities, from north to south in Baja Norte and from south to north in Baja Sur. Just keep track of whether the numbers are increasing or decreasing as you move along so you can determine if you are approaching your destination or have already passed it.

Ejidos

Some campground names include the word *ejido* or are followed by *ejido* in parentheses. These were built by the federal government many years ago to accommodate tourists on the recently paved Highway 1. All were constructed on the same plan and were turned over to the local *ejido*, a government-supported agricultural cooperative, to operate and maintain as income-producing facilities. However, since nearly all of these parks are in remote areas, the people were unable to keep the electrical, water, and sewer systems in dependable operating condition. Several are currently open for camping, but they often lack services and facilities.

Security

Many campers are as concerned about security as they are about drinking water in Mexico. We have tried to ease their minds about both. In each campground description we identify those elements that discourage noncampers from wandering among the campsites—gates, fences, guards, and resident managers.

Campground Fees

Campground fee categories are based on fees in Baja rather than U.S. standards. Throughout this book we use the following categories: Very Low: $0–3, Low: $4–7, Moderate: $8–14, High: $15–24, Very High: $25 and up.

About the Maps

This book is divided into several chapters based on established regions; an overview map of these regions precedes the table of contents. At the start of each chapter, you'll find a map of the entire region. Campgrounds are plotted on these maps by their map numbers.

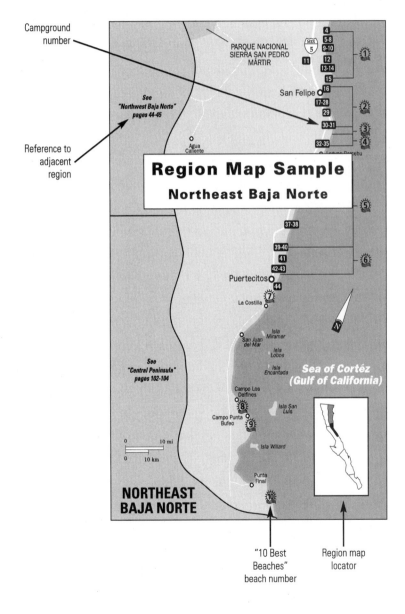

Campground number

See "Northwest Baja Norte" pages 44-45

Reference to adjacent region

PARQUE NACIONAL SIERRA SAN PEDRO MÁRTIR

San Felipe

Agua Caliente

Region Map Sample

Northeast Baja Norte

See "Central Peninsula" pages 102-104

Puertecitos

La Costilla

Isla Miramar

San Juan del Mar

Isla Lobos

Isla Encantada

Sea of Cortéz (Gulf of California)

Campo Los Delfines

Isla San Luis

Campo Punta Bufeo

Isla Willard

0   10 mi
0   10 km

Punta Final

NORTHEAST BAJA NORTE

"10 Best Beaches" beach number

Region map locator

About the Campground Profiles

Each campground in this book is listed in a consistent, easy-to-read format to help you choose the ideal camping spot. From a general overview of the setting to detailed driving directions, the profile will provide all the information you need. Here is an example:

Map number and campground name →

1 SOMEWHERE USA CAMPGROUND

Icons noting activities and facilities at or nearby the campground

General location of the campground named by its proximity to the nearest major town or landmark →

South of Somewhere USA Lake

Map name, page 4

Each campground in this book begins with a brief overview of its setting. The description typically covers ambience, information about the attractions, and activities popular at the campground.

Map the campground can be found on and page number the map can be found on

Campsites, facilities: This section provides the number of campsites for both tents and RVs and whether hookups are available. Facilities such as restrooms, picnic areas, recreation areas, laundry, and dump stations will be addressed, as well as the availability of piped water, showers, playground, stores, and others amenities. The campground's pet policy is also mentioned here.

Reservations, fees: This section notes whether reservations are accepted, and the rates for tent sites and RV sites. If there are additional fees for parking or pets, or discounted weekly or seasonal rates, those will also be noted here.

Directions: This section provides mile-by-mile driving directions to the campground from the nearest major town.

Contact: This section provides an address, phone number, and Internet address, if available, for each campground.

About the Icons

The icons in this book are designed to provide at-a-glance information on activities, facilities, and services provided that are available on-site or within walking distance of each campground. The icons are not meant to represent every activity or service, but rather those that are most significant.

 — Hiking trails are available.

 — Biking trails or routes are available. This usually refers to mountain biking, although it may represent road cycling as well. Refer to the text for that campground for details.

 — Swimming opportunities are available.

— Fishing opportunities are available.

— Boating opportunities are available. Various types of vessels apply under this umbrella activity, including motorboats and personal watercrafts (Jet Skis). Refer to the text for that campground for more details, including mph restrictions and boat ramp availability.

— Hot or cold springs are located nearby. Refer to the text for that campground for more information.

— Pets are permitted. Campgrounds that allow pets may require an additional fee or that pets be leashed. Campgrounds may also restrict pet size or behavior. Refer to the text for that campground for specific instructions or call in advance.

— A playground is available. A campground with a playground can be desirable for campers traveling with children.

— RV sites are provided.

— Tent sites are provided.

Our Commitment

We are committed to making *Foghorn Outdoors Baja Camping* the most accurate, thorough, and enjoyable camping guide to the Baja California peninsula. With this fourth edition you can rest assured that every campground in this book has been carefully reviewed so that we can provide the most up-to-date information. Be aware that with the passing of time some of the fees listed herein may have changed, and campgrounds may have closed unexpectedly. If you have a specific need or concern, it's best to call the location ahead of time.

If you would like to comment on the book, whether it's to suggest a campground we overlooked or to let us know about any noteworthy experience—good or bad—that occurred while using *Foghorn Outdoors Baja Camping* as your guide, we would appreciate hearing from you. Please address correspondence to:

Foghorn Outdoors Baja Camping, Fourth Edition
Avalon Travel Publishing
1400 65th Street, Suite 250
Emeryville, CA 94608
email: atpfeedback@avalonpub.com

If you send us an email, please put "Foghorn Outdoors Baja Camping" in the subject line.

Preface

During our many years spent traveling up and down the Baja California Peninsula, living in tents and campers, we have paid close attention to available camping spots as well as other aspects of road travel. Writing assignments from various magazines and our responsibilities in helping manage the Vagabundos del Mar Boat and Travel Club—particularly preparing the club's monthly newsletter, *Chubasco,* since 1988—have required it. We have had a continuing obligation to keep the thousands of members of Baja's oldest and largest travel club, and the multitude of people who read the magazines for which we have written, informed of all things related to Baja travel.

We have found the unbroken flow of written and oral communications from individual Vagabundos, popularly known as "Vags," to be an extremely rich font of information. This, coupled with our personal inspection of campgrounds and beaches and our experiences on the road, constitutes the source of material for this book. We wish to share the knowledge we have gained ourselves, and that distilled from such a huge number of other Baja campers, with the wide audience this book will reach.

Camping on the beach is one of the great attractions for Baja travelers. A fascination with surf washing onto mile after mile of lovely white sand, the call of seabirds and the splashing of pelicans, the spicy salt-tinged ocean air, cool breezes, seclusion, and many other special attributes draw people from all over the world to these beaches. Many are accessible only to four-wheel-drive vehicles, while others may be reached only by boat. Getting to some constitutes high adventure. We have included spots that are popular for camping and normally accessible by highway vehicles, including midsize motor homes and trailers. We also have listed the 10 best beaches for each of the five regional chapters, including some that are accessible only by off-road vehicle, boat, or foot. Information on backpacking and horse packing trips into the mountains has been included as well.

Campgrounds for recreational vehicles in Baja come in all shapes and sizes. Some are dedicated solely to annual lessees, commonly referred to as "permanents," who have installed trailers or constructed other housing. Others have some permanents but cater to overnight travelers as well. Still others have no permanents and are geared entirely toward travelers. We have included only the campgrounds that are able to accommodate transients in some way.

These campgrounds are in a continuing state of flux. New ones pop up and existing ones disappear as they are taken over for other types of development. Sometimes the owners will fill their transient spaces with permanents or simply close the park altogether. Since tourist travel is seasonal, park owners are motivated to generate the dependable income that annual leases provide.

Keep in mind that road conditions in Baja change frequently. Heavy rainfall may wipe out a road temporarily or even permanently. Never go off the beaten path without checking locally on whether your particular vehicle is suitable for driving at that particular time. Nothing is more miserable than getting stuck or breaking down in a remote spot.

Be sure your maps and source materials are reliable and current. We have helped many weary, stuck travelers out of a jam due to navigating with bad maps. The most frazzled were a Canadian couple with the wheels of their motor home buried and its rear end hung up on the bank of an arroyo on the rough coast road between San José del Cabo and Los Frailes. The map they had brought from Canada showed that road as paved, which it possibly may be some day.

In Baja there has always been an unwritten code among locals and tourists alike—that you aid anyone in trouble. We have benefited from others' helping hands on several occasions and have reciprocated. We hope in some way this book helps to keep the process going.

Introduction

Introduction

Baja History

The border between San Ysidro, California, and Tijuana, Baja California Norte, is the most frequently crossed in the world, with more than 100 million people passing through each year. It seems so much like an extension of California and the United States that visitors at first may not realize they have arrived in a foreign country. Indeed, at one time it all was part of one country, Mexico. What follows is a brief history of the peninsula.

The Name

In a popular Spanish novel published in 1500, "California" was the name of an island of women warriors who armed themselves with gold weapons. Since the Baja Peninsula was originally thought to be an island full of gold, the use of the name California appears to have been inspired by the novel in a spasm of wishful thinking.

The Early Inhabitants

Huge multicolored murals of Indians and animals exist in shallow caves in and above the deep, rugged canyons of Central Baja California. Their beauty, artistry, and mystery excite the imagination. The greatest concentration of cave murals is in the Sierra de San Francisco, north of San Ignacio. They also occur south through the Sierra San Pedro and in other small, jumbled mountain ranges to the southern end of Bahía Concepción—a total spread of about 125 airline miles.

The earliest known eyewitness report of these magnificent paintings comes from a missionary who was at San Ignacio from 1759 to 1768. There, and at the missions of Guadalupe and Santa Rosalía, the oldest Indians preserved an oral tradition about the Painters (a name coined by Harry Crosby in his definitive work, *The Cave Paintings of Baja California*), which had been passed down through generations from fathers to sons. According to the story, in very ancient times a group of men and women of extraordinary physical stature had come from the north fleeing one another. Some died due to infighting. Others were killed by ancestors of the tellers who would not tolerate such strange newcomers in their land. Research recently conducted by the Barcelona Group has placed the works at somewhere between 3,500 and 5,000 years old, ending about A.D. 350. An interesting article by Bernard M. Jones Jr., "Shamanistic Elements in Sierra de San Francisco Rock Art" (published in *Rock Art Papers*, Volume 7, by the San Diego Museum of Man in 1990), hints at a clue to the possible origin of the Painters. Mr. Jones

Indian Populations

Year	Population	Year	Population
1697	41,500	1772	5,094
1728	30,500	1775	3,972
1742	25,000	1777	5,424
1762	10,000	1790	4,076
1768	7,149		

Data from the Anthropological Museum in La Paz.

comments on the striking resemblance between a group of three huge human figures in Cueva Pintada (in the Sierra de San Francisco Mountains) and a trio of dancers used in the Hopi snake dance ceremony. Though he describes the "fascinating parallels," he stops short of hypothesizing a Hopi origin for the Painters. (Personally, we are very intrigued by the possibility that these hitherto mystery people might be linked to the Hopis.)

We have Erle Stanley Gardner, the prolific mystery writer, to thank for bringing these great art works into the public consciousness. In 1962, *Life* magazine ran a story of Gardner's, "A Legendary Treasure Left by a Long Lost Tribe." He also published a book, *The Hidden Heart of Baja*, later that year. In 1967 he published another book, *Off the Beaten Track in Baja*. Having made several expeditions into the heart of the cave painting country by Jeep and helicopter, Gardner passed on his entrancement with what he saw to a legion of avid readers. His graphic descriptions alone fired the public's imagination.

At the time Spanish explorers arrived in Baja in 1534, the peninsula was populated by several groups of Indians. The Pericús occupied the Cape region in southern Baja Sur, the Guaycuras from the Cape Region north to Loreto, the Cochimís from Loreto to San Felipe, and the Yumanos, with several subgroups, settled from the border to San Felipe.

The Spaniards estimated there were perhaps 50,000 Indians in Baja when they arrived. Successive estimates seen at the Anthropological Museum in La Paz show a steady decline. By 1790 the census estimated a population of 4,076 Indians, 235 Spaniards, six other Europeans, 183 mulattoes, and 418 Indian mestizos.

The report *Lower California and Its Natural Resources,* by Edward W. Nelson, published by the National Academy of Sciences in 1922, shows 104 Indians in Baja California in 1857. There are still a few hundred in Baja Norte today. European diseases and casualties in various uprisings essentially wiped out the Indians.

The Conquistadores

It all began with Hernán Cortéz, an adventurous plunderer who took Mexico by storm beginning in 1519. His men worked their way to La Paz in Baja California in 1534 for a short-lived stay, ending when all but one were killed by Indians. Cortéz came a year later, but the land and the Indians were too tough for even the Spaniards, who stuck it out a mere two years. Others explored the coasts and futilely tried to found colonies in order to exploit pearl oysters, which have since all but disappeared.

The Pirates

Spain was also spreading its influence across the Pacific Ocean, conquering the Philippines in 1565. Every year several Spanish galleons would set off together from Manila on a round-trip voyage across the North Pacific to Acapulco, on to Spain, and back. These ships carried the riches of the Far East—spices, silks, gold coins, and artifacts. It was necessary for them to follow the coast of North America south along the Baja Peninsula. After their long voyage from Manila, many needed to stop in Cabo San Lucas or La Paz for water and other provisions.

The valuable cargoes being transported to Spain attracted Dutch and English pirates who had been raiding Spanish settlements on both sides of the Pacific Ocean. At Cabo San Lucas it was possible to place a lookout with a spyglass on a high point of land to scan the horizon until sails were sighted, then intercept the galleon with cannon fire. The galleons that anchored in Bahía de La Paz were vulnerable to attack when the regular daytime winds blew from the north into the bay. The pirate vessels would sail in on the wind, while the galleons could not escape against it. In the evening and at night, these winds reverse, coming up from the Pacific Ocean over low hills. Called "Coromuels," these winds—which provide natural air-conditioning for La Paz during hot summers—allowed the pirates to return to their hiding spots.

Many galleons were plundered and much wealth was confiscated over a period of about 150 years until Spanish padres colonized the area in the 1700s and Spain finally gained control over Baja waters.

The Padres

No settlements took hold until the Jesuits came along. The most cherished mission in all the Californias was founded in Loreto in 1697—163 years after the first landing. Being the first, the Loreto mission is properly titled "The Head and Mother of the Missions of Baja and Alta California," and so says the inscription over the front door. The Jesuits worked their way north founding mission after mission for 70 years, until they fell out of favor with the king of Spain and were replaced by Franciscans.

Franciscan missionary Junípero Serra, a prominent figure in California's history, established only one mission in Baja, then moved on to San Diego to fulfill his destiny by creating California's mission system.

The Dominicans were handed Baja California in 1773 and set about establishing and operating more missions in Baja Norte for the next 73 years. At that point, in 1846, the reign of Spain in Mexico came to an end, and the last of the Spaniards, including the padres, were expelled.

The Mexican-American War

In 1845, contentious relations between the United States and Mexico culminated in full-scale war. Displays in the Anthropological Museum in La Paz document how the U.S. Navy blockaded Mulegé, Loreto, La Paz, and San José del Cabo. In 1847, the year the war ended, troops landed at La Paz and marched to San Antonio, Todos Santos, Santiago, and San José del Cabo, opposed by guerrillas all the way.

The United States was given Baja California, along with a good chunk of Mexico, but handed it back, not considering the land to be worth much. And that's a good thing, too. Otherwise, all the beaches would have long since been blocked by concrete and asphalt, and the Baja we love escaping to wouldn't exist.

The Modern Era

Known in Mexico as *La Frontera* (the Frontier), the Baja Peninsula was considered until recently a remote outpost. Mexico made Baja Norte a state only in 1952 and Baja Sur in 1974. With the completion of the Transpeninsular Highway from Tijuana to Cabo San Lucas in 1973, Baja initiated in earnest a new era of tourism. Currently the country is devoting great attention to developing tourism in both states. Modern transportation and communications are bringing the region into the fold.

It is difficult to determine who has conquered whom in the past 150 years. The United States has impacted Baja's economy with tourist dollars, while Baja has captivated Americans with its beauty, charm, and hospitality. We have created a marvelous symbiotic relationship—each needing the other—and we've become so assimilated that the U.S.–Mexico border is like Swiss cheese. Gringos (Americans) live in Rosarito and commute to jobs in San Diego. San Ysidro, California, has become a Mexican city in all appearances. Mexicans have repopulated California, and tourists outnumber locals in many areas of Baja.

Even the Spanish language is succumbing. In many instances it is easier to accommodate tourists than struggle with them. Mail is an example. Tourists receiving mail in Baja automatically use the familiar "P.O. Box" terminology, as at home. The term in Mexico is *Apartado Postal*, abbreviated to Apdo. or A.P. The mail goes through either way in Baja. Each year, "P.O. Box" becomes more common in advertisements by Mexican businesses.

What next?

Camping Tips
When to Go

Every camper with Baja in his or her sights has to decide when to go. The answer swings on several considerations: why you are heading south, what you plan to do, and where you hope to do it.

Many frequent visitors to Baja are "snowbirds," northerners who head south annually for the winter season. The hint of frost in their nostrils and the promise of bone-cracking, subzero temperatures and multiple feet of snow falling on any given night simplifies the planning—get out of town before it's too late. The old-timers return year after year to their favorite havens and lead the way for new migrants.

With nothing snapping at our heels, the rest of us campers have the luxury of examining all the pros and cons of seacoast versus mountains, Pacific coast versus the Sea of Cortéz, northern Baja versus southern Baja, and beach camping versus full hookups.

The most common notion is that winter is the time to go, but we are convinced this isn't always the case if you have a choice. We have bundled up in heavy jackets, knit caps, and gloves in Cabo San Lucas while singing yuletide carols around Baja Christmas trees, dried flowering stalks of century plants called *chiotes* (pronounced key-oh-tays) decorated with handmade wicker ornaments.

We have hunkered down indoors for days on end in January, watching our trailer boat bounce around at anchor under strong East Cape winds that kept us from the marlin frolicking around out there. We watched the tour promos for great East Cape winter fishing change to tour promos for winter windsurfing as the travel industry realized that the winter winds had always been there, just waiting for the clientele that desired them.

After reading scads of charts showing when each game fish is most common in each area, a common denominator became apparent—game fish follow warm water, and that means summer. There are exceptions, though—many of them. The most important one is that striped marlin can be off the tip of Baja all year, making this the greatest big-game fishing spot anywhere, no matter what time of year you come. But if you want marlin, sailfish, dorado (mahimahi), yellowfin tuna, or roosterfish up in the Sea of Cortéz, the warmer the better.

So if fishing is your thing—and it is the single most popular activity in Baja—summer is the time to go. "Wait a minute," you say. "It's hot down there then!" Unfortunately, that's true. However, hot is relative, and everyone can tolerate different temperatures. Also, various places do not have the same kind of heat.

San Felipe, in the northern Sea of Cortéz, is in the hottest and driest zone since it's behind the big windbreak of the Sierra San Pedro Mártir, which keeps cool, wet Pacific air away. La Paz, on the other hand, is east of a low dip in the central mountain chain and enjoys daily air-conditioning from the Pacific thanks to the so-called Coromuel winds (thought to be a contraction of "Cromwell," the English pirate who frequented La Paz Bay and used this daily wind to sail out of the bay). One July, we had Sonoran thunderstorms and high humidity in San Lucas Cove just south of Santa Rosalía and sweltered all night—but the lightning over the Sea of Cortéz was spectacular.

The Pacific coast is the place to be in summer if you like it cool and want to be on the water. San Quintín in the north and Bahía Magdalena in the south offer great fishing, fog, and ocean breezes.

If you prefer to find cooler weather in the mountains and have a small vehicle, try the Sierra de Juárez between the border and Highway 3. Laguna Hanson in the pine forest of Parque Nacional Constitución de 1857 is a pleasant spot on a dirt road, or try Parque Nacional Sierra San Pedro Mártir with the highest elevation in Baja California—El Picacho del Diablo at 10,154 feet. Nearby is Baja's only observatory, accessible by a rather steep dirt road. (For more information see the listing for Parque Nacional Sierra San Pedro Mártir in the Northwest Baja Norte chapter.) Places to go in the mountains are limited and are suitable only for smaller vehicles, but the pine forests and trout streams make the trip worthwhile.

Another inland destination for small vehicles is Guadalupe Canyon Hot Springs and Campground, 27 miles south of Highway 2 at the bottom of the Rumorosa Grade. (For details see the Guadalupe Canyon Hot Springs and Campground, in the Northeast Baja Norte chapter.)

Southern Baja can experience big winds *(chubascos)* in summer. From June to October, sometimes even from May to November, is hurricane season. A late hurricane in December 1982 tossed several large cruising boats onto the beach at Cabo San Lucas. But hurricanes are not all that common in any particular spot and usually do no more than bring gales and deluges of rain along the coast. The threat of one should not be enough to keep campers away if summer is when they want to travel to Baja.

Winter storms bring rain to northern Baja, and summer thunderstorms bring it to the south. The winter storms also blow all along the Sea of Cortéz, making windsurfers happy but giving anglers fits.

So what's left? You guessed it—spring and fall. The nice thing about spring is that the weather is warming up, and by Easter the winter crowds have left. Incidentally, Easter week is a great time not to be on the road in Baja. Everyone is out having fun and boosting sales of *cerveza* (beer). Police conduct safe driving campaigns and erect impressive arrays of wrecked vehicles along Highway 1 to make everyone think twice. Be even more alert if you drive during Easter week.

What is not so nice about spring is that the Sea of Cortéz is still in the grip of winter chill. Swimming, snorkeling, and scuba diving are uncomfortable without a wet suit. Also, most migratory game fish have not yet arrived.

This leaves fall. The water is still warm from heating up all summer, the air temperature has cooled off, *chubasco* season is winding down, game fish are still likely to be around, and winter tourists have not yet arrived. Take your pick.

Water

The question most commonly asked about Baja is, "Can you drink the water?" The simplest answer is yes, if you stick to the purified water *(agua purificada)* available in plastic jugs in all grocery stores. At some *agua purificada* plants they can run a hose out to your RV. We use one in Guerrero Negro and another in Mulegé. Beyond that, it's a maybe. It isn't that the water is necessarily contaminated; it's that your body may not be adjusted to the local flora and fauna. Mexicans may experience distress when visiting our side of the border, and sometimes we require an adjustment when returning home after camping in Mexico for several months. Should you get caught, Pepto Bismol is helpful, as are Lomotil and Imodium A-D. You can buy Kaopectate (kah-oh-peck-TAH-tay in Spanish) in pharmacies *(farmacias)* if you write it out or pronounce the name right; otherwise, they won't know what you are talking about.

Upon arriving at Paamul RV Park on the Yucatán Peninsula of Mexico's mainland, we inquired about the water and were told that the locals had no problem, but it might not be good for us. The water source was a *cenote* (an open pool in the limestone bedrock) into which anything could fall. Interesting enough, a jaguar also drank there. So what do you do to resolve the maybe?

The old standard for purifying water is to boil it for at least 30 minutes at sea level, longer at higher altitudes. For good measure, throw a quarter ounce or so of bleach into your dish rinse water.

A compact, lightweight, inexpensive water filter that we have used in Baja is Coghlan's (email: coghlans@coghlans.info.ca). It filters out *Giardia lamblia,* a microscopic parasite, and other organisms and particles of similar size. It can be used as a pump to take water out of a source or as a straw to drink directly from a container. Many outdoor outfitters and sporting goods stores carry some type of water filter or water purifier. If you're in an RV, there are all sorts of filters that can be installed in your water system. However, to be certain you are screening out bacteria, the filtering element must be extremely fine. Some RVers chlorinate their water tank at the rate of 8 to 16 drops of liquid bleach per gallon, then use a filter to remove the taste. Campers using jugs allow 10 drops of bleach per quart of water, then let the solution sit for at least 30 minutes to let the bleach do its work and allow the chlorine taste to dissipate.

We like Microdyn, a nontoxic product available in the produce section of Mexican supermarkets such as Gigante and in pharmacies. It destroys bacteria in water and disinfects fruits and vegetables. One drop treats two liters of water, and 10 drops treats 20 liters. Yodo and Bac-Dyn Plus are similar products.

As a practical matter, we ask people staying in a campground if they drink the water there without further treatment. If we find several who do and appear to be reasonably healthy, then we will too. If we're uneasy about taking a chance, we simply keep several jugs of purified water available for drinking and cooking and use the park water for washing up. When we're confident that the water is all right, we'll top off our water tank. We prefer the purified water for making coffee and iced tea and for brushing teeth, in any event—it just tastes better.

There are different schools of thought on purifying produce. Many people just rinse fruits and vegetables in plain water, but our Mexican friends advise purifying, especially foods that come from Guadalajara, we were told, because of the possibility of having been washed in contaminated water. But another Mexican friend said she would not purify the many varieties of beautiful fresh lettuce and herbs that come from Todos Santos in Baja Sur.

If you don't have Microdyn or Yodo, use a bleach solution for 30 minutes. For items like tomatoes, soak them for 20 minutes in one position, then turn them over for another 20 minutes. If you have room to pack a salad spinner, lettuce will last much longer. Another way to dry lettuce is to wrap it in layers of paper towels or in dish towels.

On a recent trip during the summer when shopping for groceries at a little market, we picked up a head of iceberg lettuce that had just arrived. It looked so good we wondered where it came from. To our surprise the shipping container revealed it was from Santa Maria, California. The shopkeeper said it was too hot during the summer to grow a good lettuce crop locally so they imported it from California. Even with this lettuce it was still prudent to be careful since it had been washed in local water.

When living on a boat or camping on the beach, we wash dishes in salt water. Rinse the dishes lightly in freshwater and soak any metal utensils to avoid rust. Melamine or plastic dishes hold up well with this treatment.

We also take saltwater baths. Joy liquid dish soap lathers well and does not produce a salt feeling on your skin, but leaves it soft. It is, joyfully, biodegradable. Another product for saltwater bathing is Sea Savon, a light green liquid that also is biodegradable. It is found in scuba shops in the United States. Coconut bar soap obtained in Mexico lathers in salt water, too.

Ice

Hielo (pronounced YEA-low), or ice, is sold in cube form *(cubitos)* and small blocks at most grocery stores, liquor stores, beer agencies, and some RV parks. Cubes and small blocks bagged up by companies like Diamonte are made from purified water. The plastic bag will usually say *purificada,* but if it doesn't, ask. If the cubes or blocks are made in the store where they are being sold, which often is the case in out-of-the-way places, the water used is very likely not purified.

Block ice from an ice plant *(planta de fabrica de hielo)* is not made from purified water either, and it gets dirty from being dragged around on the floor and the loading platform. A good practice is to use these big blocks only for keeping food cold (without direct contact with the food) and get bagged ice for all other purposes. If you use the big blocks, place your food in double Ziploc freezer bags to keep it from getting wet. Change the outer bag occasionally as it will leak after repeated use.

On a boat camping trip in the very remote Midriff Islands of the Sea of Cortéz, this method helped to keep fresh bread from getting moldy before it could be used. It was placed in double Ziploc freezer bags, then in two leak-proof garbage bags for good measure, then into the big ice chest with several blocks of ice that were being conserved. We put a little bleach in the water as the block ice melts.

If you are on a boat or in a remote area where freshwater is scarce, save the water off the ice for rinsing or bathing out of a portable camp shower, such as a Sun Shower. Another way to keep food from getting wet is to put water in big plastic bottles like the two-liter ones that Coke comes in, leaving some headroom, and freeze it. These make handy ice blocks that last a while, and then you have the water to drink if it's purified. One will fit in our small RV freezer over the refrigerator.

If you are going into remote areas where ice is scarce or not available, start with blocks and wrap the ice chest in quilted foil. Camping World carries a small roll called Reflectix that has two layers of aluminum separated by a 5/16-inch dead air space for insulation. The roll was enough to wrap around a five-foot-long chest and cover the top, which reflected the heat. If you don't have the insulated foil, at least place a silver-colored windshield dash saver on top of the ice chest. This works in the car also and does help conserve the ice. On a boat trip out of La Paz, we placed a big block of ice in an extra ice chest, taped the gap between the lid and the chest with duct tape, wrapped it, and didn't open the thing for three or four days. When ice was needed, there was still a sizable chunk left.

Sustenance

The Baja travel organization to which we belong and help manage, Vagabundos del Mar Boat and Travel Club, sprang from the desire of travelers to meet Baja and the Sea of Cortéz on their own terms. To us it made much more sense from a purely practical standpoint to bring our

Carnicería Talk

We have Jack Poole to thank for this helpful lexicon to shopping at Mexican *carnicerías* (meat markets); most of these terms don't show up in dictionaries. He submitted this a few years ago for use in the Vagabundos del Mar Boat and Travel Club's monthly newsletter, *Chubasco*.

Beef
- *asado de paleta:* arm roast, also chuck
- *carne molida:* ground meat; *hamburguesa* when in a bun
- *chamorro:* shank crosscuts
- *chuleta costado:* club or top loin steak
- *chuleta entera:* rib roast
- *costillas:* short ribs
- *filete de res:* filet mignon
- *flank steak:* flank steak
- *pecho:* brisket
- *pulpa bola:* tip roast
- *pulpa cuete:* eye of round
- *pulpa larga:* rolled roast—you roll it yourself. (Note: *pulpo* is octopus, so watch your tongue.)
- *pulpa negra:* top round
- *pulpa round:* To get it ground, say *"Lo muele, por favor."*
- *pulpa steak:* (pronounced more like "stek") full round
- *res de Sonora:* Sonora beef—the best
- *schuck steak:* chuck (seven-bone) steak and blade steak
- *T-bone:* Porterhouse or T-bone steak

Pork
- *chuleta de puerco entero:* pork loin
- *chuletas ahumadas:* smoked pork chops
- *chuletas de puerco:* pork chops—specify thickness.
- *costillos de puerco:* spare ribs—you may have to help by showing where to cut.
- *pierna ahumada:* smoked ham, either sliced *(rebanada)* or whole *(entero)*.
- *rebanadas de paleta:* shoulder steaks
- *tocino:* bacon

For Variety:
- *cabra:* goat, or *cabrito* (kid)—cook like lamb.
- *chorizo:* sausage
- *conejo:* rabbit
- *higado:* liver—beef *(de res)* or pork *(de puerco)*
- *pollo:* chicken
- *rinon:* kidney

friends along—we'd have more spare parts and more mechanical know-how and ingenuity, not to mention much more fun in sharing experiences.

On our first trip with a Vagabundo group many years ago, we carried enough provisions to supply a unit of the National Guard. It just seemed that this strange and wondrous remote land of mountains, deserts, and beaches wouldn't have enough food to sustain us for a whole month. The camper was packed so tight with canned goods, including canned bacon and butter, that it was difficult to determine what we had and where to find it. Much of it came home with us. Now, though, if there is extra, it's left behind with a longtime or new Mexican friend from a smaller village.

Although canned goods are necessary sometimes, especially if you are planning to be in a remote area for a period of time, they are inherently full of salt and not the healthiest for you. A trick to reduce the salt is to hold the item (particularly meats like corned beef and bacon) under hot running water. Another method is to place the meat in cheesecloth to keep it from coming apart and boil it in water for 10 minutes or so. This greatly cuts the salt taste and makes the food more palatable.

For backpacking and horseback pack trips where weight is a factor, dehydrated food found in groceries and most sporting goods stores comes in handy. Be sure you have ample purified water to rehydrate these foods.

Half the fun of traveling in Mexico is learning to exist on food found in the local markets. Of course if you like fish, you're liable to supplement your diet with all kinds of fresh seafood that you can catch or gather. Even if you don't fish, a bounty of fresh and frozen seafood is available. You don't want to miss the fresh fruits and vegetables, either, both familiar and exotic. Agriculture is big business in Baja, and the United States imports much of Baja's produce—tomatoes, melons, and much more. The tomatoes with the best flavor you can find in winter come from Mexico.

Be prudent in your provisioning and be assured that you will be able to find most of what you need in the local market. There are also many good restaurants should you need a break from shopping and cooking.

Supermarkets, many that carry much more than just food items, are found in all the major cities of Baja, and *tiendas* (small food stores) in most villages. When shopping at the *tiendas,* try to have small bills and change with you. Also take a shopping bag. The Mexican bags made of plastic mesh come in a variety of sizes and are most helpful for shopping and for many other uses, such as carrying wet bathing suits or storing garlic and onions.

Another rewarding and colorful experience is shopping at the municipal markets in larger cities like La Paz and San José del Cabo. These markets have everything. Just practice your Spanish a little and learn about metric weights and measures.

The fish displays will offer a full array of choices for fresh seafood and give you an idea of what fish are being caught at the time. If you are lucky, you might even see a leviathan being dragged in whole before it is cut up. You can bargain with the vendors. First, take a walk-through and check prices in different stalls for a particular item. The second walk-through is the time to buy. Be careful when buying shellfish—your nose is the best indicator of freshness. Seafood in the markets comes from all over Baja and is usually very fresh, but you should always be careful with shellfish, no matter where you are.

If shrimp is your fancy, keep a sharp eye for vendors. Once, on a street corner in Rosarito, a young girl with a covered basket was selling delectable shrimp. She wouldn't come down on her price, but we bought some anyway. As it turned out, her price was close to the going rate elsewhere.

In larger campgrounds, usually once a week or so, a produce truck will come through with fresh vegetables and fruits and sometimes shrimp. Don't be surprised if the shrimp market is the trunk of a car or the bed of a pickup. Just make certain the catch is fresh and negotiate a price.

For regular supplies, a good stop is a Gigante grocery store. These are found in shopping centers with plenty of parking and easy access. Gigante is a "superstore"—it has a pharmacy and carries clothes, sundries, prepared food for takeout, and baked goods at its *panadería,* or bakery. Stock up on fresh produce, lettuce, eggs, milk, and meat. Don't pass up the *bolillo,* a delicious bread that comes in large loaves or smaller rolls, and *oreja,* a flaky pastry from the *panadería.*

In these superstores that sell prepared foods and in certain shops and restaurants in larger towns, a quick and easy meal is roast chicken *(pollo rostizado)* that's been cooked slowly on a rotisserie over charcoal. This makes a very good on-the-spot meal, or you can pop it in the ice chest for lunch or dinner later.

Prices for United States' goods are higher throughout Baja. You can find almost anything in the larger supermarkets, but some of the specialty items such as low-fat, low-calorie foods will be quite a bit more. One item we priced, Lipton's decaffeinated iced tea mix with artificial sweetener, cost 25 percent more. It was a pleasant surprise to find it available at the big Centro Comercial Californiano (CCC) supermarkets in La Paz—one at Isabel La Católica and Bravo, the other at Abasolo and Colima. The first one is better stocked and has more variety, although the parking lot is smaller and tighter.

If your taste buds have been longing for something familiar, you most likely will find it at CCC. A large freezer section has pizza and frozen cakes, as well as most other frozen food you would find north of the border. We do our major provisioning here. If you need liquor, prices in the grocery stores are generally lower than in the liquor stores.

Aramburo's at Madero and Hidalgo in La Paz also stocks United States' items and has great meat, but its prices are higher than at CCC. The Aramburo's in Cabo San Lucas is a larger store with a greater selection. On each successive trip, we find a wider variety of foods available in CCC and Aramburo's.

It's best to pack things that are difficult to find everywhere—special diet items such as Nutrasweet, light or low-cholesterol mayonnaise and margarine, and favorite salad dressings and dressing mixes. Diet sodas and other diet drinks are available, but not everywhere. There is even nonalcoholic beer—a big surprise in beer-drinking Mexico.

Another invaluable item is the dry Mexican sauce packet with spices and herbs made by French's, Lawry's, and Schilling for tacos, taco salad, burritos, fajitas, enchiladas, Spanish rice, and more. Just cook up ground beef, meat strips, or whatever you like; then add the sauce packet, mix, and stir, and you're done. Dried spices that add flavor and take up precious little space are helpful in adding varied tastes—you might bring dill, thyme, minced onion, parsley, garlic powder, or paprika, among others. A friend of ours who loves to cook and travels by boat and RV to various places of abode takes along a box-shaped plastic container filled with his favorite spices.

Ziploc freezer bags are very handy for storing or freezing fish and other foods, but are not readily available. Bring them with you.

Small fruit and vegetable stores *(fruterías)* have fresh fruits and vegetables, usually a small supply of canned goods and juices, and sometimes flour tortillas. Pick up corn tortillas at special shops *(tortillerías)* where they are cranked out by the thousands and sold by the kilo.

Don't be afraid to try new and different fruits. *Guayabas* (small, round yellow guavas, pronounced guay-YAH-bahs) are very sweet. Chayote (kay-OH-tay), a hard, light-green vegetable that becomes tender and opaque when cooked, is delicious. Jicama (HE-cah-mah) is a round, hard, brown root with a firm white interior that is sweet and crunchy. The small, round *limónes* (lee-MO-naise), or limes, are found everywhere. They are great for ceviche (say-VEE-chay), or pickled fish, salsa, and iced drinks like margaritas, or just sprinkled over seafood. Limes are said to have medicinal properties and taken along with garlic ward off some intestinal problems before they begin. Mexicans use limes in numerous other ways, and in many restaurants the fruit is kept on the table beside the salsa.

Fresh cuts of meat are sold in supermarkets, municipal markets, and meat shops *(carnicerías)*. The beef is leaner than that found in the United States because cattle are allowed to roam on open range and are rarely put in feedlots for fattening. The meat is also not aged in the same way. Mexican beef is tasty and, being leaner, is better for you. Just learn the different cuts and weights so it will be easy to prepare. With ground beef, use the sauce packets designed for tacos, burritos, fajitas, and enchiladas to make an easy meal. Adolph's Meat Tenderizer or your favorite marinade helps with the steak cuts.

Conserving Provisions

After you cross the border, the special necessities you bring with you become more precious. In the cities of Baja you can find almost anything if you have the time to shop, but asking and searching can be time consuming. We find it easier to bring items that are hard to find, then save and conserve them by using greater care than we might at home.

It's not so much the money involved when special necessities are depleted or a piece of equipment breaks or is lost—more important is the feeling of deprivation over not having it while you are there and the time and energy it takes to replace something. Space is limited, so choose carefully which items you'll carry, keeping in mind where your travels will take you. When packing the 11-foot, 11-inch Lance slide-out camper we use, which has a large storage pod on the roof, we know that having an inventory list of what was packed in the pod, the many storage compartments inside and outside, and all the other nooks and crannies will save nerves and time later on. Large plastic-covered containers (Sterlite and Rubbermaid make some) are good for storing extra food items. Number the boxes, stow them in a storage pod or wherever, add to your inventory list, and note the location. It's best to keep the list up-to-date and to delete items as you use them.

After being on the road for a few days, everything seems to shake down and is easier to find.

Viewing Wildlife
Whales

By far the stars of the wild animal scene, gray whales fascinate nearly everyone. Endangered after decades of unrestricted slaughter, they have been restored to healthy population status, thanks to the laws that protect them. The dedication of the Mexican government to protecting the whales' all-important breeding and calving grounds has been critical to their recovery, as has the cessation of hunting. Scammon's Lagoon (Laguna Ojo de Liebre), Laguna San Ignacio, and Bahía Magdalena have become prime whale-watching spots in the winter months, from January through March. Arrange for guided *panga* trips in Guerrero Negro, San Ignacio, Puerto López Mateos, or San Carlos for the wildlife experience of a lifetime. (*Pangas* are tough, Mexican-designed fiberglass boats used by fishermen.) If you are moderately lucky, a "friendly" will

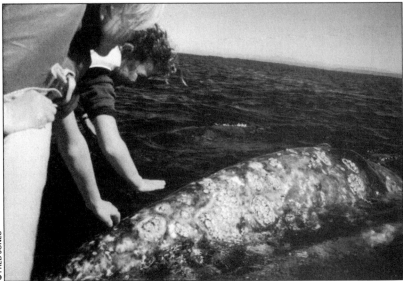

Watching and petting whales is very popular with visitors.

come alongside and you may be able to touch it. Beach campers can expect to see gray whales broaching and spouting close to shore as they swim south from the Arctic in the fall and north in the spring.

In the Midriff area of the Sea of Cortéz, you can see resident fin whales—second in size only to the monstrous blue whale. In 1999 during a La Niña season, when gray whales seemed to be fewer than normal in their usual haunts on the Pacific coast in the first quarter of the year, fin whales were present in large numbers in Bahía de Los Angeles. With luck, any number of different kinds of whales can be seen in Baja's waters: blues, sperms, minkes, killers, Bryde's, humpbacks, and perhaps others.

Fernando Arcas, who can be reached at the Visitor Center and Museum on Salvatierra in Loreto, has specialized in taking scientists out on whale-watching trips and understands their habits. He can be persuaded to take small groups out. One of our most exciting days on the water ever was spent with Fernando among huge blue and fin whales adjacent to the *panga*. He can be reached at Mex. tel./fax 613/135-0086 or email antaresgea@prodigy.net.mx.

During a Vagabundo fishing tournament at Bahía de Los Angeles, a whale leaped out of the water and crashed onto the bow of a fast-moving boat. The bow rail was broken, and the captain broke a finger as he was bashed about. The whale went on its way. We surmised that either the boat had come between a mother and her calf or else the whale had been on loco weed.

Dolphins

Several species of dolphins are commonly seen in Baja—common, bottle-nosed, long-snouted, and spotted—some frolicking in the surf and others in huge pods in the open ocean (often with yellowfin tuna). They enjoy playing around the bow waves of boats. With their grace, speed, and great beauty, these creatures are always an uplifting sight.

Big Fish

We were very fortunate on a recent trip to the Midriff area to spend an afternoon following the largest fish of all, a whale shark, around the south end of Bahía de Los Angeles with Dr. Abraham Vasquez, the owner of Gecko Camp (Campground 12, Central Peninsula). He reports that these huge, placid behemoths frequent the bay from summer through December.

The huge 20-foot manta rays have become quite scarce. Most of them, and the smaller ones as well, have wound up as dried, shredded *manta raya machaca*. What a shame.

Billfish (marlin and sailfish) sometimes will be seen jumping or snoozing on the surface. It's always a thrill to watch one of these well-crafted swimming machines come clear out of the water, often in a long series of leaps.

Sharks are not seen as often as they once were, due to heavy fishing by those who ship their fins off to Asia to be cooked up in soup. It is exciting to see one of those distinctive fins cleaving the water, however. While cruising from Bahía de Los Angeles to Bahía Kino with a group of Vagabundos, we suddenly saw a fin sticking three feet out of the water just off our starboard bow and heading across our path. There was no time to pull the throttle back and slow down. We were sure we were going to hit the shark's back, but we didn't. We passed over the fish without a bump. It had to be a whopper with a very tall dorsal fin, for our stern drive extended three feet below the surface. We wished we could have seen the entire creature.

A real oddball that we have seen infrequently is the sunfish or mola-mola. These goofy fish grow to about 1,000 pounds or so and flop around weakly on their sides, creatures of the currents with little or no movement control.

Sea Turtles

Some interesting work is going on in Baja toward the preservation of sea turtles. Traditionally a popular delicacy, turtle populations have declined severely. Today conservation groups are bringing together fishermen, scientists, and government officials to bring about a better understanding and acceptance of the need to protect these ancient creatures.

Renee Pinal, owner of San Cristobal Ranch 10 miles north of Cabo San Lucas, has supported the development of an extensive turtle egg hatchery, resulting in the release of thousands of baby hatchlings. A tour can be arranged by calling Mex. tel. 624/143-4596, fax 624/143-2313, or email bajabrechasports@hotmail.com.

Biologist Tony Resendiz has created a turtle rearing facility in Bahía de Los Angeles, from which released adult turtles with radios attached have greatly extended knowledge of migration patterns covering thousands of miles across the Pacific Ocean. Tony's email address is resendizshidalgo@yahoo.com.

Birds

By far the most engaging wild camping companions are birds. Brown pelicans give endless entertainment, their lumbering flight instantly transformed into precise dive-bombing attacks on schools of baitfish. Underwater photography discloses that they hit the water with their beaks open, ballooning out their pouches to unbelievable dimensions—which also stops them dead in their tracks. They close their beaks and squeeze the water out, swallowing the fish. They have a very solemn look when they perch with their long beaks tucked down against their breasts. With their red upper throat, bright white and glossy black stripes, and pale yellow patches on the head, the males are quite handsome.

Frigate, or man-o-war, birds circle endlessly on long wings, adroitly riding thermals. When they begin to gather over a spot in the ocean, that is the signal for fishermen to put the boat on plane and head on over, for game fish are working bait. Frigates are great thieves, outmaneuvering gulls and boobies in the air to force them to drop fish they have picked up, then gracefully snatching their booty as it falls.

On the beach, sandpipers and other shorebirds put on a constant show of feeding activity as they race to follow a receding wave, then reverse to keep just ahead of the next one. With a bird identification book in hand, you can readily identify the varied species you'll encounter. Once in a while you find a stray from somewhere far away which doesn't belong in Baja. It's like looking for a pearl in every oyster, for the thrill is in the seeking.

Gulls, of course, are always entertaining with their boldness, well-groomed coiffures, and constant mewing. They are fun to identify, too, as are the terns. On a cruise on our boat in the Midriff area of the Sea of Cortéz we visited Isla Raza, an astounding sea bird rookery. This tiny island is the only breeding ground for 99 percent of all the Heerman's gulls and elegant terns in the entire world, according to Dr. Enriqueta Velarde, who has been conducting studies there in the nesting season each year for the past 25 years. Standing among and being surrounded by that mass of thousands and thousands of raucous birds was a very special experience.

In the southern reaches of Baja, you might spy a very handsome hawk with white chest, pale patches on dark wings, black crest, and red face sitting on *cardón* cacti. This eye-catching fellow of the south is the *caracara* or Mexican eagle.

Ospreys, or fish hawks, are common and are often seen carrying a fish with the head pointed forward as it is tightly gripped with both talons. A pair has nested on a pole near the steel eagle monument at the state line north of Guerrero Negro for years. They have created a huge pile of sticks, adding to it each year. Nesting poles erected in and around Guerrero Negro have created a boom in the osprey population there—being more numerous than anywhere we've been.

Keep an eye out for a very large black bird with a prominent white patch under each wing soaring high overhead. One of these days the California condor will return to Baja's skies. In 2002 several individuals were transferred from California to holding pens in the southern Sierra San Pedro Martir. This established practice of letting them acclimate to a new habitat in "condor condos" has been successful elsewhere. Originally native to Baja California, they are being reintroduced in a joint U.S./Mexico effort.

Exotic Animals

A remnant population of 100 or so pronghorn antelope hang on in the Vizcaíno Desert south of Guerrero Negro. It is a vast area, and they are seldom seen except by biologists making aerial surveys. Once populating Baja's flatlands north into California and over to Sonora and Arizona, now they are nearly gone from Baja. There are severe penalties for killing a pronghorn antelope, which are well known among the local population, and there is hope for their survival. The antelope drink no free water, getting what they need from nightly condensation on plants and from the plants themselves, which is most unusual for an animal of their size.

Desert bighorn sheep inhabit the rougher, more remote mountains from the border south to about 40 miles north of La Paz. It has always been impossible to police the hunting of these animals, and the population is way down from its original numbers. Recently the federal government has allowed a few permits to be auctioned off in order to provide much-needed income for the *ejidos* (government-supported cooperatives) in Baja California Sur and to encourage the residents to protect the bighorn as a valuable income-producing asset. Tourists will not encounter

What to Bring

Horseback Pack Trips

We've taken horses into the Sierra San Pedro Mártir, Sierra de San Francisco, and Sierra de La Laguna. Here is what we bring on horseback pack trips:
- Two-person mountain tent with an anteroom that can be closed and a sun fly
- Nylon or plastic ground cloth to go under the tent and to serve as an apron for wiping our feet before entering the tent
- Rubber air mattresses with box sides and built-in pillows
- Sleeping bags that zip together so we can snuggle
- Small folding table
- Coleman propane three-burner stove and folding aluminum stand
- Several disposable propane bottles
- Coleman two-lamp fluorescent lantern with a new battery
- Cooking kit with pots, frying pan, plates, cups, and utensils
- Small plastic squeeze bottle of dishwashing liquid soap
- Dish rag, scrub brush, and dish towel
- Food, including dehydrated meals, canned chicken and shredded beef for tacos, etc., eggs in a plastic egg carrier, powdered iced tea mix with sweetener and lemon, cheese, salami, crackers, cookies, tortillas, and other goodies our taste buds require (several planned meals, for us *and* our guide, plus a little extra)
- Clothes, including jeans, hiking boots, lightweight tennis shoes and sandals for around camp, hats, light jackets, lightweight long-sleeved cotton or SPF Supplex shirts, T-shirts, underwear, socks, swimsuits, plastic ponchos (good for ground cloths and rain, too), and shorts
- Swiss army knife, ever present on the belt
- Pair of binoculars
- Cameras and ample slide and print film (we're photographers)
- Notebook (we're writers)
- First-aid kit in an easy-to-pack container off the shelf, prepared for the usual cuts, punctures, and abrasions
- Bug spray and squeeze bottle
- Sunglasses
- Medications and personal hygiene items

bighorn sheep unless they go out of their way to arrange for a guide. The curious can do so in San Felipe, Bahía de Los Angeles, Santa Rosalía, or Loreto.

Primitive Camping
Camping Outside of Established Campgrounds

Baja is a desert bordering on the tropics. The sun is intense, and both air and ground temperatures can be hot. The air is usually very dry, but it can also be very wet when storms set in. The Pacific coast is subject to periodic fog and frequent dew.

- Lip balm
- Sunscreen
- Flashlights with spare bulbs and batteries
- Nylon cord
- Small water filter and collapsible five-gallon plastic water jug with a spigot
- Quart canteens
- Ziploc bags for trail snacks and other unforeseen uses
- Plastic garbage bags—what goes in, goes out

Backpacking Equipment
We pare down our horseback pack-trip list and substitute more lightweight items:
- Sleeping pads instead of rubber air mattresses
- Small single-burner stove
- Fewer clothes
- No table
- No lantern
- No canned goods

Car Camping
In addition to what we'd bring on a horseback pack trip, we add:
- Water in two five-gallon collapsible plastic containers
- Ice chest
- Small propane grill
- Small folding shovel
- Tow cable
- Sun shower
- Rope
- Bungee cords—a bag full
- Duct tape, a great fixer-upper
- Field guides for birds, plants, and fish
- Fishing tackle essentials—fillet knife, spinning rods and reels, hooks, swivels, swivel snaps, sinkers, and several lures of the Rapala, Scampi, tuna feather, and jig types (if we charter a boat, we take marlin rods and Penn International 50W or Shimano two-speed reels; the rods and reels take the most room, while the rest fits in a small cosmetics case)

A basic rule in the desert is to be wary of camping in arroyos or streambeds. Infrequently a cloudburst occurs in the mountains, out of sight and hearing. A good night's sleep can be ruined by a wall of water rolling big boulders down the arroyo to scour out your campsite and you along with it. Keep in mind that these are the very forces that carved out the arroyo in the first place and they do occur periodically.

Beach Camping
When you set up camp on a beach in Baja, whether in a tent or an RV, be prepared for a primitive

experience. Camping alone is not advised. You may find yourself on one of the few beaches with improvements or in one of the handful of RV parks situated on a beach. Elsewhere you won't find picnic tables, restrooms, parking areas, trails, signs, or water spigots. You may find trash barrels.

What you certainly will find are privacy and beauty—mile after mile of pristine sand beaches, white enough to blind you, where you can walk and walk until you drop and never see another soul except your traveling companions. What looks to be a mile away will prove to be four miles. When you set off walking down a beach, it pays to bring something to drink and to go only so far that you won't be too tired to return to camp.

It also pays to plan ahead on what to do with your trash and human waste. A firm commitment to carrying out what you carried in will keep camping spots attractive and safe for all. It's worth the effort. Burn paper, cardboard, and toilet tissue, and cut up the six-pack plastic holders that secure soft drink and beer cans, slicing through the rings. There is nothing so sad as to see a helpless pelican with its bill surrounded by a plastic ring, essentially wiring it shut. Crush the rest, bag it up, and take it to the next town dump *(basurera)*.

Bring a shovel—the small folding ones take up little space. Emulate the cat by burying your personal deposits well back from the high tide line. If you settle in with an RV, drive it away when you have to dump your holding tanks. Don't put paper in the sewage tank and use discretion in selecting a spot in which to dump it, preferably the sewer system of the nearest RV park. Offer to pay for the privilege.

People who settle into a beach spot for the winter in an RV are accustomed to digging a hole, covering it with a piece of plywood, and running their sewer hose into it. Some popular spots with a high density of such campers have become noxious and badly polluted, adversely affecting adjacent beaches.

Accordingly, some beaches have been fenced off to prevent vehicular access and overnight camping. Usually a pedestrian walkway is provided for day use. All of the former camping beaches between Cabo San Lucas and San José del Cabo have been restricted in this way. Hotels and condominiums now dominate that coast, with more on the way.

The right of public access to beaches in Mexico has its limitations. There is a federal zone *(Zona Federale)* extending 20 meters back from the mean high tide line around the entire coastline of the country that is open to public access. However, adjoining landowners can be held responsible for the cleanliness of the beach in front of their property. Abuse leads to fences.

We have done considerable camping in both tents and campers on Baja's beaches over the years and have found a few security precautions to be well advised. There is nothing so effective as camping with other people to establish a comforting peace of mind. That way there can always be someone in camp to deter those who may consider appropriating your equipment and belongings. Do everyone a favor and don't create temptation.

We lost a clam fork many years ago from alongside our tent, which undoubtedly better served a local youngster. However, we weren't through chasing clams and missed it. Other campers have mentioned ice chests and other easily portable items walking off, including small boats and motors. The worst offenders are other campers, particularly those who have established semipermanent quarters on a shoestring and can use just about anything that comes their way. Your unattended campsite will look like an open bazaar to someone seeking acquisitions.

The local fishermen and ranchers are hospitable folk who work for what they have and respect the property of others, but kids will be kids—like the little shavers who peeled a magnetic sign off one of our truck doors while we were sitting inside the camper having lunch. They apparently told their mother we gave it to them. We should have caught on when she came over and politely asked if she could have the other one.

A sound practice is to completely avoid sharing alcohol with strangers. What starts out as jovial conviviality can quickly turn unpleasant and unmanageable—the more remote and isolated the area, the less inhibited people feel.

Getting Stuck in the Sand

One of the little chores you learn how to do when getting off the beaten path in Baja is how to get unstuck. Years ago we used to tent camp on Playa Santa María south of San Quintín behind the dunes, just about where the La Pinta Hotel now sits. We had a standard two-wheel-drive station wagon and loved to drive it on the beach. The drill was to reduce tire pressure to about 15 pounds, determine a path through the dunes, then make a mad dash to the beach. Once there we drove on the hard sand below the high tide line and had about eight miles of beach for a playground.

One day, full of confidence, we tried coming off the beach in a new spot and dug in. Most of the afternoon was spent jacking up the rear wheels, packing brush, driftwood, and whatever else we could find under the wheels, then surging ahead a few feet to repeat the process. It was definitely not fun.

A long time ago, our old one-ton Ford truck (the worst vehicle to get stuck we've ever had)—with nothing behind or on it, just the naked truck—buried itself in the middle of the Villa Vitta RV Park at Bahía de Los Angeles.

In another instance long ago, while towing a 5,000-pound, 21-foot boat, we turned off Highway 1 near Puerto Escondido onto what looked to be hard-sand wheel tracks. They weren't. Everything got totally buried. We had to unhook the trailer, tow the truck and camper out, then pull the boat and trailer out with a long cable. That qualified as one of the dumbest moves of

© FRED JONES

tent camping on the shore of Bahía Magdelena

all time, for which we earned the label of "Sand Crabs" from a sneaky Vagabundo who happened by and ratted on us.

Some people carry two long pieces of canvas or carpet to put under the drive wheels. Others find wetting the sand makes a difference.

Nylon tow straps can apparently be used to slingshot the stuck vehicle out of its hole by a second vehicle. Have that vehicle run out to the limit of stretch (about another one-fifth the length of the strap), then slam on the brakes. As the brake lights come on, step on the gas to the stuck vehicle. We haven't seen this done, but we've been told of the technique. It presents a pleasant mental image of the stuck vehicle simply shooting forward like a rocket. When you're stuck, you'll try anything, right? We'll just keep on with the old jack-it-up-and-stuff-it method.

One more stuck story. Once, during the year we spent in Iran, we ventured out on a dry lake bed in our standard station wagon, decided we had gone far enough as the bushes were petering out, stopped, and tried to back up. We dug in. We jacked up the rear wheels, stuffed thornbrush under them, went back a couple of feet, got stuck, and repeated the process numerous times. A sheepherder steered his flock over our way to see what these goofy foreigners were up to, gave us an enormous toothless grin, put one finger on the top of his six-foot-long staff, and gently pushed it all the way down. When he pulled it out, wet muck was clinging to it. Goggle-eyed, we realized the station wagon was resting on a very thin crust over mushy goop. With renewed vigor and a sense of the whole shebang slowly sinking out of sight, we jacked and stuffed in a frenzy to the limit of our endurance. Once we had traction, the pedal went to the floor, the wagon shot up and over a six-foot-tall thornbush in reverse, and finally reached solid ground.

Moral: Getting stuck isn't such a big deal. It's what you do next that counts.

Backpacking

Unless you have a great deal of experience backpacking in the desert, we do not recommend backpacking in Baja. If you get too far away from the car, even in the mountains, you can encounter a water problem. It is easy to forget that this is an arid peninsula that has very limited water sources, and finding them may take local knowledge. It is also dry and can be numbingly hot.

Read *Into a Desert Place* by Graham Mackintosh before you think about backpacking in Baja. Mackintosh walked the entire coastline on both sides of the peninsula, carried all the water he could, including a gallon plastic jug in each hand, and tried several types of water distillation devices. He still had some close calls. It is an unforgiving, harsh environment and not to be approached lightly.

Having said that, the mountains do offer some challenging backpacking opportunities. The Sierra San Pedro Mártir in Baja Norte is a massive mountain range with a high forested plateau some 40 miles long and 10 miles wide between roughly 6,000 and 8,000 feet in elevation. Jeffrey pine is the dominant forest tree, alongside some sugar pine and incense cedar. At higher elevations you will find lodgepole pine and white fir. There also are huge meadows on which cattle graze.

Off to the east is the highest peak in Baja—El Picacho del Diablo—at 10,154 feet elevation. Climbing it is a major event and is usually done from the eastern base of the steep escarpment of the Sierra San Pedro Mártir because of the 3,000-foot-deep Cañon del Diablo separating the plateau of the main range from El Picacho. This canyon is a rather weird geological quirk—as if extra effort was expended to isolate El Picacho from mankind.

Trails were established long ago by Indians and have been further delineated by vaqueros (cowherders). Unlike what we are accustomed to in the United States, there are no signs, no trail markers, and no good maps. Trails peter out. You can get lost. You can fail to find water. Before setting out, drive to the Meling Ranch and talk to the people there about where to go, how to find your way, and other lifesaving advice you can't leave without. Hire a guide if you feel the slightest bit doubtful about your outdoors expertise. We packed out of there on horseback many years ago with a guide and packer and had a great experience. You can, too, on foot or horseback, if you go about it right.

If you're an angler, you can enjoy fishing for Nelson rainbow trout, native to Arroyo San Antonio and later introduced into Arroyos San Rafael and La Zanja. They are not big—up to a foot long—but catching one in such an unlikely place is fun. There is also a scenic waterfall in Arroyo San Antonio.

To get to the Meling Ranch, drive about 6.5 miles south of Colonet or about eight miles north of Camalu on Highway 1. Turn east toward San Telmo and continue beyond it to the ranch—a total distance of about 31 miles. The road is dusty and has some fairly steep grades, which were all we wanted to handle with our big camper.

At the other end of the peninsula, the Sierra de La Laguna rises high in the sky above the desert. Surrounded by the tourist centers of La Paz, Los Cabos, and the East Cape, its isolated lushness is unsuspected by visitors in the popular resorts fronting the ocean. The heart of the sierra can be reached only by arduous effort over rugged, steep, centuries-old trails that are unsigned and difficult to find. They have been beaten two to three feet into the rock by thousands of hooves and feet over the past 200 years or more.

The sierra's rugged peaks can be seen from the surrounding circle of Highways 1 and 19. An especially striking vista is from Highway 1 between Buena Vista and San José del Cabo, from which jagged peaks loom to nearly 7,000 feet.

The area's most startling feature is the dense forest of 60-foot pine and oak trees with trunks up to three feet in diameter, a scattering of huge red-trunked *madroños* with large, glossy, bright-green leaves, and the bizarre *sotol* with clusters of long, slender yuccalike leaves atop tall thin trunks.

The pines are Mexican *piñón,* others of which are found far away in northern Mexico and adjoining Arizona and Texas. The massive black oaks and *madroños* are species unique to the Sierra de La Laguna. The *sotol* occurs elsewhere only in a few widely scattered groups farther north in Baja. In a moister, cooler climate in the far distant past, the progenitors of all these species found their way out of northern Mexico and down the Baja Peninsula. When the climate grew drier and warmer, they became isolated in the higher, moister reaches of the Sierra de La Laguna. As time went on, most were supplanted by new species.

Up in the sierra, level land is hard to find. The one sizable meadow, about one mile by a half mile, is known as La Laguna. Local lore has it that originally there was a lake here, which broke out of its confines 100 years or so ago.

The shortest route to it is from Rancho La Burrera at a 1,600-foot elevation out of Todos Santos. Some maps show Rancho La Burrera as San Juan del Asserradero. Start at the microwave dish on the south side of Todos Santos on Highway 19. Drive 1.3 miles south just past Km 54 and turn left on a sandy road across a cattle guard at the top of a hill. Starting from zero on the odometer, ignore a road to the left at 2.2 miles. Continue straight ahead toward the fire lookout tower. At 4 miles, take the left fork. Cross a cattle guard at 5.4 miles, pass a dam on the left at 6.4 miles, and cross another cattle guard at 7.2 miles. At 8.8 miles, continue straight past a signed road on the left to San Martín, then pass another road to the right. At 12.3 miles, marked by a gate, the road makes a steep descent down the north bank of an arroyo to the ranch at 13.3

Basic Steps to Cleaning a Fish: First, slit belly from anal vent to gills. Then sever lower junctions of gills. Next, pull out innards and gills. And last but not least, run thumbnail along cavity to clean out dark matter.

miles. Find a place to park and start walking. At the ranch you may be able to arrange for horses and to have the gate opened. If you are able to drive in, remember to build momentum to traverse the drifted humps of sandy soil on the return out of the arroyo. Our conventional one-ton pickup, which has a propensity for digging in, handled it easily. Motor homes and trailers should not make the drive in from the highway, however.

The trail heads easterly from La Burrera up the big wash coming out of the mountains, then climbs up the north slope. The 4,000-foot ascent of seven miles to La Laguna took us about four hours on horseback. A shaded water source about midway affords refreshment.

At La Laguna, a two-room *casita,* or little house, in the trees at the meadow's edge is used by "forest guards" who keep an eye on things and gauge rainfall in the meadow. Another two-room *casita* in the open can be used for shelter and cooking. Cattle and pigs forage over the land, watering in the stream that runs east into Cañon San Dionisio. The trail continues down that canyon to a ranch of the same name.

Backpackers have used two other trans-sierra routes with hard-to-find ancient trails. South of Rancho La Burrera, the next trail goes from Rancho Santo Domingo on the west to Rancho Boca de La Sierra on the east. Another trail farther south goes from Rancho El Guerigo on the west to Rancho El Salto on the east. Farther south yet, the iffy Naranjas Road crosses from its junction with Highway 19 at a sign to El Saltito de Los Garcia to Highway 1 at a point 9.5 miles south of the turnoff to Miraflores. You can go up it partway from either side, but a hurricane wiped it out higher up.

Boat Camping

Camping either in a boat or in a tent on shore has a great deal of potential in several sections of the Sea of Cortéz. The many islands around Bahía de Los Angeles, Puerto Escondido, and La Paz have attractive coves and beaches. Since stretches of open ocean must be crossed, small open boats like inflatables and cartop aluminum models are not suitable. Strong winds can whip up on short notice, churning the ocean into a maelstrom. Trailer boats of 20 feet or so in length can handle rough seas, although the open-cockpit, center-console designs can get awfully wet. Cuddy cabins give protection and are adequate for sleeping. Camper canvas to the stern makes a cozy home for living on board.

We have lived aboard our old 21-footer for several weeks at a time, though our present 27-footer is far more comfortable with its aft-cabin layout. We have lived in it for four months while on the road to and from Florida and cruising in the Bahamas as comfortably as in our big camper. We have spread mosquito netting across the deck and slept peacefully under the stars in a double sleeping bag. Recently we circumnavigated all the islands in the Midriff section of the Sea of Cortéz in the 27-footer. It was better able to take the rough seas and substantial rip tides we encountered, which create whirlpools and undertows.

We once set up a tent camp on the beach on Isla Partida north of La Paz for a week with some dive buddies who had a small compressor. We had a great time exploring the underwater world there.

Boats require special equipment. It is much tougher to get help having broken down on the water than having broken down on the highway. You must be more self-sufficient with tools and parts. Having a buddy boat may mean the difference between getting back to shore and being stranded. There are times when being towed is unavoidable. Necessary items in addition to those listed for vehicles and for primitive camping are:

- Towing bridle
- Propeller
- Water pump impeller
- Hoses
- Belts
- Marine alternator
- Distributor parts
- Spare gas

Protection Against Insects, Sea Life, and Cactus

Mosquitoes and gnats can make your life miserable. Sooner or later you will run into both of them, so have plenty of bug spray on hand at all times. Read on for tips on how to deal with these and other annoying creatures and plants.

Mosquitoes

These ubiquitous pests can be controlled with any of the commercial compounds containing DEET (N, N-diethyl-metatoluamide), the one chemical that can be counted on to do the job. We have a squirt bottle of U.S. Army-type repellent with 71 percent DEET, and it works well. It is recommended that DEET be washed off, and there is some controversy about the safety of the higher strengths. It might be best to use the lesser strengths most of the time and save the heavy-duty stuff for when you are in an area where lots of pests are out at dawn's first light and dusk. We haven't been able to find the Army type lately, but there are various brands of DEET out; Muskol is effective and comes in 100 percent strength and lesser amounts, too, like 40 percent.

A different type of product, called After Bite, made by the Tender Corp, Littleton, New Hampshire, helps relieve the itch and pain from mosquito and gnat bites, and we always carry it with us when outdoors. Be sure to read the labels.

Keep covered up and spray or rub the repellent on exposed skin. Also spray clothing. DEET melts certain kinds of plastic, like watchbands and eyeglass frames, so be careful with the stuff.

Gnats

The most vicious biting bug in Baja is the *jejene* (hay-HAY-nay). Everyone likes to call this teeny-weeny gnat a no-see-um, but you can see um, though barely. They walk right through mosquito netting. The first thing you'll notice is that something is biting you and you are beginning to sting and itch all over. Soon you'll have scads of little welts that itch even more. We have a photo of one of our friends in which he looks as if he has a bad case of measles. Talk about an unhappy camper.

In our experience DEET repellents aren't as effective on *jejenes* as on mosquitoes, but if you keep slathering on the stuff it helps a lot. People are usually happier when they depart the *jejene* encampment. If you can find a breezy spot, the winds should blow them away. Fortunately they are not troublesome in many places, but when you are among them, they will drive you crazy. Since they breed in cracks in mud created by tidal waters coming and going over shallow areas, such as mangrove swamps, it pays to avoid spending the night in these spots.

Many people swear by Avon Skin-So-Soft as a bug repellent. We haven't found that to be so, but it may be just the right combination for you.

Stingrays

This fish can whack you with its whiplike tail if you wade around carelessly in salt water. Stingrays are common off Baja and should be kept in mind, for their barb can inflict a painful wound. The best thing to do is shuffle your feet or keep thrashing a stick ahead of you. They bury themselves in the sand and can't be seen, but as they don't relish being stepped on, they will swim away if alerted. Be particularly cautious when stepping down off a surfboard or sailboard or out of a boat or snorkeling in shallow water.

If you are unlucky enough to get hit, the standard advice is to cleanse the wound with cold salt water and extract all pieces of the barb or its sheath. Soak the injury in hot water at as high a temperature as can be tolerated for 30 to 90 minutes. (Dr. Abraham Vasquez, the doctor in Bahía de Los Angeles who has treated hundreds of stingray victims, prescribes 110°F water for one hour plus taking Tylenol.) Disinfect and bandage it as you would any other puncture.

Some people swear that the pain can be relieved by zapping the spot with a stun gun or a live spark plug. We have no experience with these stunning techniques, which reportedly also neutralize the effects of snakebite and other venoms.

Sea Urchins

Some sea urchins with long, slender spines are present in both the Pacific Ocean and the Sea of Cortéz. These spines penetrate booties, sneakers, or bare skin like needles and are difficult to remove because they are barbed. It is important to try to extract all pieces of broken spines. Local remedies may involve frequently dousing the skin with citrus juice to help eliminate any unremoveable bits. Disinfect the punctures and keep them clean.

Jellyfish

Tiny jellyfish, whose stings encourage you to leave the water, are found in Baja. Rub in meat tenderizer—Adolph's is considered good. Other recommended treatments are ammonia and urea. After Bite, in a pen form, is mainly ammonia. Tentacles on the skin can be covered with dry sand, then scraped off after a few minutes.

Cactus

It was an exciting moment. Fred was assisting other biologists in Arizona on a desert bighorn sheep project. While hiking up an arroyo, he spotted a big ram climbing out on one side. He plunked down to a restful sitting position for a steady look with the binoculars and nailed his Levi's to his butt by landing on a jumping cholla cactus ball. The ram was forgotten so that total attention could be devoted to getting unstuck. A wadded-up handkerchief held around the spiny ball gave sufficient leverage to pry it loose without impaling his fingers. These little devils are barbed and resist being pulled out.

On a similar expedition in Baja, Gloria brushed too close to a cactus alongside a steep, rough trail and collected a cactus spine in her leg. One of the Mexican biologists whipped a pair of tweezers out of his shirt pocket and removed that rascal in an instant.

If you walk around where cacti live, it is best to be fully clothed, pay them serious respect, and carry a pair of tweezers. Carelessness can be painful.

Cactus spines are also disrespectful of automobile tires. We have received flats in big truck tires after four-wheeling on desert roads and have had to endure the big grin of the tire guy (the shop is a *llantera,* yawn-TEAR-uh) as he holds up a little spine in his pliers and says, *"Espina!"* We now watch out for chunks of cactus branches across the road and get out and remove them. That takes less time than changing a tire.

Problems with Sun, Heat, and Cold
Sunburn

People are a lot wiser today than they used to be about taking it easy in the sun. If you want to avoid getting burned when you hit Baja, give yourself only a half hour of exposure the first day, then a half hour more for each of the four or five days it takes to start tanning. Use sunscreen or sunblock ointments all the time. Sun protection factors (SPFs) range from 2 to 50 or higher. An SPF of 15 or higher will block 93 percent of the sun's UVB rays and is the minimum rating recommended by the Skin Cancer Foundation of New York. An SPF of 30 or higher provides only 4 percent more protection, but may be recommended for highly sensitive individuals. Some sunscreens are rated as "broad-spectrum," meaning they also protect against ultraviolet-A (UVA) rays, but the SPF standard measures only UVB protection, not UVA. Sunscreen should be applied about one-half hour before becoming exposed—really rub it in, and be sure it's absorbed. Reapply often, especially if you get wet or sweat a lot, at a maximum of every two hours.

Exposure may occur anyway, and you can develop some bright red spots. For instance, switching to a smaller swimsuit can uncover white skin that needs extra protection. Light-skinned people burn very quickly and are better off completely covered. At the other end of the spectrum are those who tan readily but will burn if they push it too fast. Everyone should determine how they react and protect themselves accordingly.

If you become sunburned, get out of the sun, cover yourself up, and apply a soothing ointment such as Solarcaine or Noxema. Suffer as silently as possible and be wiser the next time.

For our most recent trip we bought shirts and pants that were rated SPF 30, made from a synthetic material called Supplex. These have mesh inserts that can be opened to allow ventilation and buttons on the sleeves so you can roll them up and button at various lengths. They worked very well. When you are in and out of the water, it is easier to grab the SPF 30 clothes than put on sunscreen every time you get out.

Heat Exhaustion

We were having a great time fishing in a friend's *panga* off of Isla San José north of La Paz. It was hot, but Fred was comfortable in a swimsuit and cap. After several hours, we headed back to San Evaristo, where he became a little nauseated and couldn't eat the delicious *taquitos* our friend's wife had prepared. During the long drive back to La Paz, Fred became more uncomfortable. He climbed right into bed, feeling disoriented and woozy.

Some years before, while hiking strenuously on a July day for a desert bighorn sheep survey in Death Valley National Monument, Fred became overheated from the exertion. His legs ceased to function, and drinking copious amounts of water and pouring it over his head had no effect. He was able to move to a nearby spring by lifting each leg by hand from behind the knee, swinging the leg forward, then doing the same thing with the other leg. Finally at the spring, he fell headlong into a pool. The rising steam blotted out the sun, and he was soon able to stagger to the car.

Both of these events were cases of heat exhaustion, which is caused by loss of fluids and salt. Hot, dry desert air sucks moisture out of the body at a high rate. One may experience muscle cramps and headaches, pale and clammy skin, and dizziness and fainting.

Here's what the *American Medical Association (AMA) Family Medical Guide* says to do: Lay the person down in a cool, quiet place with feet raised a little. Loosen any tight clothing and give the victim water to drink, adding a teaspoon of salt to each quart.

In order to avoid heat exhaustion, it is important to maintain adequate moisture in your body and to limit your activity level. We have learned from United States Army studies (made when General Patton's tank corps was undergoing training in the California desert) that people performing strenuous activity in the desert require at least two gallons of liquid a day to offset fluid losses. It was also demonstrated that water by itself is not sufficiently palatable to consume in such quantities. You can guzzle it every time you have the slightest desire and still not take in enough. It is necessary to improve it by adding flavoring—citrus juice, chocolate, powdered tea, whatever you can do to make it more interesting. We have adopted the attitude that it is foolish to carry water around with you when you could be drinking it. It only functions in your stomach, not in a canteen. Just be sure you have enough.

Fred took two college students into the Santa Rosa Mountains of California one July to make bighorn counts at water holes. When it's hot, desert bighorn stay close to water, so it's a good time to count them. Prospectors warned Fred that they couldn't survive in those hot, hot canyons at that time of year. However, armed with the findings of Patton's troops, they guzzled water like it was going out of style and had no problems. The prospectors were right about one thing: those canyons were like ovens, with rocks so hot they blistered the skin.

Heatstroke/Sunstroke

Heat exhaustion can lead to heatstroke under prolonged exposure to very hot conditions. Body temperature can become very high, the skin can turn flushed, hot, and dry, and the pulse can grow strong and rapid. The *AMA Family Medical Guide* says to remove clothing and wrap the sufferer in a cold, wet sheet or sponge him or her with cold or lukewarm water. Fan the person by hand or with a fan until the body temperature comes down; then turn him or her face down in a comfortable sleeping position with upper arms and one leg at right angles to the body, bent at the elbows and knee. Cover the person with a dry sheet and continue to fan. If the body temperature starts to rise, repeat the cooling process.

Hypothermia

Baja really does have everything. If you work it right, you can freeze and fry in the same place on the same day.

After a hypnotic night sleeping to the rhythmic slosh of waves on the beach at San Pedrito RV Park south of Todos Santos, Fred decided the surf must be full of a great many fish. At dawn, he donned his swimsuit, firmly grasped his surf-casting rod, and plunged in waist deep for a couple hours of fruitless casting. Deciding it was time for breakfast, he gave it up to return to the camper.

Funny thing! He was shaking so badly he could barely navigate up the slope of the beach. Inside the camper, he went into a frenzy of shivering and shuddering and felt like an ice cube through and through. Gloria whipped up hot chocolate, wrapped him in a blanket, and sweetly told him what a horse's patootie he was. There was nothing he could say, as it was true.

For such cold Pacific Ocean water all the way south to Cabo San Lucas, you can blame the Japanese current, which sweeps north past Japan, across the frigid North Pacific, then south along the North American coast without warming up a whole lot.

Even in the Sea of Cortéz the water can be too cold for long immersion, except in the shallows where it warms up nicely. When we dive in the Cortéz, we always wear a wet suit or jeans and a long-sleeved cotton shirt, depending on the water temperature. It's true that we have never won any awards for sartorial elegance among the diving crowd, but it's also true that we enjoy our dives. One thing about wet clothes is that you need to get them off as soon as you're back in the boat. Nothing robs heat from the body faster than wet Levi's.

On an early spring raft trip on the Yampa River in Utah, Fred nearly did it again with the hypothermia by wearing wet Levi's. A few rapids soused his trousers, clouds blocked the sun, and he went into that deep shivering mode. Gloria forcibly pulled his pants off, to the delight of our Vagabundo friends, and with dry legs he warmed right up. We had wondered why all the oarsmen wore nothing but shorts and sandals—they got wet all the time but dried off quickly.

When prolonged exposure to cold drops the body temperature more than four degrees below normal, hypothermia has hit. Our source, the *AMA Family Medical Guide,* says to get the person into warm, dry clothes and administer warm drinks. Hey, that's just what Gloria did at San Pedrito! Hypothermia can become very serious if it's allowed to progress, so catch it at the first shiver.

Medical Care

Gloria once developed an infected finger while in La Paz, so we asked our Mexican friends where to go. There are several hospitals to choose from. We went to the closest one, displayed the finger, and were ushered right into a doctor's office. He specified an antibiotic (no prescription needed), which we obtained at a pharmacy. A good source for information on administering medications, their side effects, contraindications, etc., is the *Nursing Drug Handbook,* published by Springhouse Corporation, Springhouse, Pennsylvania. It is printed in a small, handy format and is very informative.

Clinics are available in small communities and will handle minor scrapes and cuts. The cities have hospitals where treatment for more serious ailments can be obtained. Prices are minimal compared to what we are accustomed to.

Major problems may require transport back home, which can be very expensive if a special medical airplane must be flown in with a doctor and nurse. But if it is a life-threatening situation, that is what must be done. Elderly people in particular may secure peace of mind by subscribing to one of several air evacuation programs ahead of time for a fee.

Travel Tips

Mexico has a different legal system, different customs, a different culture, and is, well, different. That is why we all go there—to get away from the treadmill at home and have fun. Here are the most important things to do and become accustomed to before your trip.

Licenses and Permits

Permits and documents are essential for traveling in Baja California, and even more so when you enter the mainland of Mexico from Baja.

Tourist Cards

The first thing to think about is a tourist card. Most tourists call it a visa or visitor permit. The formal identification is Form FM-T. Everyone who will be in Baja for more than three days or south of San Quintín or San Felipe needs one. You can obtain one at any immigration *(migración)* office in Baja. You will need a valid passport, birth certificate or naturalization paper, and a photo identification card.

Once you fill out the form, you must go to any bank in Mexico to pay a 190-peso fee then have it validated in Mexico at an immigration office. It is much more convenient to purchase a prepaid FM-T from the Vagabundos del Mar Boat and Travel Club office at U.S. tel. 800/474-BAJA (800/474-2252).

The easiest immigration office to locate, as well as the easiest to deal with, is in Tijuana just across the border. Pull into the far right-hand lane signed for Declaration Only, park, and go to the immigration office behind the row of buildings to the right to obtain the FM-T form. Then go to the adjacent bank to pay, and return to immigration to have it validated. Have a passport, copy of your birth certificate or naturalization paper, and photo identification card. Both the immigration office and bank are open 24 hours a day, seven days a week (in the current acronym jargon—24/7).

Vehicle Permits

If you are taking a vehicle to the mainland by ferry from Santa Rosalía (to Guaymas) or La Paz (to Topolobampo or Mazatlán), a Temporary Vehicle Importation Permit is necessary. Do not count on obtaining one in Santa Rosalía. Either procure it at a customs *(aduana)* office at the border, in La Paz at the customs office in the Treasury *(Hacienda)* building across from the city dock *(Muelle Fiscal)* in the center of town, or at the vehicle control booth at the customs office at the Pichilingue Port, where the ferry dock is located.

To obtain the permit, you'll need a tourist card; vehicle registration; a leasing contract (if the car is leased or rented) in the name of the individual importing the car; if it's a company car, a document certifying that you work for the company; and an international credit card (American Express, Diner's Club, MasterCard, or Visa) in the name of the owner or driver of the vehicle.

You must pay a 100-peso fee, by credit card only, for three items: a six-month Temporary Vehicle Importation Permit, a form on which you promise to take the vehicle back out of the country, and a windshield sticker. Cash is not accepted. If you don't have a credit card, you must go to the nearby Mexican bonding agency, which is the Bank of the Army *(Banjército)*. The bond will cost one to two percent of the Blue Book value of the vehicle, plus tax and processing costs. If you are going only to Baja and will not be on the Mexican mainland, you will not need the vehicle permit.

If you will be leaving your house trailer, boat, or boat trailer behind when you exit Baja, you must obtain a free 20-year Temporary Vehicle Importation Permit from a customs office. Bring all documents that will establish who you are, that you own the vehicle, and that it is currently registered somewhere other than Mexico.

Fishing Licenses and Boat Permits

These are much simpler to deal with than those for vehicles. Regulations state that in order to operate a boat in Mexican waters, it is necessary to hold a boat permit and personal fishing license for everybody aboard the boat, regardless of age and whether or not they're fishing. These can be obtained from Mexican Fisheries *(Pesca)*. You can get one in Mexico, but locating a *(Pesca)* office can be a chore. Contact the U.S. office at 2550 Fifth Avenue, Suite 101, San Diego, CA 92103, U.S. tel. 619/233-4324. For faster service, phone the Vagabundos del Mar Boat and Travel Club at U.S. tel. 800/474-BAJA (800/474-2252).

U.S. Fish and Wildlife Service agents confiscate fish being brought into the country by people who don't possess Mexican fishing licenses. Don't trust *panga* or charter boat operators to have a license to cover you; instead get your own by the week, month, or year.

Pets

If you have a pet, obtain an International Health Certificate from your veterinarian as close to your departure date as possible and bring it with you. Be sure rabies and distemper shots show on the certificate. We were never questioned about this matter in Mexico when we brought our cat, but we have been asked to show the certificate when crossing back into the United States.

Insurance
Liability

Mexican law is considerably different from that in the United States. In the event of an accident, both parties are detained until it is determined who is responsible for what, including damage to the highway, and how the debt is to be paid. Liability coverage with a Mexican company takes care of your end of things. Liability coverage with companies other than those in Mexico is not recognized, *regardless of what your insurance agent may tell you*. Without Mexican coverage, you may wind up in jail if you're involved in an accident.

Mexican vehicle liability policies include coverage for anything towed, including boats and trailers, which must be listed on the policy. For an additional moderate fee, liability coverage can be purchased to cover boats while on the water. Although the risk of a boat accident is less than for vehicles, the same consequences can follow if there is no insurance coverage. Liability-only coverage for vehicles for a full year is very inexpensive, also.

Physical Damage

Coverage for damage to your vehicle and boat can also be purchased from a Mexican company.

Attention Travelers

You are entering a fruit fly–free area.
Do not bring the following products without authorization:
Oranges, grapefruit, *zapote,* plum, guava, mango, *tejocote, mamey,* fruit or ornamental plants or other restricted plant products, potato gold nematode.
B.C.S. (Baja California Sur) is free of hog cholera and is eradicating avian salmonella and exotic Newcastle disease from poultry.
Do not bring live pigs or pork products (fresh meat, sausage, etc.) or live birds or poultry products (fresh meat, eggs, bird dung, etc.) without corresponding zoosanitary documentation.
For further information call Mex. tel. 612/122-3311 and 122-2219 in La Paz.

—from a sign at the Guerrero Negro inspection station

Call the Vagabundos del Mar Boat and Travel Club at U.S. tel. 800/474-BAJA (800/474-2252) for competitive rates. Some United States companies extend coverage for a short distance into Mexico, up to about 75 miles south of the border, which doesn't take you very far.

Legal Aid
If an accident results in being held or in incarceration, it is advisable to have Legal Aid accompanying your vehicle insurance. The coverage offered by the Vagabundos del Mar Boat and Travel Club at U.S. tel. 800/474-BAJA (800/474-2252) covers legal assistance, payment of fines and administrative fees, payment of bail bond premium, assistance in filing the police report, payment of attorney fees, and assistance in administrative procedures with a 24-hour claims hotline.

Toll Roads
All of the services below, including insurance, are free once you've paid the fees at each toll booth.

Tijuana to Ensenada
Services along this route include mechanical services for emergency calls to repair vehicles, medical services in Tijuana and Ensenada, clean restrooms, public phones, a free accident insurance policy, and emergency radio communications at 15 stations 1.5 kilometers apart. The toll road insurance covers liability for third parties, final costs, medical costs, and damage to the roadway. It does not cover legal costs and bonds.

Tijuana to Tecate
Services on this route include emergency call boxes approximately every kilometer, tow service to the entrance of the toll road, additional night surveillance, medical service, and ambulance service.

Customs
Mexico
You are allowed to bring in any of the following:

- Personal items, e.g., clothing, footwear, toiletries, all in reasonable quantities according to the trip duration
- Books and magazines
- Medicine for personal use, with medical prescription in case of psychotropic substances
- Used or second-hand sporting equipment
- One portable TV set, one laptop computer, and one portable typewriter
- Up to 20 CDs, records, or cassettes
- A musical instrument
- Fishing equipment, a pair of skis, and two tennis rackets
- Three liters of alcohol or wine, if over 18 years old
- 400 cigarettes or 50 cigars, if over 18 years old
- One movie camera and one regular camera and up to 12 rolls of film

The first $50 worth of dutiable items is free. Campers may have their vehicles searched, but unless a tourist is carrying commercial quantities of marketable goods, furniture, or household appliances, there should be no problem. If asked what you have, the simple answer "things to camp with" will usually suffice.

You may be searched for fruits and vegetables at Guerrero Negro going either way across the Baja Norte–Baja Sur state line, or you may simply be asked what you have. Sometimes they will take things; other times they won't. Lately they have been spraying malathion under all vehicles for a small mandatory fee (about $1) to kill fruit fly eggs and larvae. Baja California Sur is a fruit fly–free zone. The station is located a few hundred yards south of the big steel eagle at the state line. Another such inspection station is north of La Paz at Centenario, but rarely do they require tourists to stop.

United States

Clearing customs is not a particularly pleasant experience upon returning home from an idyllic sojourn in Baja, but informed travelers can ease the strain. Customs officials state that in order to get across the border quickly, you must take an active role. It is your responsibility to be prepared, to be cooperative, not to be offended by their questions, and to have necessary documents ready to be presented.

Your attitude has a lot to do with how quickly or slowly you get across. If you cooperate with the inspector, it speeds things up. Answer questions fully. Don't come with all your purchases wrapped. Have them in the cab with you as you arrive at the gate. Bring a list of everything you have purchased in Mexico with the value of each item. If you will be bringing new dutiable items (cameras, lenses, binoculars, radios, etc.) into Mexico, avoid possibly having to pay duty on them when returning to the United States by taking them to a customs office beforehand. There they will record serial numbers for each item and prepare a "Certificate of Registration for Personal Effects Taken Abroad." Keep these documents with you.

It helps to understand how customs inspectors perceive the people with whom they are dealing. Protecting national sovereignty is their main concern. What we normally consider our constitutional rights were deliberately excluded by the framers of the Constitution for citizens crossing back into the United States. We can be detained legally, strip-searched without probable cause, or examined without the usual need for prior information. The only right we have is to be treated courteously. Approach customs with the attitude that you have rights, and you're starting out on the wrong foot.

It helps to accept that the burden is on us and to realize that the questions are not meant to be personal, demeaning, or degrading. Rather, they are designed to help us get across the border by sorting out what the inspectors need to know.

A lot of people react very negatively to the questions. Beyond certain questions that must be asked, each inspector must determine what to ask you personally in order to get a sense of you and speed up the process. Sometimes the best way to do this is to ask a question deliberately intended to spark a reaction, like "What are you smuggling?" A lot of people smile and laugh. Some peoples' knuckles go white or other parts of the body respond involuntarily. For instance, the carotid artery can jump under stress. We were told of one fellow who crumbled and opened the trunk to show the inspector what he was smuggling.

Consider the process from the viewpoint of the inspectors, who work under very difficult circumstances. An eight-hour shift may run 16 hours. At the San Ysidro–Tijuana port of entry, they average about 100 cars per hour with three people per car, so they talk to 300 people per hour. Of these the usual 10 percent are on the fringes of sanity. Rain, heat, cold, and noxious fumes take their toll. Inspectors move from lane to lane at the primary gates and to the secondary gates or the pedestrian area and are on their feet for most of the day.

Immigration and Naturalization Service (INS) and Customs Service inspectors each staff half of the primary gates. Their purpose is to sort out the arrivals who merit further scrutiny at secondary, but also to keep the primary lanes moving. We were told there's about a 20 percent increase in traffic each year and that inspectors handle upward of 100 million crossings annually at San Ysidro–Tijuana—more people than all but a few nations have.

Customs and INS inspectors receive cross training and do their jobs at the primary gates in the same way. The people at the secondary gates perform specialized work—Customs, INS, or Agriculture.

Despite years of study, the problem of long customs lines has not yet been—and may never be—solved. The weather has more to do with it than anything else. If it is pleasant in San Diego, everyone heads for Tijuana. In spite of how long a line seems, though, the typical crossing is complete in 45 minutes.

Intercepting smuggled goods is the major goal of our border people. Smugglers watch the border constantly to see if inspectors are easing off near the ends of their shifts. They even have nicknames for each inspector.

Smugglers have become very sophisticated, building compartments in drive shafts and otherwise manufacturing cars with invisible joints so inspectors can't tell where things are hidden. They hire and use grandpa and grandma types or 30-year-old clean-cut couples with a child. Since smugglers go to great lengths to blend in, the customs game is to keep a few moves ahead and intercept as many of them as possible. Those of us who make up the 90 percent who are plain old tourists can contribute to the effort by submitting gracefully to the necessary inconveniences.

You can expect to be sent to the secondary gates if you have been in Mexico any length of time. Permitted fruits available in Mexico are bananas, blackberries, blueberries, grapefruit, dates, lemons, limes, pineapples, prickly pears, raspberries, strawberries, and tangerines. All other fruits are prohibited and will be confiscated. This may change, and you can check current available information at www.aphis.usda.com.

Most vegetables are permitted, except sugar cane and sweet potatoes.

Also prohibited are meats (including pork and raw poultry). Be aware that when crossing into the United States at Mexicali, inspectors make periodic checks of whitefish fillets to assure that they are not the protected totuava fish. Unless the meat can be identified by patches of skin, it may be taken for laboratory identification. If it's totuava, you will be hearing from them. If not, you have lost your fish.

Each U.S. citizen is allowed $400 of dutiable items. Canadians are allowed $300 if they have been out of Canada for at least seven days. This allowance may be claimed every 30 days into the United States but only once a year into Canada. Be sure to include on your list all fruits, vegetables, and alcoholic beverages (up to one liter duty-free into the United States or Canada; in some U.S. states additional bottles may be brought in if duty is paid and you are at least 21 years of age), whether purchased in Mexico or brought down with you. At this point the inspector can only assume it all came from Mexico. Before leaving home, obtain the booklet *Know Before You Go* from a U.S. Customs office. Be cautious of endangered species by-products that you may unknowingly be bringing back to the United States. The most common items include turtle products and alligator bags.

Aside from the 24-hour San Ysidro–Tijuana port of entry on U.S. I-5 and Baja Highway 1, there are five other Baja ports of entry:

- Otay Mesa, on the east side of Tijuana near the airport, is usually faster than the San Ysidro–Tijuana port, but it requires too much driving in heavy traffic through Tijuana to suit us. We had to change a traffic-side boat trailer tire on an overpass in Tijuana after sunset (with no place to get off the road) and have had no further desire to use Otay Mesa. It is open from 6 A.M. to 10 P.M.
- Tecate, off Highway 94 and on Baja Highways 2 and 3, is very quick to get through. It is open from 6 A.M. to midnight.
- Mexicali, on Highway 111 and Baja Highway 5, is open 24 hours.
- Mexicali east, about seven miles east of Calexico on Highway 98 and south on Highway 7, and east of Mexicali on Madero Avenue along the border fence, is open 6 A.M. to 10 P.M.
- Algodones, about 47 miles east of Calexico on I-8 and three miles south on Highway 186, and about 19 miles east of Mexicali on Baja Highway 8, is open from 6 A.M. to 8 P.M.

Firearms and Drugs

Save yourself inestimable grief by leaving these seriously illegal items home. Pistols are an absolute no-no. Don't bring boxes of .22 shells for trading stock either. If they are found, it will be assumed that a gun is close at hand, and your vehicle may be demolished in the search. If you are expecting to hunt, be sure you obtain all firearm permits as well as hunting licenses and permits beforehand.

Expect to be stopped several times at military roadblocks checking for firearms or drugs. The soldiers are uniformly polite and usually do not search tourists' vehicles. If they do, one person should accompany the soldier inside. There is a permanent roadblock a few miles south of Maneadero.

Bring prescriptions for all medications that require them at home to satisfy U.S. Customs and for painkillers, tranquilizers, many diet pills, and other controlled substances purchased in Mexico to satisfy Mexican authorities. Have no street drugs or funny cigarettes. A Mexican jail is not a pleasant place to spend your vacation. Once you break the law, you cease to be a tourist, and any assistance that tourists are entitled to disappears.

Vehicle Preparation

Mexico is full of good mechanics who are very inventive in fixing things using what they have to work with. However, they are not into on-board computers, turbochargers, and other

Safety on the Road

Pre-travel Service Items
• Tune-up
• Oil and filter change
• Air filter change
• Gas filter change
• Lubrication
• Check and/or pack wheel bearings
• Inspect all hoses under the hood and replace if unduly soft or brittle
• Inspect all belts and replace if frayed
• Check wiper blades and replace if necessary
• Check shock absorbers and replace if necessary
• Check and clean battery terminals (fluid level and general condition)
• Check front-end alignment
• Check tires for condition and pressure, including spares
• Check turn signals
• Check wheel lug nuts for tightness (periodically recheck in Baja, too)

Spare Parts
• Belts, one for each under the hood
• Air filter, one
• Points and plugs, one set each
• Tire, one mounted on a wheel (many sizes of tires for RVs are not available in Mexico, so play it safe and bring your own)
• Hitch ball, one (if you are pulling a trailer)
• Hoses, one for each under the hood
• Keys, one spare set
• Oil, enough for a change plus extra for an emergency
• Oil filters, two
• Gas filters, two (if you have a gasoline-burning vehicle)
• Diesel filters, two (if you have a diesel-burning vehicle)
    Obtaining spare parts in Mexico for vehicles and boats from the United States has become very difficult. Currently it is necessary to carry them by hand instead of having them shipped. Carriers are not willing to hassle with the required customs duty.

Toolbox
We carry a simple metal toolbox holding:
• 22-piece socket set with 1/4- and 3/8-inch drives in a carrying case, including 6- and 12-inch extensions
• 3/4-inch socket set
• 8- and 12-inch crescent wrenches
• Four-piece SAE flare-nut wrench set
• Nine-piece combination wrench set
• Distributor wrenches
• Monkey wrench

- Pipe wrench
- Oil filter and gas filter wrenches
- Regular pliers
- Vise-grip pliers
- Channel-lock pliers
- Lineman's pliers
- Needle-nose pliers
- Wire cutters
- 18-piece hex key set
- Claw hammer
- Hacksaw
- Keyhole saw
- Battery terminal cleaning tool
- Tape measure
- Half-round file
- Round file
- Half-round wood rasp
- Pry bar
- Two putty knife scrapers
- Wire stripping/crimping tool
- Spark plug tool
- Five blade and four Phillips screwdrivers from small to large sizes
- Brake-adjusting tool
- Drive pins
- Assorted taps
- Cold chisel
- Scissors
- 12-volt test light
- Alligator-clip test leads
- Steel wool
- Spool of fine copper wire
- Duct tape
- Plastic ties

Other Essential Items
- Jack, heavy enough for your vehicle
- Lug wrench
- Flashlights, two, plus extra batteries
- Jumper cables
- Small shovel
- Small ax
- Volt meter
- 110-volt tire-inflating compressor
- WD-40 spray lubricant
- Siphoning hose
- Red flag (as used by waterskiers) to wave off traffic in an emergency

high-tech innovations. The simpler the workings of your vehicle, the better your chances of getting it repaired. The government also provides a safety net for travelers in need in the form of the Green Angels.

These green utility trucks are manned by English-speaking mechanics and cover each section of most paved highways in Baja California. They carry spare gasoline, for which you pay, and a few tools. Most important, they have short-wave radios linked in a network by numerous microwave towers. If they can't get you going, they can call a tow truck to take you to a shop. Tips are appreciated, but seldom offered by tourists. Feel free to help these lifesavers out in return for their assistance.

Of course, prevention is always best. Have your vehicle serviced and checked over thoroughly before leaving home, and stock some basic spare parts that might come in handy if you break down in a remote area.

Driving Safely

Keep firmly in mind that Baja Highway 1 from Tijuana to Cabo San Lucas and all the other paved roads in Baja were built for the trucks and buses that keep the necessities of life flowing. The highways were not designed for tourists accustomed to zipping around on freeways.

Also consider before your trip what you will do if your vehicle stops moving down the highway (for one of innumerable unpredictable reasons) and you have to go for help. Who goes and who stays with the vehicle? This amounts to a major decision fraught with conflicting imperatives.

Aside from the companionship, there is much to be said for traveling with others. On one of our trips on which we towed a boat and trailer behind our camper, the tongue broke, and the boat and trailer had to be left alongside the highway while one of us drove off for a tow truck.

driving along scenic Highway 1

Assuming that the boat would attract the curiosity of passersby and generate a desire to see what it contained, we were convinced that someone had to stay with it. Gloria volunteered, feeling a sense of security because a group of field workers was just across the highway. If they had not been there, we could not have left her alone.

It would have been much simpler if we were traveling with another couple who could have parked alongside the boat while we went off to get help.

Something else to keep in mind is that turn signals are used differently in Mexico. A driver ahead of you will use a turn signal to notify you that it's OK to come ahead and pass. You have to decide if it is safe to do so, but don't count on him turning left. However, if an intersection is coming up, it is wise to wait to see if the driver will turn. Keep this in mind when you use your left turn signal in the usual fashion—or else you may turn into someone who misread you and tried to pass.

If you want to become an old Baja hand, adhere diligently to two simple lifesaving rules:

Rule 1: Don't Drive over 50 Miles per Hour

Baja's roads are narrower than we're used to and don't have shoulders. Trucks and buses drive fast. You are certain to meet one just where the highway is narrowest—where concrete abutments for culverts pinch in on the pavement on each side. This is when you must have precise control of where your right wheels are, even more so if you are towing something. Slowing quickly from 50 miles per hour allows precisely controlled evasive action—safely.

Take it for granted that sooner or later you will enter a curve to meet an oncoming truck or bus taking part of your lane, but you won't be able to pull to the right because a row of boulders is in your way. Instead of flares or reflective markers, the locals use boulders to steer others away from their stalled vehicles—then often leave the rocks in place when they move on. You must be able to stop or slow down enough to let the truck or bus go by.

Rule 2: Don't Drive at Night

The dangerous situations discussed in Rule 1 become impossible to deal with safely at night. Then there are the black cows, horses, and burros that roam on open range and are not visible until you are right on them. They love to feed on the side of the highway where the vegetation grows lush from rainfall sliding off the pavement and, of course, will usually stand right in the middle of the highway to contemplate their next move.

If you are thinking of driving to Cabo in two days from the border, have your affairs in order—it's suicidal.

One of Parkinson's laws of management is that work expands to fill the time available in which to do it. The corollary is that grand vacations are compressed into the limited time available in which to take them. If your Scrooge of a boss will give you only a week off and you have been dying to spend it in Cabo, forget driving—fly, that's what airplanes are for. If you must drive, forget Cabo. Settle for some other destination you can reach comfortably without violating the above rules, like San Felipe, San Quintín, or Bahía de Los Angeles. After a day of driving, take a cool, refreshing shower and kick back. This gives you more time to get into the Baja mind-set and have a stress-free, relaxed stay in mañana land.

Fuel

Gasoline and diesel fuel are readily available from Pemex service stations on the Transpeninsular Highway and in all cities at prices above those in the United States. Pemex stations do not

The Mexican Government's Green Angels assist tourists stranded on the highway.

take credit cards—pay in cash (pesos preferably)—and are usually open 24 hours a day, including Christmas Day.

Gasoline comes in two grades: unleaded Magna Sin rated at 87 octane, and unleaded Premium at 92 octane. Some people feel that these ratings are a few points higher than the U.S. rating system. Diesel is readily available.

The vehicles that we use run on unleaded regular gasoline in the United States and run just fine on Magna Sin. Vehicles that need premium gas in the United States should get by fine with Premium in Baja.

One of the precautions we exercise in Baja is to drive off the top one-quarter of our total two tank supply, which is one-half of one tank. We top off when one tank is half empty. As soon as you pass a Pemex station with less than three-quarters of your fuel supply left, you can count on finding the next two stations temporarily out of gas. We have had to take gas out of our boat to help get stranded optimists on their way after having waited a day or two for a gas truck to arrive. This is where a realistic understanding of the word "mañana" comes in handy—rather than "tomorrow" it really means "not today."

Several games are played at gas stations to extract more money from you than you owe. It pays to have locking gas caps so that no one can start pumping until you are standing there. Otherwise the pump may not be reset to zero. You also have to watch to see that the attendant does not suddenly reset the pump, then restart it without your knowing what you had on it. At least know the maximum number of liters your tank will hold so you can refuse to pay for more than that. Have your own calculator, since many pumps have inoperable total-price indicators. We pay in pesos to avoid varying dollar exchange rates.

Losing a little at these low-stakes games once in a while keeps us on the lookout for new variations. Look at them as contests that enliven the tedium of steady driving. On the other side of the coin, we have had some amazing experiences with attendants returning substantial overpayments when both of us later realized what happened. One fellow had written the calculations on the palm of his hand and referred right to it when we came back for a recount. Fortunately he had not needed to wash his hands in the interim.

Some vehicles run on propane *(gas butano)*, which is sparsely available. On the Transpeninsular Highway, there are plants only in Ensenada, Colonia Vicente Guerrero, Guerrero Negro, Santa Rosalía, Ciudad Constitución, La Paz, and Cabo San Lucas. Propane is provided for household use rather than vehicles. Although it can be obtained for vehicles, doing so is difficult.

Ferries

There is ferry service from Baja to the mainland between Santa Rosalía and Guaymas, La Paz and Topolobampo (Los Mochis), and La Paz and Mazatlán for passengers and vehicles. Fares and departure times are subject to change without notice. Arrival times depend upon the weather. If you are towing something, bring it with you when obtaining your ticket so overall length can be determined.

Departures from Santa Rosalía are at 11 P.M. Tuesday and Friday, arriving in Guaymas about nine hours later. Departures from Guaymas are 8 A.M. Tuesday and Friday. The Santa Rosalía terminal is on the pier in the middle of town on Highway 1.

The ferry office in La Paz is at Cinco de Mayo and Guillermo Prieto. The departure and arrival terminal is north of town at Pichilingue. Departures from La Paz for Topolobampo are at 11 A.M. daily except Sunday, arriving about eight hours later. Departures from Topolobampo are at 10 P.M. daily, arriving about 10 hours later.

Departures from La Paz to Mazatlán are at 3 P.M. daily, arriving about 18 hours later. The reverse trip is at 3 P.M. daily, arriving about 18 hours later. Fares increase periodically.

A "salon" has numbered seats. "Tourist" fare is for a stateroom with two to four berths, with a washstand inside and bathrooms and toilets outside. "Cabin" fare is for a stateroom with two berths with complete bathroom facilities inside. A "special cabin" is a suite with a living room, a complete bathroom, bedrooms, and a closet.

Baja Ferry Rates

Routes and rates subject to change

Class	Guaymas–Santa Rosalia	Topolobampo–La Paz	Mazatlán–La Paz
Salon	$46	$36	$46
Tourist	$104	$81	$104
Cabin	$127	$104	$127
Special cabin	$150	$127	$150
Autos to 16.5 ft.	$220	$220	$355
Autos to 21.5 ft.	$283	$283	$460
Auto/trailer to 29.7 ft.	$645	$389	$645
Auto/trailer to 56.1 ft.	$1,196	$730	$1,196
Bus/motor home	$605	$460	$605
Motorcycle	$60	$48	$60

Information and reservations can be obtained at a central source in Mazatlán by calling SE-MATUR at their toll-free number, 800/696-9600, from inside Mexico, or at these departure points:
- Muelle Fiscal, Apartado Postal 72, Santa Rosalía, Baja California Sur, Mexico, Mex. tel. 615/152-0013 or 0014.
- Guillermo Prieto y Cinco de Mayo, La Paz, Baja California Sur, Mexico, Mex. tel. 612/125-2366 or 2346; Pichilingue Terminal Mex. tel. 615/122-5005 or 5213, fax 615/125-5717.
- Muelle Fiscal, Guaymas, Sonora, Mexico, Mex. tel. 622/222-2324 or fax 3393.
- Muelle Fiscal, Topolobampo, Sinaloa, Mexico, Mex. tel. 668/862-0141 or fax 0035.
- Terminal Transbordadores, Mazatlán, Sinaloa, Mexico, Mex. tel. 669/981-7021 or fax 7023.

On-board services include an information and passenger assistance office; a cafeteria; a kiosk selling magazines, film, pharmacy items, and gifts; free medical service (medications must be paid for); projection of video films; a cellular telephone; toilets; and lockers.

Additional information can be obtained at www.ferrysematur.com.mx. A reservation form is also provided on this website, but tourists report that it is not effective and also that reservations made by phone may not be either. It is best to present yourself to the appropriate office a couple of days ahead of time and make your reservations in person. If you are taking a vehicle to the mainland, review the preceding section on Vehicle Permits.

A fast trimaran also goes between La Paz and Topolobampo for passengers only. It goes every day except Wednesdays. Departure time from La Paz is 8:30 A.M., arriving in Topolobampo at 12:30 P.M. Departure time from Topolobampo to La Paz is 3:00 P.M. arriving at 7:30 P.M. Tourist Class costs $45 per person one-way and includes air-conditioning, comfortable seating salon style, TV, and video. Tourist Class Plus costs $55 per person one-way and includes air-conditioning, larger seating, table, refrigerator, TV, and video. This is a good way for Baja campers to take a bus to Los Mochis from Topolobampo and the train to the Copper Canyon for an interesting side trip, while leaving the RV in La Paz.

Money

Dollars are universally accepted, but we like to have sufficient pesos to use at gas stations and other businesses with prices in pesos to avoid losing on the exchange. We stop in San Ysidro on the United States side of the border to pick up a few hundred dollars' worth at an exchange house named "Baja Mex" on Border Village Road at East San Ysidro Boulevard, which doesn't charge a fee or commission. Once in Baja we rely on obtaining more at ATM machines. Many banks do not take traveler's checks due to extensive fraud. Many businesses do take traveler's checks, however.

Telephones

There are several ways to make long distance phone calls from Baja, either to another country or within Mexico. The simplest and cheapest method is to purchase a phone card at home and use it in Mexico. The next best is to purchase a TELNOR or TELMEX telephone card from any of numerous shops throughout Baja for 25, 35, 50, or 100 pesos. These are inserted in any of a multitude of pay phones on sidewalks labeled *Ladatel–Red de Telefonia Publica* (look for the card slot in the upper left-hand corner). Insert the card, dial 001, the area code, then the number, and start talking. When 20 seconds are left on the card, a countdown appears in the readout window.

Unfortunately many shops displaying *Larga Distancia* signs no longer offer the operator assistance that used to be the cheapest way to call, but now entice you to use one of the privately owned blue or black phones mentioned below. These should be avoided at all costs.

Privately owned blue or black phones with signs offering calls to be paid for by international credit cards are found mounted on walls everywhere. You simply pick them up and dial the operator to place your call. The charge is exorbitant, as you might expect, since the establishment gets a big cut from the private company providing the service.

You can also sign up for Mexican cellular service and use your cellular phone—but this is also a very expensive way to go.

If your pocketbook can stand it, a satellite phone allows you to call from anywhere.

Email

Internet cafés can be found in all cities. Since they are small businesses and often come and go, just ask the management of the campground where you are staying where the nearest one is.

PocketMail is a mobile email service that enables you to send and receive email and send faxes from virtually any telephone world-wide, and a computer is not required. Just compose your messages on the PocketMail device, dial the international access number, hold the device up to the telephone, and send and receive your email in seconds. It works with *Ladatel* phones, *Larga Distancia* services, private phones, or cell phones. Used in conjunction with prepaid phone cards from home, or a *Ladatel* phone card, it is an efficient and fairly inexpensive way to keep in touch with family and friends while in Mexico.

The new PocketMail devices have a 6,000-character/message capacity and are PC compatible; you can receive 60,000 character messages by "splitting" them.

Time Zones

Both Baja Norte and Baja Sur now observe daylight saving time. Baja Norte is in the Pacific time zone, and Baja Sur is in the mountain time zone.

Tourists have been known to miss a whale-watching reservation in Guerrero Negro by failing to set their clocks ahead an hour when crossing the state line.

© FRED JONES

Chapter 1

Northwest Baja Norte

Pacific
Ocean

Río San Antonio

MEX 3

8
33

Cabo Colonet

Colonet

Valle de
Trinidad

MEX 1

San Telmo de Abajo

Río San Rafael

San
Telmo

34

Camalu

Río San Telmo

PARQUE
NACIONAL
SIERRA SAN
PEDRO
MÁRTIR

42

43

9

35 Colonia Vicente
Guerrero

Isla
San
Martín

Laguna
Figueroa

See "Northeast Baja Norte" pages 76-77

Valle de San Quintín

36
37
38-39

Lazaro
Cardenas

Cabo
San
Quintín

N

40

10

Río Santa María

41

0   10 mi

0   10 km

© AVALON TRAVEL PUBLISHING, INC.

Punta
Baja

See
"Central Peninsula"
pages 102-104

NORTHWEST
BAJA NORTE

Northwest Baja Norte

The Pacific coast from the border to where Highway 1 turns inland near El Rosario is very popular with tourists because of its proximity to the United States. It is easy to throw some things in a car or rig on the spur of the moment and head south for a few days of relaxation and decompression from the hustle and bustle of life in Southern California.

People suffering from summer heat in inland areas can hole up on a cool southern beach and dunk themselves in the nippy Pacific waters, still carrying overtones of the frigid Arctic via the Japanese current. Accordingly, summer is the high season.

Fishing can be very good in the surf and even better offshore. Pismo clams lurk beneath the sand at low tide, and the waters draw surfers and scuba divers. Travelers with agile vehicles can make forays inland to hot springs, mountain national parks, an observatory, and other hideaways.

Those who prefer the urban scene can knock about in glitzy Tijuana and the somewhat more sedate Ensenada. Golfers will find ample opportunities for teeing off. In short, there is something for everyone in northwest Baja Norte.

Getting Through Tijuana

The first thing you have to do is wend your way through Tijuana without getting off course. As you approach the border from the north, get in the second lane from the right (not the far right lane, which is for Customs Declarations). Once you're through the border gate into Mexico and cleared out of secondary inspection, stay in the lane going up the overpass ahead beneath the sign indicating "Highway 1D" and "Rosarito, Ensenada, Scenic Road." The next signs over that lane say the same thing as the road swings left in a circle to deposit you along the south side of the border fence. Don't change lanes until you are along the fence.

Drive carefully and don't let the local speeders rush you along. Stay to the right as you climb

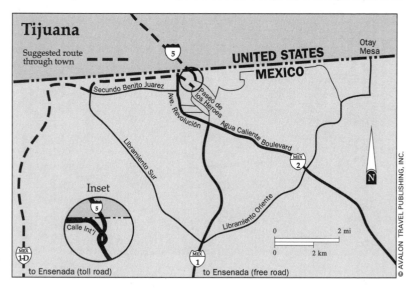

a big hill. After the road swings left and drops down into an arroyo, exit to the right, following the sign to Rosarito-Ensenada. You will come onto a wider thoroughfare heading west up a steep grade. If you are towing anything, maintain your momentum. Keep following signs to Rosarito-Ensenada. A left turn over the last hill puts you onto the *cuota* (toll) road. Current tolls as of the time of writing at each of the three toll booths are 22 pesos for a passenger car and 43 pesos for all other vehicles.

Rosarito–La Misión Area
(campgrounds 1–9)

Rosarito is almost a suburb of Tijuana, but not quite, with less than 10 miles between them. For tourists it offers the first beach-town environment south of the border and thus is very popular.

Developers are building up this stretch of coast with hotels and condominiums. Still you'll find quite a cluster of RV parks in and around Rosarito. Several in town have been around for many years and are mostly full of permanently dug-in trailers that show the debilitating effects of sitting for years in a salt-air environment. If you favor this area, look over your options before settling in to be sure you have found the spot that suits you best. The high season is summer.

Sporting Events

Bullfighting is a traditional Mexican spectacle. Every summer Sunday from May to September, a *corrida de toros* is held in one or the other of Tijuana's two bullrings: the old Plaza de Toros downtown on Agua Caliente Boulevard or the newer ring by the beach against the border. Tickets can be obtained at the ring or from the ticket office downtown. Prices depend on whether you want to sit in the afternoon sun *(sol)* or shade *(sombra)* and how far you are from ringside. *Sombra* is definitely more comfortable.

Like bullfighting, the game of **jai alai** is never dull. The action can be riveting, as the hard little ball flies around almost faster than the eye can see. The skill and agility of the players are astounding. You can bet on each match, and the program tells you about every player. In the evening when you're tired of shopping on Avenida Revolución, simply walk up the street to Calle 7, enter the palatial *fronton* (jai alai arena), sit down, and watch the athletes with the long basket on one hand do their work.

Horse and dog racing fans can head to the Agua Caliente Racetrack. It's been around seemingly forever, and every map shows it as a landmark. Just go east of downtown on Agua Caliente Boulevard. Greyhounds race during the week, then horses take to the track on weekends.

Shopping

Shopping in Tijuana is a major event and can be both exciting and rewarding. Tijuana is no place to shop for day-to-day necessities, though. For that, head to Rosarito.

The center of commerce in Tijuana for traditional Mexican wares is Avenida Revolución from Calle 1 to Calle 9, plus all the side streets and alleys that branch off. There are many, many shops offering everything you can imagine. Storekeepers are fairly aggressive about herding potential customers into their establishments. That's fine—go on in and look around and ask about prices for any items that appeal to you. Feel the storekeeper out on what price he might accept, then go on your way and start comparing prices at other shops. You'll find identical items all along the street and will gradually get an idea of what price is fair to both of you. Don't be afraid to haggle. Haggling is part of the enjoyment for seller and buyer alike. Keep a smile on your face and talk softly. Develop a rapport, taking care to admire the workmanship and quality of the goods. Politely make an offer. If you bid too low, it may be considered an insult. Developing a feel for the "real" price is important.

Tijuana is a manufacturing center for many goods, including those fashioned from leather, onyx, wood, and metal. Accordingly you can buy these items cheaper here than in other cities because there are no freight costs to factor in. We once purchased some little onyx carvings near El Mármol, nearly 300 miles south of Tijuana. Since the onyx came from there, we thought it was the best place to purchase the manufactured product. Then the lady told us they would send the uncarved blocks to Tijuana and have the finished items shipped back. We would have fared better on Avenida Revolución.

Be wary of leather goods made from unfamiliar animal skins. If United States Customs officers suspect they are from endangered species, they might relieve you of the items for closer inspection, and you may never see them again.

A more modern shopping area is Plaza Río Tijuana, the site of large department stores and upscale shops. We have made several pre-Christmas forays here armed with shopping lists for everyone in the family and always left knowing we saved a bundle. Many groups of people come across the border from the United States for a fun day of shopping here.

Be careful of the flea markets you'll encounter around Tijuana. Customs officials have found that many things sold there, particularly electronic items such as stereos and TVs, were heisted in the United States. Obtain receipts to prove that you did not purchase items at one of the flea markets that is "hot" at the moment.

Rosarito has some nice shops, particularly in the arcade at the Rosarito Beach Hotel. The free road south of Rosarito is lined with pottery shops and a few small pottery factories. Check out the prices in the factories—they're generally lower, as this is where the shops buy their products. We often stop on the way home from a Baja trip to add to our collection of Mexican pottery.

Sightseeing

The Tijuana Cultural Center in the Zona Río at Paseo de los Héroes and Avenida Independencia houses a museum, an Omnimax theater with a 180-degree wraparound screen on which special films are shown, and a performing arts theater that features changing performances. There is also a shopping arcade. The cost of admission to the theater depends on the performance. The Cultural Center is open from Monday to Friday from 11 A.M. to 7 P.M. and on weekends from 11 A.M. to 8 P.M. If you get a chance to see "Los Voladores de Papantla," don't miss their act. These men climb a tall pole, attach themselves to long ropes, then swing down to the ground in a breathtaking spiral.

Covering a city block, Mexitlan on Calle 2 and Avenida Ocampo in Tijuana displays more than 150 scale models of Mexico's pyramids, colonial churches, and modern buildings. There are also shows featuring music and dances from the country's various regions. After dark, hidden lights dramatically illuminate the model buildings. Mexitlan is open daily except Tuesday, from 10 A.M. to 8 P.M. and in summer from 10 A.M. to 10 P.M. Hours are extended on holidays and weekends.

Dining

If you have ever enjoyed a Caesar salad, you might want to stop in at Caesar's Hotel on Avenida Revolución and Calle 4 to have another. This is supposedly where it was invented.

There are lots, and we mean lots, of restaurants in Tijuana, so many that we won't even try to sort them all out here. However, we do highly recommend one that we have considered special for decades—the Coronet on Calle 7 off Avenida Revolución. The quail entrée has brought us back again and again.

The village of Puerto Nuevo, south of Rosarito, specializes in lobster. If you're in town for lunch or dinner, try one of the smaller restaurants where the atmosphere is more homey and the prices a bit lower. We like Nachos on Chinchorro, located on the second street on the left as you enter town.

Ensenada Area
(campgrounds 10–31)

Ensenada is not quite a border town, but since it's only 68 miles south of the United States via the fast toll road, many people from Southern California flock to the area for weekend visits. Another popular route, only four miles longer, is south from Tecate on Highway 3. Though this option takes a half hour more, it's a very pretty drive through mountains and valleys lush with vineyards, orchards, and other agricultural communities. An exceptional benefit of reentering the United States through Tecate instead of Tijuana is much lighter traffic and ease in clearing customs. Be sure to arrive before midnight, as the border crossing is closed from midnight to 6 A.M.

Fishing

Fishing can be good out of Ensenada off Islas de Todos Santos and Punta Banda for albacore, barracuda, bonita, mackerel, kelp bass, lingcod, and other rockfish. Several fishing fleets operate out of the sportfishing dock just east of the fish market. Access and parking is very tight, as you have to thread your way around and between buildings. As you come into Ensenada, go through the first two lights and turn at the first street to the right (the Hotel Santo Tomás is across the street). Go a very short block toward the fish market and take the first left turn in front of the fish market. Continue and take the first right turn and then head left to the sportfishing fleet offices on the waterfront. Passenger cars and pickups do much better than motor homes on this route. Look it over before committing yourself. It may be wise to take a

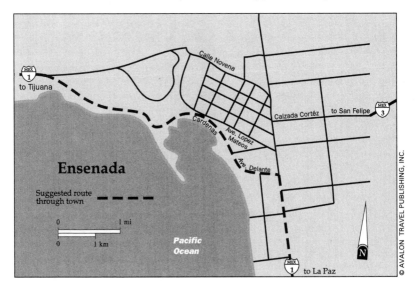

cab from wherever you are staying. It is best to purchase tickets at the offices, for you can be cheated on the street.

Smaller boats can be engaged at the docks or at Punta Banda from independent sportfishing operators or *panga* fishermen who sometimes rent their boats and hire themselves out as guides. Punta Banda is about 25 miles from Ensenada and takes about one hour to reach by car.

Shopping

Ensenada is one of the best places to shop in Baja, and Avenida Lopez Mateos is the center of the action. Just strolling down Lopez Mateos and window-shopping is a delight. Bargaining is enjoyed by both shoppers and shopkeepers, provided the haggling is kept light with a tinge of humor and respect for both the merchandise and the vendor. Don't be shy about bargaining—you can be certain there is no way you will purchase an article for less than bottom price. One shop we stop at, Galeria Mexicana, on the left before the entrance to the Estero Beach Resort and RV Park (see listing in this chapter), always has a variety of unique items from all over Mexico.

The Ensenada fish market is an interesting place to shop, dine, or just look. The displays of fish are colorful and attractive, and food stalls serve up wonderful fish products. We particularly enjoy the deep-fried *vieja*. The promenade along the waterfront in front of the fish market is pleasant for strolling and feeding the sea lions that hang out there. Fish for them can be purchased there. Follow directions to the sportfishing dock listed above.

Sightseeing

There is much to see and do in Ensenada. Take a tour of Mexico's oldest winery, Bodegas Santo Tomás, at 666 Avenida Miramar between Calle 6 and Calle 7 in Ensenada. Wine tasting and a tour costs $2. Tours are given at 11 A.M., 1 P.M., and 3 P.M. every day.

Be sure to drive out to Punta Banda and see La Bufadora (the Blowhole) spout its geyser of seawater up the cliff face.

Dining

One of our favorite dining spots is El Rey Sol, at 1000 Avenida Lopez Mateos, a famous French restaurant in business since 1947. The original owner came here from Santa Rosalia when the French-operated copper mines there folded up. It is open from 10 A.M. to 10 P.M. Haliotis, at 179 Avenida Delante (also known as Avenida Sangines), is a good choice for seafood.

Another good restaurant is KAIA, on Avenida Moctezuma between Calle 4 and Calle 5. It specializes in Basque cuisine, and the paella is among the finest around.

San Quintín Area
(campgrounds 33–41)

This portion of northwest Baja Norte's Pacific coast, while a bit farther south, is still within easy reach of Southern California. It is a popular destination for long weekends and extended vacations. Many people have established residences here for temporary use. For those traveling to or from southern parts of the peninsula, it also makes a convenient overnight stopping point before or after a day spent shopping in Ensenada.

Fishing

This is the preeminent activity that draws tourists to the area. Isla San Martín, Roca Ben, and other high spots in the ocean off the mouth of Bahía San Quintín offer good enough fishing to attract long-range boats from San Diego, even though it is a time-consuming and expensive boat ride. Now that anglers can get out there easily in their own boats using the concrete launch ramps at the Old Mill RV Park (see listing in this chapter)—or on a charter boat from Pedro's Pangas, Tiburon Pangas or Don Eddie's Landing next door, El Capitan Sportfishing, or Cielito Lindo Sportfishing at Cielito Lindo Motel and RV Park (see listing in this chapter)—they can enjoy the same great fishing at a fraction of the cost and have the satisfaction of doing it on their own. Offshore there are yellowtail, tuna, and bonita; on the high spots, ample lingcod and rockcod can be found. Inshore waters behind the surf harbor sand bass, corvina, halibut, perch, and other species that can also be taken in the surf from shore. In the bay there are white sea bass, halibut, and others. Bahía San Quintín also has large blue crabs, the same critters that are considered a delicacy on the East Coast of the United States. Large Pismo clams inhabit the beaches.

To reserve a spot with Pedro's Pangas, call U.S. tel. 562/599-5106 or U.S. tel. 888/568-2252 in the United States; Tiburon's Pangas, call Mex. tel. 616/170-0821; Don Eddie's Landing, call Mex. tel. 616/162-3143, 2722, or 1244; and El Capitan Sportfishing, Mex. tel. 616/162-1716. Cielito Lindo Sportfishing can be reached by email at Book4fish@aol.com.

Boating

Keeping in the channel to the mouth of the bay requires local knowledge. Guides move or remove markers so as to protect their income. Inexperienced boaters have been known to spend the weekend stuck on mudflats. For cheap insurance hire a guide to take you out if you cannot contrive to follow one of the commercial boats in the morning.

Bird-Watching

Bahía San Quintín is one of Baja's prime estuaries for wintering migratory waterfowl. A growing number of dedicated bird-watchers are focusing their attention here to ensure the future health of the estuarine system. Fish populations use the bay for breeding, as do many birds, and other birds make this their winter grounds during their migrations.

Hunting

Waterfowl hunters find brant goose hunting to be very good in the marshes at the north end of Bahía San Quintín in winter. Quail hunting on the surrounding ranches can be very good, too.

Surfing

Surfers favor the beaches on the Pacific Ocean to the west, south to the mouth of Bahía San Quintín, and along Bahía Santa María.

Off-Roading

Off-roaders find great enjoyment following wheel tracks on the peninsula between Bahía San Quintín and the Pacific Ocean. The volcanic cones that spread their lava and ash across this rugged terrain are prominent landmarks. There is much to see—and many flat tires to fix—when exploring here. Pristine campsites suitable for tent campers, vans, or small truck campers can be found on the remote Pacific shores, though it is best to camp in groups rather than singly.

Sightseeing

One side trip is to the ruins of Misión Santo Domingo de la Frontera. The Dominicans established the original mission in 1775 at a site two miles downstream from where the ruins now stand. It was moved in 1798 to obtain a more constant water supply. Aside from the usual cultivation of fruits, beans, and grains, it generated additional income through the sale of salt from San Quintín and sea otter pelts to Russian and United States traders. Epidemics struck down the native population eventually, and the mission was abandoned in 1839. Partial adobe brick walls from about five buildings are all that remain.

To get there, drive north from Colonia Vicente Guerrero on Highway 1 for about 1.5 miles. Take the signed turnoff and continue 2.5 miles east. The trip involves several crossings of Río Santo Domingo, a mere trickle, adding an adventurous note to the journey.

For a longer junket, try the Meling Ranch, about 31 miles east of Highway 1 through San Telmo. This historic, operating cattle ranch, originally known as Rancho San José, has developed facilities for tourists, including a pool. Pack trips on horses and mules can be arranged into the vast reaches of the Sierra San Pedro Mártir—a trip we have made. The ranch was founded in 1910 by Harry and Ella Johnson, only to be destroyed in 1911 during the Mexican Revolution and then rebuilt. Gold from placer deposits at Socorro was an important source of income. One of the Johnson daughters, Alberta, married Salve Meling, and the couple acquired the ranch in 1919.

The dusty dirt access road turns off Highway 1 about 6.5 miles south of Colonet, or eight miles north of Camalu. Heavy vehicles should not be taken, as there are steep grades. We drove up once with our 20-foot Born Free camper, which has its own axle behind the truck to support its rear end. One of the ladies at the Meling Ranch looked at us in wonder and asked, "You drove that up here?" We didn't know how to respond. Another 25 miles over steeper grades gets you to the National Observatory high in the pine forest of the Parque Nacional Sierra San Pedro Mártir. We wisely decided not to tackle that with our heavy rig. The ranch can put you up for the night in a room. They serve great meals.

Mountain Area
(campgrounds 32, 42–43)

The northern mountains of Baja Norte have several campgrounds that offer cool refuge from the summer heat, including two national parks in which camping is allowed at undeveloped sites. The northernmost park, Parque Nacional Constitución de 1857 (see listing in this chapter), covers 28,000 acres in the Sierra de Juárez and features conifer forests and a lake, Laguna Hanson. The other is Parque Nacional Sierra San Pedro Mártir (see listing in this chapter), covering 160,000 acres. Its main features are conifer forests, trout streams, the highest peak in Baja—El Picacho del Diablo, at 10,154 feet in elevation—and the National Observatory. Los Manzanos Campground (see listing in this chapter) is just outside the western border of this park.

Campgrounds

■ ROSARITO CORA RV PARK
🛏️ 🚐 ⛺

In San Antonio

Northwest Baja Norte map, page 44

You might have guessed that the first campground you would encounter while heading south on Highway 1 is a KOA. Though it is not up to KOA's usual standards, it is comfortable and attractive. There are lots of small trees, and the site slopes to the west so that each space has a distant ocean view. When asked what people do here, the manager said the permanents do nothing and most overnighters arrive late in the evening to stay over before crossing the border the next day. There are many things to keep you occupied, however, if you are inclined to be active. Unfortunately Tijuana is difficult to drive around, due to hectic traffic, unless you know where you are going. If you are towing anything, it isn't worth the aggravation. For RVers, the best way to do Tijuana is from one of the parks in San Ysidro or Chula Vista, California. You can get to the border by taxi or the Tijuana Trolley, which runs frequently from San Diego. Walk across the border, then catch a cab. Summer is the time to visit, as winter is chilly. For things to do in Tijuana and the surrounding area, see the Rosarito–La Misión Area, earlier in this chapter.

Campsites, facilities: There are 40 campsites with water and electricity, but no sewer hookups. Flush toilets, hot showers, laundry facilities, a dump station, and a small store are on the premises. Don't drink the well water, which is mineralized. The park is secured with a night watchman from 9 P.M. to 6 A.M. Tent campers are welcome. Obtain limited supplies here and go to Rosarito for the rest.

Reservations, fees: Reservations are accepted. Fees are high—$18 per night. Long-term rates are $80 per week and $185 per month.

Directions: Take the San Antonio exit off Highway 1D (the toll road) about 7.5 miles south of the Tijuana tollgate. Cross over the toll road to the east and drive up a cobblestone driveway to the hillside site.

Contact: Rosarito Cora RV Park, P.O. Box 430513, San Ysidro, CA 92143.

■ COCO LOCO TRAILER PARK
🌊 🛏️ 🚐

In Rosarito

Northwest Baja Norte map, page 44

The park is clean, and the location—right on Playa Rosarito—is choice. But the price tag is high, especially given the lack of facilities. Summer is the time to visit, as winter is chilly. For things to do here, see the Rosarito–La Misión Area, earlier in this chapter.

Campsites, facilities: There are nine campsites with full hookups and concrete pads. No facilities are available, not even toilets or showers. Don't drink the water. The park is secured with a gated wall, and the manager lives on the premises. Tent campers are not welcome. Obtain supplies in Rosarito.

Reservations, fees: All sites are first come, first served. The fee is very high—$25 per night.

Directions: Turn west off the main street of Rosarito at Quinta Plaza, which is one-quarter mile north of the big orange building, and head to the beach. A prominent sign at the corner says "Restaurant Bar La Hacienda de Villa." Look for the trailer park sign after driving one block.

Contact: Drive up and knock on the door.

❸ CHUY'S TRAILER PARK
🏊 🐕 🚐

In Rosarito

Northwest Baja Norte map, page 44

This trailer park is crowded, and space is limited for maneuvering a rig. Summer is the time to visit, as winter is chilly. For things to do here, see the Rosarito–La Misión Area, earlier in this chapter.

Campsites, facilities: There are 26 campsites with full hookups and concrete pads. Flush toilets, hot showers, and a restaurant are on the property. Don't drink the water. A guard provides security at night. Obtain supplies in Rosarito.

Reservations, fees: Reservations are accepted. The fee is high—about $20 per night, varying according to the season.

Directions: Turn west off the main street of Rosarito at Thrifty's, which is 100 yards north of the big orange building, and head to the beach.

Contact: Chuy's Trailer Park, Costa Azul 75, Rosarito, Baja California, Mexico. There is no phone.

❹ PLAYA ENCANTADA NO. 2
🏊 🐕 🚐 ⛺

South of Rosarito

Northwest Baja Norte map, page 44

Park on level land on a bluff above the very nice little beach nestled between two points of land. You can lie back and enjoy the ocean just below, but you had better come fully prepared for primitive camping as the facilities are limited. Summer is the time to visit, as winter is chilly. For things to do here, see the Rosarito–La Misión Area, earlier in this chapter.

Campsites, facilities: Pit toilets are provided, but there are no other facilities. No water is available. Security is provided by a resident manager. Tent campers are welcome. Obtain supplies in Rosarito.

Reservations, fees: Camping is first come, first served. The fee is moderate—$8 per night.

Directions: The beach is at Km 30 on Highway 1 (the free road), about one mile south of Rosarito.

Contact: Drive in and talk to the owner.

❺ POPOTLA TRAILER PARK
🏊 🐕 🚐

South of Rosarito

Northwest Baja Norte map, page 44

Though primarily a residential facility, this trailer park does have some spaces for overnighters in a separate area. Campsites are near the ocean with a little beach, which creates a pleasant setting. Summer is the time to visit, as winter is chilly. For things to do here, see the Rosarito–La Misión Area, earlier in this chapter.

Campsites, facilities: There are 33 campsites with full hookups and concrete pads. Clean, tiled restrooms with flush toilets and hot showers, a pool, and a restaurant are on site. Don't drink the water. The park is secured with a guarded gate. Obtain supplies in Rosarito.

Reservations, fees: Reservations are accepted. Fees are high—$15 per night. Long-term rates are $84 per week and $300 per month.

Directions: The park is at Km 33 on Highway 1 (the free road), about three miles south of Rosarito.

Contact: Popotla Trailer Park, Kilometro 33 Carretara Ensenada, Rosarito, Baja California, Mexico. There is no phone.

❻ TECATE KOA ON RANCHO OJAI
🚶 🚵 🐕 🪑 🚐 ⛺

East of Tecate on Highway 2

Northwest Baja Norte map, page 44

In years past Rancho Ojai was a working cattle and horse ranch, but it has now been converted to a campground. Some beautiful hiking and nature trails weave throughout the property. Nearby is a nine-hole golf course at the Rancho Tecate Country Club and Resort. A greater distance away are the Valle de Guadalupe wineries, Ensenada, Tijuana, and the beaches in between. Summer is the time to come to escape the heat at lower elevations. It is cold in winter. For things to do in Tijuana and the surrounding area, see the Rosarito–La Misión Area, earlier in this chapter.

Campsites, facilities: The 40 full-hookup RV campsites, 15 of which are pull-throughs, are interspersed with some small trees and are near huge, old oaks. There also are 15 tent campsites under oaks and a large overflow area without hookups. Facilities include tiled restrooms with flush toilets and hot showers, a dump station, central barbecues, tables, a heated pool, laundry facilities, a store, a restaurant, a clubhouse, volleyball, basketball, horseshoe pits, a playground, miniature golf, hay rides, bicycle rentals, horse rentals, ranch animals for viewing and petting, and horseback riding and hiking trails. There are 14 camper cabins and cottages available for rent, along with a camper kitchen. The water is good to drink. Security is provided by a resident caretaker, with a fence and gate that's closed at night. Obtain supplies in Tecate.

Reservations, fees: Reservations are accepted. Fees are high—$17 per night, $100 per week, and $300 per month for RVs; $12 per night, $60 per week, and $200 per month for tents.

Directions: From Tecate drive 13 miles east on Highway 2 to the camp on the north side of the road.

Contact: Tecate KOA, P.O. Box 280, Tecate, CA 91980, Mex. tel. 665/655-3014, fax 665/655-3015, email: Rojai@telnor.net, website: www.tecatekoa.com.

7 ALISITOS TRAILER PARK

In La Misión

Northwest Baja Norte map, page 44

This is primitive camping on a flat area above a nice beach. The ocean is right below, creating a pleasant ambience. Summer is the time to visit, as winter is chilly. For things to do in the Rosarito area, see the Rosarito–La Misión Area, earlier in this chapter.

Campsites, facilities: Pit toilets are provided, but there are no other facilities. No water is available. The manager lives on the premises, so security is good. Tent campers are welcome. Obtain supplies in Rosarito.

Reservations, fees: Camping is first come, first served. The fee is very low—$3.50 per night.

Directions: The park is at Km 59 on Highway 1 (the free road), just north of the Hotel La Misión.

Contact: Drive in and talk to the manager.

8 MAL PASO TRAILER PARK

South of La Misión

Northwest Baja Norte map, page 44

This is one of the few places where you can camp right on the beach—and a marvelous beach it is. They have hauled in soil on top of the sand to allow for driving out to the high-tide line. The beach extends a short distance north and a long, long way south. We spent a very enjoyable night here. Summer is the time to visit, as winter is chilly. For things to do in the La Misión area, see the Rosarito–La Misión Area, earlier in this chapter.

Campsites, facilities: Facilities include mediocre flush toilets and cold showers. Don't drink the water. The owners live at the entrance of the compound, so security is good. It is ideal for tent camping. Obtain supplies in Rosarito.

Reservations, fees: Camping is first come, first served. The fee is low—$4 per night.

Directions: From La Misión drive 2.5 miles south on Highway 1D (the toll road). Cross the big creek bottom and the low ridge, then look for palms, trailers, and cabins to the right of a pedestrian overpass. Slow down and turn onto a dirt road into the RV park at Km 71, just before the overpass.

Contact: Drive in and talk to the owner.

9 BAJA SEASONS VILLAS AND RVS

South of La Misión
Northwest Baja Norte map, page 44
Here is a first-class resort with all the amenities and a prime location on a long, long beautiful beach. We spent one night here just to experience the posh way of camping. Summer is the time to visit, as winter is chilly. For things to do in the La Misión area, see the Rosarito–La Misión Area, earlier in this chapter.

Campsites, facilities: There are 137 campsites with concrete pads and full hookups, including satellite TV. Facilities include clean, tiled restrooms with flush toilets and hot showers, steam rooms and saunas, laundry facilities, a pool and spa, a restaurant and bar, a store, a clubhouse, a recreation room, a game room, a reading room, two night-lighted tennis courts, a volleyball court, a horseshoe pit, horses to rent, a putting green, and miniature golf. Also available are RV storage, safe-deposit boxes, and transportation to Ensenada. The well water is brackish, but you can get purified water in the restaurant. There is a fence around the park, a guarded gate, and 24-hour security inside. Tents are prohibited. Obtain supplies at the park store.

Reservations, fees: Reservations are accepted. Fees are very high—oceanfront sites are $30 per night, $165 per week, and $545 per month in winter; $35 per night, $231 per week, and $775 per month in summer. Sites inside the park are $24 per night, $132 per week, and $330 per month in winter; $30 per night, $198 per week, and $545 per month in summer. Holiday rates are higher.

Directions: From La Misión drive about three miles south on Highway 1D (the toll road). You can't miss the park to your right on a long unobstructed stretch of highway at Km 72.

Contact: Baja Seasons Villas and RVs, 4492 Camino de La Plaza, Suite TIJ-1031, San Diego, CA 92173, U.S. tel. 800/754-4190, fax 619/422-5953.

10 PLAYA SALDAMANDO

North of Ensenada
Northwest Baja Norte map, page 44
Surfers, scuba divers, kayakers, hikers, and anglers frequent this beach. There is a rather sharp turn off the toll road onto the dirt road, which must be taken slowly. The dirt road descends the precipitous slope of the mountainside with switchbacks. Small motor homes can make it, but trailers and larger motor homes are not recommended. Fireworks (except on Fourth of July and New Year's Eve), motorcycles, three-wheelers, dune buggies, quads, nude bathing, and drugs are prohibited. Summer is the time to visit, as winter is chilly. For things to do here, see the Ensenada Area, earlier in this chapter.

Campsites, facilities: There are 10 RV campsites, all without hookups, as well as 400 tent sites with *palapas,* tables, barbecues, water, and fire rings. Facilities include both flush toilets and outhouses and cold showers. The water is not potable, so bring your own. They rent boogie boards and trailers with flush toilets, showers, and stoves. Security is provided by three resident watchmen, a single entrance road into the fenced property, watch dogs, and solar lights. Tent campers are welcome. Obtain supplies in El Sauzal.

Reservations, fees: All sites are first come, first served. The fee is low—$10 per night for RVs and $8 for tents.

Directions: Take the steep, half-mile-long dirt road off the southbound side of the Tijuana-Ensenada toll road (Highway 1D), eight miles north of Ensenada at Km 94. The exit is marked with a sign. Heading south, start watching for the sign after passing El Mirador viewpoint on the right side of the toll road.

Contact: Playa Saldamando, P.O. Box 120224, San Diego, CA 92112, U.S. tel. 619/857-9242, email: saldamando@k-online.com, website: www.mexonline.com/playasal.htm.

11 VILLA DE SAN MIGUEL
🏊 🐕 🚙 ⛺

In El Sauzal
Northwest Baja Norte map, page 44
The site is on a plateau above a rocky beach
with great waves for surfing. The price is right,
and the park is reasonably close to Ensenada.
Summer is the best time to visit, as winter can
get cold. For things to do here, see the Ensenada Area, earlier in this chapter.

Campsites, facilities: There are 500 campsites
for tents with barbecues, electricity, sewer, a
dump station, and water, plus 40 pull-through
RV sites with full hookups. Flush toilets, hot
tiled showers, a restaurant, a bar, and a gift
shop are available. Don't drink the water.
Guards are on duty around the clock, so the
place is secure. Obtain supplies in El Sauzal.

Reservations, fees: Reservations are accepted.
Fees are moderate—$8 per night for tents or
$10 per night for full-hookup sites, $60 per
week, $150 per month, and $1,500 per year.

Directions: From the southern tollbooth on
the Tijuana-Ensenada toll road (Highway 1D),
drive one-half mile south on Highway 1D.
From Ensenada drive eight miles north on
Highway 1.

Contact: San Miguel Village, Apartado Postal
55, El Sauzal, Baja California, Mexico,
Mex. tel./fax 646/174-7948, email: villadesan
miguel@yahoo.com, website: villadesan
miguel.com.

12 PANCHO'S RV PARK
🚶 🚲 🏊 🐕 🚙 ⛺

North of El Sauzal on Tecate Highway 3
Northwest Baja Norte map, page 44
The park is shady, with sites set beneath large
oak trees. It is a pleasant enough place to stay,
particularly for tent campers, but it is not a
destination spot. Old mines in the area can be
explored. Summer is the preferred time to visit.
For things to do here, see the Ensenada Area,
earlier in this chapter.

Campsites, facilities: There are 20 pull-through
campsites with full hookups. Facilities include
flush toilets, hot showers, a pool, barbecue pits,
a playground, and a restaurant. Don't drink
the water. There is no security. Tent campers
are welcome. Obtain supplies in El Sauzal.

Reservations, fees: All sites are first come, first
served. Fees are low—$5 per night and $80 per
month for a site with hookups, or $3 per night
for tents. Hot showers cost $1.

Directions: From Ensenada drive six miles north
on Highway 1, then follow Tecate Highway 3
north for nine miles. The camp is at Km 93.

Contact: Drive in and talk to the owner.

13 RANCHO SORDO MUDO RV PARK
🚶 🚲 🏊 🐕 🚙 ⛺

North of El Sauzal on Tecate Highway 3
Northwest Baja Norte map, page 44
The owners of this campground also run a
school for deaf children, and all camping fees
are donated to the school. The school can be
toured. A Frisbee golf course is nearby. Staying here puts you within walking distance of
the Domecq Winery and near the L. A. Cetto
Winery. Tours of the wineries are available by
prior arrangement through the operators of
the campground. A Russian colony museum
is nearby in Guadalupe and hot springs are
close by. Don't drink the water. Summer is
the preferred time to visit. For other things
to do here, see the Ensenada Area, earlier in
this chapter.

Campsites, facilities: There are 20 pull-through
RV campsites and 10 others, of which 10 have
full hookups and 20 have electricity and water.
There are 10 tent sites with water, sewer, a
dump station, and electricity. Small trees are
planted at each site. Facilities include flush
toilets and hot showers. The water is not safe
to drink. A resident manager with
large dogs provides security. Tent
campers are welcome. Obtain supplies in Guadalupe.

Reservations, fees: Reservations are accepted. Fees are moderate—$10 per night for RVs and $7 per night for tents.

Directions: From Ensenada drive six miles north on Highway 1, then follow Tecate Highway 3 north about 19 miles to the campground. It's at Km 75 in the Guadalupe Valley, near the Domecq Winery.

Contact: Rancho Sordo Mudo RV Park, P.O. Box 1376, Chula Vista, CA 91912; messages can be left at U.S. tel. 619/660-2236, email: ranchosordo@hotmail.com, website: www.ranchosordomudo.org.

⑭ CALIFORNIA TRAILER PARK AND MOTEL

In El Sauzal

Northwest Baja Norte map, page 44

An old, rundown RV place next door to the north is under the same name and ownership. Don't confuse it with the nice new RV facilities within the motel compound. Summer is the preferred time to visit. For things to do here, see the Ensenada Area, earlier in this chapter.

Campsites, facilities: There are 45 campsites with full hookups, some with concrete pads. Flush toilets, hot showers, and laundry facilities are available. Don't drink the water. The park is secured with a gate. Tent campers are not welcome. Obtain supplies in El Sauzal.

Reservations, fees: Reservations are accepted. Fees are moderate—$10 per night or $150 per month.

Directions: The park is on the ocean side of Highway 1 just north of the Pemex plant. From Ensenada drive six miles north on Highway 1.

Contact: California Trailer Park and Motel, Apartado Postal 262, Ensenada, Baja California, Mexico, Mex. tel./fax 646/174-6033.

⑮ RAMONA BEACH RV PARK AND MOTEL

In El Sauzal

Northwest Baja Norte map, page 44

Campers stay in an unattractive setting, a big, level area on the north side of the motel and store. Summer is the preferred time to visit. For things to do here, see the Ensenada Area, earlier in this chapter.

Campsites, facilities: There are 60 pull-through campsites for RVs, 40 with full hookups and concrete pads and 20 with no hookups. A store, restaurant, and tiled restrooms with flush toilets and hot showers are on site. Don't drink the water. At night there is some lighting for security. Tent campers are welcome. Obtain supplies in El Sauzal.

Reservations, fees: Reservations are accepted. Fees are high—$14 per night, $95 per week, $250 per month, and $2,700 per year.

Directions: The park is on the ocean side of Highway 1 directly across from the Pemex plant. From Ensenada drive three miles north on Highway 1.

Contact: Ramona Beach RV Park and Motel, Apartado Postal 513, Ensenada, Baja California, Mexico, Mex. tel. 646/174-6045.

⑯ KING'S CORONITA TRAILER PARK

On the north side of Ensenada

Northwest Baja Norte map, page 44

The park is occupied primarily by permanents and has a residential atmosphere. Boat storage is available on site. Summer is the preferred time to visit. For things to do here, see the Ensenada Area, earlier in this chapter.

Campsites, facilities: There are 65 campsites adjacent to the Pacific Ocean, of which 15 are pull-throughs with trees, full hookups, and concrete pads. Twenty campsites with trees, tables, and barbecues are available for tent camping. Flush toilets and hot showers are available in tiled restrooms, which have become rundown. Don't drink the water. The park is secured with a locked gate and security guard, and you must ask the manager, who lives next to the gate, to unlock it for you. Obtain supplies in Ensenada.

Reservations, fees: Reservations are accepted. The fee is high—$15 per night, $75 per week, $160 per month, and $1,920 per year for RVs, and $5 per night or $25 per week for tents.

Directions: The park is on the ocean side of Highway 1 three miles south of the last tollbooth. It is on the north side of the Marina Coral, just before the road turns to the right into Ensenada around the waterfront. Watch for the sign south of the overpass to the CICESE school.

Contact: King's Coronita Trailer Park, Apartado Postal 133, Ensenada, Baja California, Mexico, Mex. tel./fax 646/174-4540.

▮17▮ CAMPO PLAYA RV PARK
🛏 🚐 ⛰

In Ensenada
Northwest Baja Norte map, page 44

This is the best place to stay for fishing, dining, and sightseeing in Ensenada. If you don't want to unhook your rig and drive around town, you can call a cab. Restaurants are within walking distance, as is the Gigante Supermarket. The prominent landmark you passed, the 12-foot-high busts that people call the "three heads," represents the Mexican heroes Benito Juárez, Venustiano Carranza, and Miguel Hidalgo y Castillo. Summer is the preferred time to visit. For things to do here, see the Ensenada Area, earlier in this chapter.

Campsites, facilities: There are 90 pull-through campsites with full hookups and concrete pads. Clean, tiled restrooms with flush toilets and hot showers are available. Don't drink the water. The park is fenced, but people can wander through. Tent campers are welcome. Obtain supplies in Ensenada.

Reservations, fees: Reservations are accepted.

Fees are high—$16 per night, $98 per week, and $200 per month for RVs and $10 per night for tents.

Directions: The park is on the corner of Las Dunas and Delante and a few blocks west of the Gigante Supermarket where Highway 1 takes a sharp right turn to the south. Street signs in this area are hard to find, and map makers disagree on what streets are called. As you go through Ensenada, past the statue of the so-called three heads in the Civic Plaza, take the left turn at the light across from the naval base with one of the biggest Mexican flags ever made and keep looking to the left for Campo Playa in a couple of blocks. You can't miss it—really.

Contact: Campo Playa RV Park, Apartado Postal 789, Ensenada, Baja California, Mexico, Mex. tel./fax 646/176-2918, email: camplaya@telnor.net.

▮18▮ JOKER HOTEL, RV PARK, AND RESTAURANT
🛏 🚐 ⛰

In Ensenada
Northwest Baja Norte map, page 44

The campsites are narrow, short, and difficult to get into. They are suitable only for vehicles under 23 feet long without trailers. Summer is the best time to visit. For things to do here, see the Ensenada Area, earlier in this chapter.

Campsites, facilities: There are 12 pull-through campsites with full hookups, including television. Flush toilets, hot showers, a pool, whirlpool tub, satellite TV, and a restaurant/bar are available. Do not drink the water. The park is secured with a guard. Tent campers are welcome. Obtain supplies in Ensenada.

Reservations, fees: Reservations are accepted. The fee is moderate—$12 per night.

Directions: Take Highway 1 to the south side of Ensenada. The park is south of the military base on the east side of Highway 1.

Contact: Joker Hotel, RV Park, and

Restaurant, Apartado Postal 2069, Ensenada, Baja California, Mexico, U.S. tel. 800/2-JOKER-2 (800/256-5372), Mex. tel. 646/177-5151, fax 646/177-4460.

19 CORONA BEACH TRAILER PARK

South of Ensenada
Northwest Baja Norte map, page 44

This is a large, flat site behind residences on the beach of Bahía Todos Santos, which normally has very mild surf. It is a nice place to camp. Horses can be rented for rides on the beach; the going rate is $10 an hour. Try a gallop in the surf—it's fun! Summer is the preferred time to visit. For other things to do here, see the Ensenada Area, earlier in this chapter.

Campsites, facilities: There are 60 pull-through campsites with electricity and water. Flush toilets, cold showers, and a recreation hall are provided. Don't drink the water. The park is secured with a fence, and the owner lives on the premises. Tent campers are welcome. Obtain supplies at shops along Highway 1.

Reservations, fees: Reservations are accepted. Fees are moderate—$10 per night and $260 per month.

Directions: Take the Estero Beach Hotel turnoff from Highway 1 about six miles south of Ensenada. Go west on the paved street toward the beach and turn right on the first paved road. When the pavement becomes dirt, look north for a yellow water tower with "Corona Beach" painted on it.

Contact: Corona Beach Trailer Park, Apartado Postal 1149, Ensenada, Baja California, Mexico. There is no phone.

20 PLAYA MONALISA

South of Ensenada
Northwest Baja Norte map, page 44

A homey atmosphere pervades this very nice, neat, small compound with cobblestone streets.

Rules require you to arrive with an empty holding tank, so as not to overload the septic system. The owner will turn you away if he suspects you are packing a full load. Many people prefer to visit in summer, since winter can be cold. It is, however, less crowded in winter and the fishing is good. For things to do here, see the Ensenada Area, earlier in this chapter.

Campsites, facilities: There are 15 RV campsites with full hookups, concrete pads, *palapas*, fire rings, and trees. There are 20 tent campsites with some *palapas*, tables, trees, and central water for washing. On the property are clean, tiled restrooms with flush toilets and hot showers, a restaurant, motel rooms, satellite TV, and horse rentals. Don't drink the water; purified bottled water is available. The park is secured with a gated fence, and the owner lives on the premises. Obtain supplies at shops along Highway 1.

Reservations, fees: Reservations are accepted. Fees are high—$17.50 per night, seventh day free per week, and $225 per month for RVs. Tent sites are $14 per night and seventh day free per week.

Directions: Take the Estero Beach Hotel turnoff from Highway 1 about six miles south of Ensenada. Go west on the paved street toward the beach and turn right on the first paved road. When the pavement becomes dirt, you'll see Monalisa to your left on the beach. Signs will direct you to the park.

Contact: Playa Monalisa, Apartado Postal 607, Ensenada, Baja California, Mexico, Mex. tel./fax 646/177-5100.

21 EL FARO BEACH MOTEL AND TRAILER PARK

South of Ensenada
Northwest Baja Norte map, page 44

This is a crowded place, and as such it can get fairly noisy. It is right on the beach, however, and we spent a very pleasant night at one of the attractive sites. Summer is the preferred time to visit. For things to do here, see the Ensenada Area, earlier in this chapter.

Campsites, facilities: There are 20 RV campsites with electricity and water on the beach below the restaurant and room for 150 tent campers with no hookups. Facilities include tiled restrooms with flush toilets and cold showers, a store that's open in the summer, satellite TV, horse rentals, and a dump station. Don't drink the water, which comes out of a cistern. The park is secured with a fence and patrolmen. Tent campers are welcome at the beach campsites. Obtain supplies at shops along Highway 1.

Reservations, fees: Reservations are accepted. Fees are moderate—$12 per night for RVs, $70 per week, $210 per month, and $1,500 per year; for tents it's $7 per night, $42 per week, $150 per month, and $1,000 per year.

Directions: Take the Estero Beach Hotel turnoff from Highway 1 about six miles south of Ensenada. Go west on the paved street toward the beach about two miles and continue west when the road turns to dirt. You will see El Faro.

Contact: El Faro Beach Motel and Trailer Park, Apartado Postal 1008, Ensenada, Baja California, Mexico, Mex. tel. 646/177-4630, fax 646/177-4620.

22 ESTERO BEACH RESORT RV PARK
🏃 🚴 ⛱ 🏊 🎣 🐎 💧 🚐

South of Ensenada
Northwest Baja Norte map, page 44

This is our favorite RV park in the Ensenada area. All the amenities are available at this fullfledged resort. The RV park has many shade trees and is on the edge of the huge Estero de Punta Banda Reserve, home to a wide variety of aquatic birds, including loons, grebes, pelicans, cormorants, herons, egrets, hawks, and coots. Estero de Punta Banda is about 4.5 miles long and shaped somewhat like a dumbbell, with the north end about one mile wide and the south end about two miles wide. Punta Estero separates the *estero* from Bahía Todos Santos. A one-half-mile gap lies between the north end of Punta Estero and the point of land housing the Estero Beach Hotel. Beneath this gap is a shallow bar that creates breakers at low tide and during storms.

The resort rents equipment for all manner of water sports—you can get lessons if you want. Windsurfing is one of the more popular pursuits in the *estero*. In awe we watched an elderly couple adroitly mount their individual boards at the ramp and sail off together with great aplomb. Fishermen launch their trailer boats here for a modest fee and brave the entrance sandbar for offshore fishing around Islas de Todos Santos, but they are careful to cross it at high tide each way. It can be dangerous, as friends of ours learned when they bounced on the bottom between large swells. Summer is the best time to visit. For things to do here, see the Ensenada Area, earlier in this chapter.

Campsites, facilities: There are 38 RV campsites with full hookups, concrete pads, and trees. The tiled restrooms are clean, with flush toilets and hot showers. Also available are a laundry, a restaurant, a launch ramp into the *estero,* tennis courts, horses, bicycles, volleyball courts, a recreation center with billiards, Ping-Pong, and games, a children's playground, shops, and an exhibit center and museum displaying treasures from various Mexican cultures. A beach club offers sailing, windsurfing, waterskiing, snorkeling equipment, and personal watercraft. Don't drink the water. The park is secured with a guarded gate and 24-hour guard service. Obtain supplies at shops along Highway 1.

Reservations, fees: Reservations are accepted. The fee is high—$20 per night for RVs or tents.

Directions: Take the Estero Beach Hotel turnoff from Highway 1 about six miles south of Ensenada. Go west on the paved street and follow signs to the office, where you will register. The RV park is on the bay a little farther ahead.

Contact: Estero Beach Resort RV Park, PMB 1186 482 West San Ysidro Boulevard, San Ysidro, CA 92173, Mex. tel. 646/176-6225, 6230, or 6235, fax 646/176-6925, email: reservations@hotelesterobeach.com, website: www.hotelesterobeach.com.

23 LA JOLLA BEACH CAMP
🏃 🚲 🏊 🛶 🚌 🐴 🚐 ⛺

In Punta Banda

Northwest Baja Norte map, page 44

On holidays this park is jammed with tourists. It's a large place with lots of activity at any time of year. Small boats can be launched into the surf of Bahía Todos Santos for fishing and scuba diving around the Punta Banda Peninsula. On the south side of the peninsula, you should visit La Bufadora (the Blowhole). Park in the cluster of curio shops at the end of the road and walk 100 yards to the viewing area. Every wave forces water into a narrow slot and upward onto the face of the cliff with a resounding boom. Summer is the best time to visit. For other things to do here, see the Ensenada Area, earlier in this chapter.

Campsites, facilities: There is plenty of room to camp on the beach without hookups in front of permanent residences. Flush toilets, hot showers, a restaurant, a dump station, a launch ramp, and horse rentals are available. Don't drink the water. The park is secured with a guarded gate. Tent campers are welcome. Obtain supplies in Punta Banda.

Reservations, fees: All sites are first come, first served. Fees are low—$6 per night for two people or $140 per month.

Directions: Heading west from Maneadero on the paved road to La Bufadora, drive eight miles. The camp is on the beach at Bahía Todos Santos at Km 12.5.

Contact: Mex. tel./fax 646/154-2004.

24 VILLARINO RV PARK
🏃 🚲 🏊 🛶 🚌 🐴 🚐 ⛺

In Punta Banda

Northwest Baja Norte map, page 44

Each space has its own tree in this well-tended camping area that is generally not as crowded as neighboring La Jolla Beach Camp. See the description of that listing to learn about all the action on the Punta Banda Peninsula. Summer is the best time to visit. For things to do here, see the Ensenada Area, earlier in this chapter.

Campsites, facilities: There are 35 campsites with full hookups. Facilities include flush toilets, hot showers, a restaurant, a full-service store, boat rentals, tables, fire rings, grills, a playground, a volleyball court, a horseshoe pit, motorbike and hiking trails, horse rentals, a launch ramp, and large tents with cots to rent for $5 per night. Don't drink the water. The park is secured with a guard gate. Tent campers are welcome. Obtain supplies in Punta Banda.

Reservations, fees: Reservations are accepted. Fees are moderate—$10 per night per person. Discounts of 25 to 40 percent per week are available, depending on the number of people in your party. The monthly rate is $240.

Directions: Heading west from Maneadero on the paved road to La Bufadora, drive eight miles. The park is on the beach at Bahía Todos Santos at Km 12.5, next door to La Jolla Beach Camp (see listing earlier in this chapter).

Contact: Villarino RV Park, Apartado Postal 842, Ensenada, Baja California, Mexico, Mex. tel. 646/154-2045, fax 646/154-2044.

25 OCEAN VIEW RV PARK
🏃 🚲 🐴 🚐 ⛺

In Punta Banda

Northwest Baja Norte map, page 44

This park has a great view of Ensenada Bay to the north. For things to do in the Ensenada area, see the Ensenada Area earlier in this chapter. For things to do on the Punta Banda Peninsula, see La Jolla Beach Camp in this chapter.

Campsites, facilities: There are 20 campsites with full hookups. There are no facilities and no security. Don't drink the water. Tent campers are welcome. Obtain supplies in Punta Banda.

Reservations, fees: Reservations cannot be made. Fees are moderate, $50 per week, $160 per month, and $1,400 per year.

Directions: Heading west from Maneadero on the paved road to La Bufadora, drive 10 miles. The park is on a slope above the road. Signs will direct you.

Contact: There is no address or phone number.

26 EJIDO CAMPO NO. 5

West of Punta Banda
Northwest Baja Norte map, page 44

This primitive campground perched above the water of Todos Santos Bay is rather difficult for large RVs to reach on the steep access road, but is delightful for smaller vehicles. Summer is the best time to visit. For things to do in the Ensenada area, see the Ensenada Area, earlier in this chapter. For things to do on the Punta Banda Peninsula, see La Jolla Beach Camp in this chapter.

Campsites, facilities: This is a primitive camping area with no facilities or security. Water is not available. Obtain supplies in Punta Banda.

Reservations, fees: Camping is first come, first served. Fees are very low.

Directions: From Punta Banda drive about 1.5 miles west on the paved road to La Bufadora.

Contact: Drive in to the entrance station.

27 EJIDO CAMPO NO. 7

West of Punta Banda
Northwest Baja Norte map, page 44

The paved road to Punta Banda has climbed high on the intervening ridge, and the dirt road leading down the mountainside to this primi-

tive campground close to the ocean is very steep. Tent campers in small vehicles will find the camping to be quite pleasant, but most drivers with larger rigs would not risk the hazard of getting here. Summer is the best time to visit. For things to do here, see the Ensenada Area, earlier in this chapter. For things to do on the Punta Banda Peninsula, see La Jolla Beach Camp in this chapter.

Campsites, facilities: This is a primitive camping area with no facilities or security. Water is not available. Obtain supplies in Punta Banda.

Reservations, fees: Camping is first come, first served. Fees are very low.

Directions: From Punta Banda drive about three miles west on the paved road to La Bufadora.

Contact: Drive in to the entrance station.

28 EJIDO CAMPO NO. 8

West of Punta Banda
Northwest Baja Norte map, page 44

This third rustic campground on the Punta Banda Peninsula overlooking the Pacific Ocean to the south also has a steep access road and a great view for campers in smaller vehicles. Summer is the best time to visit. For things to do in this area, see the Ensenada Area, earlier in this chapter. For things to do on the Punta Banda Peninsula, see La Jolla Beach Camp in this chapter.

Campsites, facilities: This is a primitive camping area with no facilities or security. Water is not available. Obtain supplies in Punta Banda.

Reservations, fees: Camping is first come, first served. Fees are very low.

Directions: From Punta Banda drive about 4.5 miles west on the paved road to La Bufadora.

Contact: Drive in to the entrance station.

29 LAS CAÑADAS BALNEARIO

🚶 🚲 🏊 ⛴ 🏕 🐕 ♿ 🚐 ⛺

South of Maneadero

Northwest Baja Norte map, page 44

This is far more elaborate than any other *balneario* in Baja and would be a fun place to spend a couple of nights. It is certainly a convenient spot to pull into if darkness is coming. The RV campground is on a small, bare hill in open country, with little to distinguish it. Perhaps some landscaping will be forthcoming. Summer is the best time to visit. For things to do in the area, see the Ensenada Area earlier in this chapter.

Campsites, facilities: There are 11 pull-throughs with full hookups, concrete pads, tables, and barbecues, which can also be used by tenters. Facilities include tiled bathrooms with flush toilets and hot showers, pools, and a store. The park is secured by a guard gate and a chain at the entrance. This is an exceptionally large recreation complex with a lake with fish, a water slide, pedal boats, volleyball, basketball, football, kayaks, bicycles, and cabins. It is designed as a day-use facility for people from Ensenada, but it has camping facilities, as well. It is open from March 20 to October 20.

Reservations, fees: Reservations are accepted. Fees are high—$15 per night.

Directions: From Ensenada drive south on Highway 1 through Maneadero to the military checkpoint at Km 31.5 (about 20 miles). Las Cañadas is on the west side of the highway.

Contact: Las Cañadas Balneario, Mex. tel. 646/153-1055, fax 646/153-1056, website: www.lascanadas.com.

30 EL PALOMAR

🚶 🚲 🏊 🏕 🚐 ⛺

In Santo Tomás

Northwest Baja Norte map, page 44

This park is set in a recreation area *(balneario)* for people from Ensenada who flock here on weekends for picnics, swimming, and other activities. As the years go by, more and more attractions are developed. Quail hunters come to hunt on ranches up the valley of the Río Santo Tomás, and anglers come to fish in the ocean down the valley. At the north end of the olive grove below the highway, there is a small pile of melted adobe marking the last remains of the Misión de Santo Tomás de Aquino, which was built by the Dominicans in 1794. Summer is the preferred time to visit. For things to do here, see the Ensenada Area, earlier in this chapter.

Warning: The entrance road down into the RV park is steep, and the drive coming up can be difficult since you must look out for trucks and buses whizzing by on Highway 1. We had to go into four-wheel drive once to crawl slowly out into traffic while dragging our 10,000-pound boat behind us.

Campsites, facilities: There are 42 campsites, of which 12 are pull-throughs with full hookups; the other 30 have just electricity and water. Facilities include concrete pads, *palapas,* trees, tables, a dump station, tiled restrooms with flush toilets and hot showers, a pool, a waterpark (including a gondola, water slide, and paddleboats), tennis, volleyball, hiking, biking, a restaurant/bar, a curio store, barbecue pits, an area for off-road motorbikes, satellite TV access, a motel, a gas station, and hunting and fishing guide services. Don't drink the water. The park is secured with a chain across the entrance road. Tent campers are welcome. Obtain supplies in Maneadero.

Reservations, fees: All campsites are first come, first served. Fees are moderate—$12.50 per night or $60 per week.

Directions: From Maneadero drive 18.5 miles south on Highway 1. The campground is on the north side of the road. Register at the office in the store across the road.

Contact: El Palomar, Avenida Ruiz #339 Interior, Ensenada, Baja California, Mexico, Mex. tel./fax 646/178-8022 or 153-8002.

31 MALIBU BEACH SUR RV PARK

🏕️ 🚴 🏊 ⛵ 🏠 🚐 ⛺

South of Puerto San Ysidro
Northwest Baja Norte map, page 44
The park has a delightful location on a bluff above a very nice beach. We pulled in one afternoon planning to check it out, then continue on to Ensenada, but we couldn't tear ourselves away. We spent a most pleasant night serenaded by the surf. Castro's Camp, at Puerto San Ysidro four miles north of the village of Erendira, is known for good fishing in the kelp and on the bottom. You can charter a *panga* there if you'd like to try your luck. Summer is the preferred time to visit. For things to do here, see the Ensenada Area, earlier in this chapter.
Campsites, facilities: There are 14 pull-through campsites with full hookups and concrete pads. Electricity is provided by a generator from 5 P.M. to 10 P.M. Facilities include laundry and tiled restrooms with flush toilets and hot showers. Don't drink the water. The owner lives on the premises, so security is good. Tent campers are welcome. Obtain supplies in San Vicente.
Reservations, fees: Camping is first come, first served. The fee is moderate—$10 per night for RVs or tents.
Directions: Drive south of Santo Tomás on Highway 1 for 17 miles and then follow a very rough paved road 12 miles west to Erendira on the ocean. Continue three miles south across the river on a rough dirt road winding through tomato fields.
Contact: Drive in and talk to the owner.

32 PARQUE NACIONAL CONSTITUCIÓN DE 1857

🏕️ 🚴 🏊 🏠 🚐 ⛺

East of Ensenada
Northwest Baja Norte map, page 44
Parque Nacional Constitución de 1857 offers an uncrowded, relaxing camping experience. Sleeping in the cool mountains in a forested setting is a different way to enjoy Baja, which is usually identified by its coastal attractions. Folks with a yen for exploring will enjoy tramping around among the park's pine trees. Spring, summer, and fall are the times to visit.
Campsites, facilities: This is primitive camping with no developed facilities or services. There is no water. Security is not a problem due to the remote location. Obtain supplies in Ensenada.
Reservations, fees: All sites are first come, first served. There is no fee.
Directions: You can access the park from the north or south, but the preferred route is from the south. Take Highway 3 southeast from Ensenada toward San Felipe about 25 miles to Ojos Negros. Turn left (north) on a short paved road into the village. At its end, turn right onto a graded dirt road. Continue eight miles, then turn right at the junction. Go another 12 miles and turn left. The park is about 27 miles farther, a drive of approximately two hours. Proceed through the pines to Laguna Hanson, which may be dry, and pick a campsite. This road may be impassable after a rain. Pickup trucks are advised. Don't try this in a motor home or trailer without scouting it out.

The northern route has some rough stretches and is less traveled. From Tecate drive east on Highway 2 about 32 miles to El Condor, where a graded dirt road heads south about 37 miles to the park. After 16 miles it joins another graded dirt road coming in from La Rumorosa on Highway 2, about 10 miles east of El Condor. The main road bears east passing El Topo Rancho, climbs a steep grade, and enters the park. Pickup trucks are advised.
Contact: Drive in and camp.

33 SAN ANTONIO DEL MAR BEACH

🏕️ 🚴 🏊 ⛵ 🏠 ⛺

Northwest of Colonet
Northwest Baja Norte map, page 45
The beach and dunes are extensive and well suited for vehicles that can traverse soft sand. There is nothing here for travelers with motor homes

or trailers. Summer is the preferred time to visit. For things to do here, see the San Quintín Area, earlier in this chapter.

Campsites, facilities: It is possible to camp on the beach with four-wheel-drive vehicles. There are no facilities. With the right vehicle it is a great spot for tent camping. Obtain supplies in Colonet.

Reservations, fees: Camping is first come, first served. The fee is very low—$3 per night, assuming someone comes to collect it.

Directions: On the north side of Colonet close to the bridge over the river, turn west at the San Antonio del Mar sign onto a good dirt road and drive seven miles. Beach access is among several beach houses.

Contact: Drive in and camp.

34 PUNTA SAN JACINTO TRAILER PARK

🥾 🚴 🏊 ⛴ 🐕 🚐 ⛺

North of Camalu
Northwest Baja Norte map, page 45

This is a popular spot for surfers. The 1981 wreck of a large ship is just offshore, and there is a small fish camp and a few permanent trailers. Summer is the preferred time to visit. For things to do here, see the San Quintín Area, earlier in this chapter.

Campsites, facilities: There are 12 semideveloped RV campsites, plus room for RV and tent camping along the beach. Pit toilets and one hot shower are provided. Don't drink the water. There is no security, and problems have been reported. Obtain supplies in Camalu.

Reservations, fees: Camping is first come, first served. The fee is low—$5 per night.

Directions: At Km 150 on Highway 1 between Colonet and Camalu (about five miles north of Camalú), turn west on a graded dirt road and drive 4.5 miles to the beach.

Contact: Drive in and camp. The manager will come around and collect the fee.

35 POSADA DON DIEGO

🥾 🚴 🏊 ⛴ 🐕 🚐 ⛺

South of Colonia Vicente Guerrero
Northwest Baja Norte map, page 45

The park covers a good deal of ground, with big spaces and lots of room for large groups. We have stayed here many times when traveling south with groups of Vagabundos. Summer is the preferred time to visit. Anglers and surfers use nearby Playa San Ramon, which is 2.5 miles west of the campground on a sandy road. Fishing can be good for perch and corbina. In and around San Quintín there's a large agricultural community dedicated to growing tomatoes and strawberries, most of which are shipped north to the United States. For things to do here, see the San Quintín Area, earlier in this chapter.

Campsites, facilities: There are 100 campsites (20 pull-through) with concrete pads, tables, and trees, of which 40 have full hookups and 60 have only electricity and water. Facilities include tiled restrooms with flush toilets, hot showers, fire rings, tables, laundry facilities, a restaurant with a banquet/meeting room, a bar, a gift store, a dump station, a volleyball court, and a horseshoe pit. Don't drink or cook with the water, which is brackish and comes from a well. The owners live on the premises and there is a night watchman; in addition, police officers pass through hourly, so there are no problems with security. Obtain supplies in San Quintín.

Reservations, fees: Reservations are accepted. Fees are moderate—$11 per night, $205 monthly, and $2,480 yearly.

Directions: Head one mile south of the stoplight in Colonia Vicente Guerrero on Highway 1 to the dirt access road adjacent to the propane plant 100 yards south of the Mesón Don Pepe RV Park sign. There is no sign for Don Diego's from the north, though there is a sign on the roof of a shed visible from the south. The park is one-half mile west, past Mesón Don Pepe restaurant.

Contact: Posada Don Diego, Apartado Postal 126, Colonia Vicente Guerrero, Baja California, Mexico, Mex. tel. 616/166-2181, fax 616/166-2248, email: posadadondiego@hotmail.com or posadadondiego@yahoo.com, website: www.posadadondiego.com.

36 OLD MILL RV PARK

South of San Quintín
Northwest Baja Norte map, page 45

Yes, there really is an old gristmill, the remains of a failed attempt at farming by English settlers in the late 1800s. In front of the park, the embankment of an abandoned railroad trestle narrows the tide through a raceway going into the upper bay. The road in from Highway 1 has deteriorated badly. Summer is the best time to visit. For things to do here, see the San Quintín Area, earlier in this chapter.

Campsites, facilities: There are 20 camping spots (five pull-through), all with full hookups and concrete pads. An overflow area with no hookups is also available. The restrooms are clean and tiled with flush toilets and hot showers. Facilities include fire rings, grills, and a free launch ramp. Rental boats with guides are available nearby, as well as a restaurant and bar. Don't drink the water. There is no security. Tent campers are welcome. Obtain supplies in San Quintín.

Reservations, fees: Reservations are accepted. Fees are high—$10 per night for tents and $15 for RVs.

Directions: At the sign about 2.5 miles south of the military camp, which is south of San Quintín, turn off Highway 1 and follow the signs 3.5 miles west on a graded dirt road to the shore of Bahía San Quintín.

Contact: Drive in and talk to the manager.

37 OLD PIER MOTEL AND RV PARK

South of San Quintín
Northwest Baja Norte map, page 45

An old cemetery used by English settlers in the 19th century is nearby to the south, and just to the north is a reconstruction of an original house and outbuildings from that era. This is an ideal place for tent camping, as it sits on the edge of a bluff under trees with a grand, long view of Bahía San Quintín and the rugged peninsula on the far side. Bird-watching in the marshes around the bay can be magnificent. A staircase down the 20-foot-high bluff gives access to the shoreline. Summer is the most popular time for camping. For things to do here, see the San Quintín Area, earlier in this chapter.

Campsites, facilities: There are seven campsites with no hookups. Tiled flush toilets, cold showers (hot showers are available in the motel rooms), concrete fire pits, and a restaurant are available. Don't drink the water. Security is not a problem due to the remote location and access to the campground being routed through the motel and restaurant entrance. Tent campers are welcome. Obtain supplies in San Quintín.

Reservations, fees: All sites are first come, first served. The fee is very low—$3 per night. Weekly discounts can be negotiated.

Directions: Driving down Highway 1, ignore the Old Pier sign. Turn off at the Old Mill sign about 2.5 miles south of the military camp, which is south of San Quintín, then head 2.5 miles west to the Old Pier sign pointing south. Turn left and continue 1.5 miles.

Contact: Mex. tel. 616/163-4206, or drive in and talk to the owners.

38 CIELITO LINDO MOTEL AND RV PARK

South of San Quintín
Northwest Baja Norte map, page 45

A short one-quarter mile hike toward the ocean brings you to the outstanding Santa María Beach with miles to explore. Summer is the preferred time to visit. For more information, see the San Quintín Area, earlier in this chapter.

Campsites, facilities: There are 15 campsites, of which six are pull-throughs; eight have full hookups and seven with *palapas* are for tent and van campers. Trees, a good restaurant/bar, a barbecue area, Kiddieland, a motel, a TV lounge, stables with horseback riding, a mini-zoo, and a charter boat business with a small tackle shop are on the property. Facilities include clean tiled restrooms with flush toilets and hot showers. Don't drink the brackish water. Security is provided by resident managers and a resident night guard. Obtain supplies in San Quintín.

Reservations, fees: Reservations are accepted. Fees are low—$8 per night for RVs and $5 per night for tents.

Directions: Drive about seven miles south of San Quintín on Highway 1 to the La Pinta Hotel sign. Turn west about 3.5 miles past the hotel to Cielito Lindo. Watch for the signs.

Contact: Cielito Lindo Motel and RV Park, Apartado Postal 7, San Quintín, Baja California, Mexico, U.S. tel. 619/593-2252 ext. 2 for reservations, email: cielito@telnor.net, website: www.bajasi.com

39 GYPSYS BEACH CAMP
🏃 🚴 🏊 ⛵ 🎣 🐴 🎿 🚐 ⛺

South of San Quintín
Northwest Baja Norte map, page 45

The campground is in a lovely spot behind the dunes and close to the surf on one of Baja's truly great beaches. Playa Santa María extends several miles to the south and offers good fishing for perch and corbina, as well as lots of Pismo clams. In years past we were able to pluck big ones off the beach every morning after the waves of the previous night's high tide had scooped them out of the sand for us. Fishing can be just as satisfying. While fishing one evening on the point between the beach and the inner bay, a dolphin came close to shore, caught a large leopard shark, and proceeded to toss the shark high in the air, catch it, and toss it again.

In one hour there that night, we caught a leopard shark, an angel shark, a bat ray, a stingray, and a guitarfish. All in all, it was a very memorable evening. Summer is the preferred time to visit. For more information, see the San Quintín Area, earlier in this chapter.

Campsites, facilities: There are 38 dry campsites, of which 15 are pull-throughs. There are tiled bathrooms with flush toilets and hot showers, a clubhouse with electricity available for slide shows, an enclosed camping building, and a two-story building with a bar and snack bar commanding a great view of the Pacific Ocean. Security is provided by a resident guard. Full amenities are available at Cielito Lindo, one-quarter mile away.

Reservations, fees: Reservations are accepted. Fees are low—$5 per night. Caravan staff camp free.

Directions: Drive about seven miles south of San Quintín on Highway 1 to the La Pinta Hotel sign. Turn west for about 3.5 miles past the hotel to Cielito Lindo (see listing earlier in this chapter). Watch for the signs. Drive past the Cielito Lindo Restaurant and turn right on a dirt road to Gypsys Beach Camp, which is visible one-quarter mile away.

Contact: Gypsys Beach Camp, Apartado Postal 7, San Quintín, Baja California, Mexico, U.S. tel. 619/593-2252 for reservations, email: gypsys @bajasi.com, website: www.bajasi.com.

40 EL PABELLÓN RV PARK
🏃 🚴 🏊 🎣 🐴 🚐 ⛺

South of San Quintín
Northwest Baja Norte map, page 45

Tent campers revel in this place, a choice spot on magnificent Playa El Pabellón, which runs for miles in both directions. When we first asked the attendant where to park, he gave a wide sweep of his arm and with a huge smile bellowed, "Anywhere!" If you can, camp between the widely spaced rows of shrubs on the leveled-off area at the edge of the dunes. The shrubs break the wind and afford a little privacy. It is the best-run park operated by an *ejido* in Baja. Interesting enough, it is not one of the old parks built for them by the government. *Pangas* can be chartered for fishing trips behind the breakers or out to Isla San Martín. The fishermen sell Pismo clams, stone crab claws, lobster, and fish from their *pangas,* which operate through the surf in front of the campground. Surf fishing can be good for perch and corbina. Summer is the preferred time to visit. For other things to do here, see the San Quintín Area, earlier in this chapter.

Note: Some confusion in locating the access road has resulted from erection of a similar El Pabellón sign one mile south on Highway 1. When you are driving north, this will be the first sign you see, but ignore it. Competing individuals in the *ejido* are trying to divert you to their operation, which is at the south end of the actual El Pabellón RV Park. Unfortunately the access road at the south end leads you across soft sand, which has trapped unwary RVers.

Campsites, facilities: In addition to the many places to park at the edge of the dunes and farther back, there are 14 campsites with water faucets and sewer hookups. The two restroom buildings are clean and have flush toilets and hot showers. Concrete outdoor sinks and fish cleaning tables are available. Don't drink the water. There is no security. It's ideal for tent camping. Obtain supplies in San Quintín.

Reservations, fees: All sites are first come, first served. The fee is low—$5 per night.

Directions: Proceed about nine miles south of San Quintín on Highway 1 and look for the El Pabellón sign one mile south of the junction of Highway 1 with the old highway—it comes in at a sharp angle on the right. Follow the dirt road one mile to the park on the beach.

Contact: Drive in and talk to the attendant.

41 PLAYA DE TRANQUILO

South of San Quintín
Northwest Baja Norte map, page 45

The Pacific Ocean is on the western edge of the property, which looks down at the water from bluff tops. Steep access leads to a nice beach. There is also a big sand dune on the bluff. Summer is the time to visit. For things to do here, see the San Quintín Area, earlier in this chapter.

Campsites, facilities: There are 10 pull-through campsites with full hookups. Facilities include restrooms with flush toilets and cold showers. Don't drink the water. There is security if someone is living on premises. Otherwise, being right on Highway 1 presents temptation to passersby.

Reservations, fees: All sites are first come, first served. The fee is moderate, $10 per night.

Directions: It is on the west side of Highway 1 at Km 30, about 18 miles south of San Quintín.

Contact: Drive in and camp.

42 PARQUE NACIONAL SIERRA SAN PEDRO MÁRTIR

Southeast of Ensenada
Northwest Baja Norte map, page 45

Hiking, fishing, mountain climbing, even the National Observatory—the Sierra San Pedro Mártir National Park has it all. Tent camping in this mountain setting far from the crowded coastal areas of Baja is a delight. Just set up camp in any of six designated campgrounds. A particularly attractive campsite is in a pine forest at the base of the observatory access road. The upper elevations of the mountains are covered with conifer trees interspersed with meadows (and aspen) generating year-round streams harboring a unique trout species—the Nelson rainbow. From the high points, sweeping views may be had of the desert plain around San Felipe, the Sea of Cortéz, and the Sonoran coast on the Mexican mainland. It is pleasant to settle back against a towering Jeffrey pine and contemplate that arid region baking in the summer heat so far below you.

Spring, summer, and fall are the best times to visit.

Note: Some steep grades must be

tackled en route to the Meling Ranch and even steeper ones beyond that. Motor homes and trailers are not suited for the drive. The road in from Highway 1 can be incredibly dusty, up to several inches deep, and vehicles become enveloped in clouds of the stuff, which penetrates every crack.

Campsites, facilities: This is primitive camping with no developed facilities or services except for pit toilets at the base of the access road up to the observatory. There is no water. Security is not a problem due to the remote location. Obtain supplies in Ensenada.

Reservations, fees: All sites are first come, first served. There is no fee.

Directions: The best way to access the park is to turn east off Highway 1 about eight miles south of Colonet at the village of San Telmo de Abajo. A sign for San Telmo (about six miles) and the Meling Ranch (about 21 miles) marks the start of a graded dirt road that leads approximately 60 miles to the park, a drive of three hours.

Contact: Drive in and camp.

43 LOS MANZANOS CAMPGROUND

Southeast of Ensenada near Parque Nacional Sierra San Pedro Mártir

Northwest Baja Norte map, page 45

An ideal location for tent camping, this forested mountain setting offers seclusion far from the crowds that you are more likely to encounter while staying on the coast. However, at last report there was no one in attendance at Los Manzanos. You might want to head up the road two miles to Parque Nacional Sierra San Pedro Mártir (see listing earlier in this chapter), which is open to camping in designated locations and has more attractive campsites with pit toilets.

Campsites, facilities: There is room under giant oak trees for 10 to 25 vehicles with no hookups, but only three designated spaces. Flush toilets and hot showers are available, and a generator provides electricity to the common facilities. The spring water is good to drink. Security is not a problem due to the remote location. Obtain supplies in Ensenada.

Reservations, fees: Reservations are accepted. Fees are low—tents are $5 per night, vans and campers are $7, and motor homes and trailers are $8.50, with discounts available for longer stays.

Directions: The best access is from Highway 1 about eight miles south of Colonet in the village of San Telmo de Abajo. A sign for San Telmo (about six miles) and the Meling Ranch (about 21 miles) marks the start of a graded dirt road that leads about 60 miles to the Parque Nacional Sierra San Pedro Mártir, a drive of three hours. Los Manzanos is two miles before the park. Motor homes and trailers are not recommended due to steep grades.

Contact: Drive in and see the manager.

10 Best Beaches

① PLAYA ROSARITO
In Rosarito

Northwest Baja Norte map, page 44

Both Coco Loco Trailer Park and Chuy's Trailer Park (see listings in this chapter) are on this long beach, the best known feature of Rosarito. The wide, clean stretch of sand is good for surfing and fishing. Although it is an urban spot and as such is heavily used, it is highly regarded by the people who flock to Rosarito because it's the first good beach south of the border. Southern California beaches are so horribly crowded that Rosarito is greatly appreciated by those eager to spend a weekend in a more attractive setting. Rosarito has everything you might need in the way of services or supplies. Summer is the preferred time to visit, as winter is chilly. For things to do here, see the Rosarito–La Misión Area, earlier in this chapter.

Directions: The beach runs along the front of the city of Rosarito.

② CANTAMAR DUNES
South of Rosarito

Northwest Baja Norte map, page 44

There is a nice beach on the ocean below the dunes. The big activity here is driving all-terrain vehicles on the dunes. Obtain supplies in Rosarito. Summer is the preferred time to visit, as winter is chilly. For things to do here, see the Rosarito–La Misión Area, earlier in this chapter.

Directions: The dunes are next to Highway 1 (the free road) and extend for three miles between Km 47 and 52, about 13 miles south of Rosarito. Exit the toll road at Cantamar.

③ PLAYA LA FONDA
South of Rosarito

Northwest Baja Norte map, page 44

From the bluffs above, you'll catch your first view of this beach as it curves enticingly around the irregular projections of the coastline. The sand is fine and clean. Spending a night at Alisitos Trailer Park (see listing in this chapter), which sits on the bluff, allows you to take full advantage of the setting. Watching the moon's reflection on the sea and sand below is a romantic experience for any couple. This is a great place to stroll barefoot, letting the sand ooze between your toes, and to dash out into the receding wetness of the last wave. Get the things you need in Rosarito. Summer is the preferred time to visit, as winter is chilly. For things to do here, see the Rosarito–La Misión Area, earlier in this chapter.

Directions: The beach is at Km 59 on Highway 1, about 20 miles south of Rosarito. Take the Alisitos exit off the toll road.

④ PLAYA LA MISIÓN
At La Misión

Northwest Baja Norte map, page 44

We have enjoyed this wide, soft sand beach while visiting friends who have a house in La Misión. The rocky prominence blocking the north end affords elevated spots for sitting and scanning the ocean for the plumes of gray whales as they migrate south in the fall and north in the spring. During weekends the beach can be very crowded near the south end. It is especially popular with locals. Surf fishing can produce perch and corbina. Obtain supplies in Rosarito. Summer is the preferred time to visit, as winter is chilly. For things to do here, see the Rosarito–La Misión Area, earlier in this chapter.

Directions: The beach extends for about one mile north of the Río Guadalupe at Km 69 on the toll road (the free road goes inland at La Misión, just to the north). At La Misión, 24 miles south of Rosarito on Highway 1D, the free road (old Highway 1) crosses under the toll road (Highway 1D). Drive two miles south on the toll road to the parking area on the west side of the highway in the arroyo of the Río Guadalupe.

5 PLAYA MAL PASO
South of La Misión

Northwest Baja Norte map, page 44

This is one of the most spectacular beaches in all of Baja, with a wide strip of sand that sweeps in an unbroken line from one end to the other. Since there are only three access points, a little walking will yield as much solitude as a person could need. The sand is clean and soft, and the beat of the surf is soothing and relaxing. At Mal Paso Trailer Park it is possible to drive out on imported clay soil and camp close to the surf line. In fact, few beaches in Baja allow vehicular access so close to the surf. The song of the sea lulls campers into a peaceful, restorative sleep.

Beachgoers might see grunion here during the fishes' frenzied nocturnal mating ritual—a startling sight for those who have never witnessed the hilarious spectacle. These seven-inch smelt spawn through the spring and summer only on three or four nights following each full or new moon and then for a one- to three-hour period immediately after high tide. Females swim onto the beach accompanied by several males, dig themselves into the sand, and lay their eggs. The males discharge their milt on the sand near the female and go back to the water. The female then frees herself and returns to the sea. The eggs remain buried in the sand for about 10 days, until the next series of high tides washes them out. As the baby grunion hatch and immediately swim off, fishermen dash about, scooping them up after each wave and filling their buckets. Grunion are good broiled or battered and deep-fried.

The nearest supplies are in Rosarito. Summer is the preferred time to visit, as winter is chilly. For things to do here, see the Rosarito–La Misión Area, earlier in this chapter.

Directions: The beach extends about 2.5 miles. Access it from Mal Paso Trailer Park (see listing in this chapter) at Km 71, Baja Seasons (see listing in this chapter) at Km 72, or La Salina (the salt pan) at Km 73.

6 BAHÍA TODOS SANTOS BEACHES
South of Ensenada

Northwest Baja Norte map, page 44

Even though we use the plural, this is really one long beach. Various segments have different names, depending upon what is behind them: Playas Hermosa, Corona, Mona Lisa, and Estero. The bay is polluted near Ensenada but farther south, toward the estero, it is cleaner. We have had a great deal of enjoyment on these very wide beaches, whether riding horses, walking, wading in the surf, or just sitting and watching the gulls and shorebirds as the waves roll in. Supplies can be picked up out on Highway 1 or on the side streets. Visit in summer, as winter gets chilly. For things to do here, see the Ensenada Area, earlier in this chapter.

Directions: Starting from Corona Beach Trailer Park (see listing in this chapter) on the north, the beaches extend about 1.5 miles past Playa Monalisa (see listing in this chapter) and El Faro Beach Motel and Trailer Park (see listing in this chapter) to Estero Beach Resort and RV Park (see listing in this chapter).

7 PLAYA PUNTA BANDA
In Punta Banda

Northwest Baja Norte map, page 44

The beach in front of La Jolla Beach Camp and Villarino RV Park (see listings in this chapter) is very popular with campers. Small boats can be launched into the surf of the bay for fishing and diving along the point. Obtain supplies in Punta Banda or back in Maneadero. Visit in summer, as winter gets chilly. For things to do here, see the Ensenada Area, earlier in this chapter.

Directions: The beach runs along the north side of the Punta Banda Peninsula. From Maneadero on Highway 1, take the Punta Banda road for about eight miles to the beach.

⑧ PLAYA SAN ANTONIO DEL MAR
Northwest of Colonet

Northwest Baja Norte map, page 45

There are dunes behind the large beach and plenty of room for camping. (See San Antonio del Mar Beach campground in this chapter.) People like to cruise in their all-terrain vehicles in the dunes, surf, and cast into the surf for perch and corbina. The road in is best handled by pickups or four-wheel-drive vehicles. Colonet has the basic supplies. Summer is the time to visit, as winter is chilly.

Directions: Access is by a seven-mile dirt road leaving Highway 1 near the north end of the Colonet bridge at the San Antonio del Mar sign. It is about 65 miles south of Maneadero.

⑨ PLAYA SAN RAMON
Northwest and west of San Quintín

Northwest Baja Norte map, page 45

Surfers like this wide sand beach that extends for about 12 miles south of the Río Santo Domingo, ending at some cliffs. There are lots of Pismo clams to dig for, and the surf fishing for perch and corbina is good. Obtain supplies in San Quintín. Summer is the time to visit, as winter is chilly. For things to do here, see the San Quintín Area, earlier in this chapter.

Directions: Access the beach west of Posada Don Diego RV Park (see listing in this chapter) on a soft sand road that leads to the dunes or by rough four-wheel-drive roads west of San Quintín.

⑩ BAHÍA SANTA MARÍA BEACHES
South of San Quintín

Northwest Baja Norte map, page 45

This magnificent, wide beach extends unbroken from the mouth of Bahía San Quintín for about 10 miles south to Arroyo Socorro. Many sand dollars dot the beach, and if you dig around in the sand, you'll find Pismo clams. Surf fishing can be good for perch and corbina, and the waves attract surfers. San Quintín has a full array of supplies. Summer is the time to visit, as winter is chilly. For things to do here, see the San Quintín Area, earlier in this chapter.

Directions: The northern beach, Playa Santa María, is reached at Cielito Lindo Motel and RV Park and Gypsys Beach Camp (see listings in this chapter). The southern beach, Playa Pabellón, is reached at El Pabellón RV Park and Playa de Tranquilo (see listings in this chapter). Access is also possible via sandy roads off the road into Cielito Lindo and off Highway 1.

Chapter 2

Northeast Baja Norte

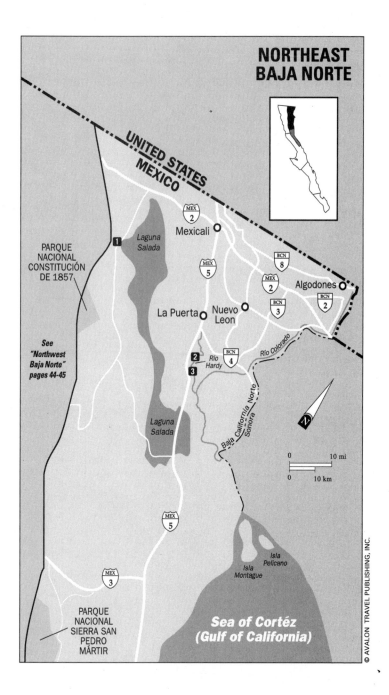

NORTHEAST BAJA NORTE

UNITED STATES
MEXICO

MEX 2

Mexicali

Laguna Salada

PARQUE NACIONAL CONSTITUCIÓN DE 1857

1

MEX 5

BCN 8

MEX 2

BCN 3

Algodones

BCN 2

La Puerta

Nuevo Leon

See
"Northwest
Baja Norte"
pages 44-45

2 Río Hardy

3

BCN 4

Río Colorado

Baja California Norte Sonora

N

Laguna Salada

0   10 mi
0   10 km

MEX 5

Isla Pelicano

Isla Montague

MEX 3

© AVALON TRAVEL PUBLISHING, INC.

PARQUE NACIONAL SIERRA SAN PEDRO MÁRTIR

**Sea of Cortéz
(Gulf of California)**

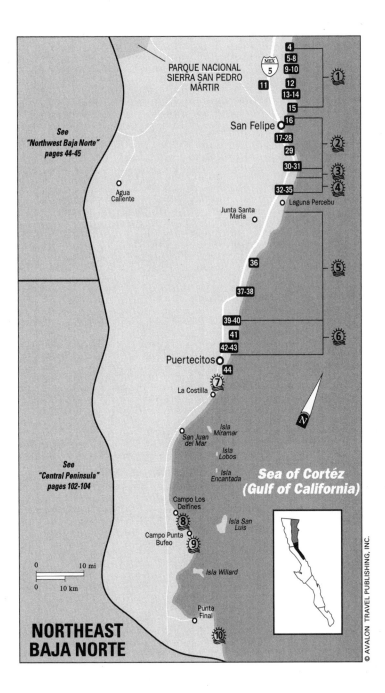

PARQUE NACIONAL
SIERRA SAN PEDRO
MÁRTIR

MEX 5

4
5-8
9-10
12
13-14
15

11

1

San Felipe

16
17-28
29
30-31
32-35

2
3
4

See
"Northwest Baja Norte"
pages 44-45

Agua
Caliente

Junta Santa
María

Laguna Percebu

36

37-38

39-40
41
42-43

5

6

Puertecitos

44

7

La Costilla

Isla
Miramar

San Juan
del Mar

Isla
Lobos

Isla
Encantada

N

Sea of Cortéz
(Gulf of California)

See
"Central Península"
pages 102-104

Campo Los
Delfines

Isla San
Luis

8

Campo Punta
Bufeo

9

Isla Willard

0   10 mi

0   10 km

Punta
Final

10

NORTHEAST
BAJA NORTE

© AVALON TRAVEL PUBLISHING, INC.

Northeast Baja Norte

Readily accessible from Southern California through Mexicali, this stretch of the Baja California Peninsula is very popular. Winter is the prime season, while summer is the most uncomfortable with high desert temperatures. The area is easy to get to for long weekends, and even for short ones if you are willing to push it. San Felipe, the center of activity, is a mere 124 miles south of the U.S.–Mexico border on Highway 5–the nearest Baja resort on the Sea of Cortéz.

From San Felipe the paved road leading 54 miles south to Puertecitos has its limitations. It is badly marred with potholes and has numerous small *vados* (dips into stream channels). Unlike elsewhere in Baja, these *vados* are not always announced to drivers by warning signs. The waterways they drop into are mostly narrow, creating a sudden plunge and an equally sudden ascent on the other side. Popping into one at high speed could be disastrous. This road must be taken at moderate speed, preferably in daylight.

The large tourist population disperses itself into a huge collection of *campos, playas,* and RV parks on the water between Río Hardy on the north and Puertecitos on the south. Pavement ends at Puertecitos, and the rugged dirt road on south to Bahía Gonzaga and ultimately Highway 1 at Laguna Chapala is suitable only for high-clearance vehicles.

Sierra de Juárez Area
(campground 1)
The Sierra de Juárez tilts gradually upward to the east, then drops precipitously down a 5,000-foot escarpment to the desert floor at sea level. The Rumorosa Grade on old Highway 2 is steep, curvy, and scenic, with startling vistas of the desert far below. A parallel toll road with an easier gradient is also available. The eastern slope has several palm-lined streams cut through solid rock, with water running from pool to pool. Exploring is best done in winter, as the rock-lined canyons become ovenlike in the summer heat.

Río Hardy Area
(campgrounds 2–3)
The Río Hardy is about 40 miles south of the border and 80 miles north of San Felipe. It is not on the Sea of Cortéz and, accordingly, people go there for different activities—freshwater fishing, game-bird hunting, and waterskiing. The river is fed mainly by agricultural drain water.

San Felipe and Puertecitos Areas
(campgrounds 4–44)
Originally a fishing village, San Felipe has had 50 years since the arrival of paved roads to stimulate development of a strong tourist clientele. With the totuava fish population depleted and currently protected, the shrimp fishery all but moribund, and commercial fishing in the northernmost reaches of the Sea of Cortéz closed by presidential decree, tourism, including sportfishing, now supports the local economy. The growth of hotels, campgrounds, and resort developments is continuous. Great beaches are the main attraction.

Starting about 10 miles north of San Felipe and continuing another 54 miles south to Puertecitos, there is a series of campos and *playas* on the Sea of Cortéz, each with its own sign and access road off Highway 5. Even when they adjoin each other, they have separate access roads. Along some stretches of highway, such roads appear every quarter mile.

While most of these *campos* lease sites by the year and do not serve overnight travelers, some indicate on their signs that they have camping facilities. These vary from nothing except a place to pitch a tent or park a rig to full-service establishments. Frequent campers check them all out, settle into a favorite, and return year after year. Newcomers with nothing to guide them are completely befuddled and can exhaust all their available time driving down one access road after another.

The Puertecitos camping experience is out of the ordinary, requiring an attitude adjustment. The large number of visitors who seek out this area desire the simplicity and tranquillity of desert living on a beach far from the trappings of urbanized society. Sunrises and sunsets take on special significance; the comings and goings of the extreme daily tides become endlessly fascinating. The satisfying pleasures of life are oriented to natural phenomena rather than contrived amusements. There is much opportunity for intriguing activities, yet there is no need to do anything. Camping here can touch on the essence of mañana-land and foster a great refreshing of the spirit, or it can be the epitome of privation in a primitive existence.

Fishing

In the vicinity of Puertecitos, anglers will find corvina, bay bass, triggerfish, barracuda, sierra, pargo, and grouper. Around San Felipe you can expect corvina, croaker, and various types of bass. If you don't have your own boat, you can usually rent a *panga* wherever there are local commercial fishermen. Ask other campers who have been there awhile how the fishing is, as it comes and goes.

Alex's (Alejandro's) Sportfishing in San Felipe has a good reputation with foreign residents. His office is on the city's *malecón* (waterfront), and he is usually nearby. He speaks good English and charges fair prices for half-day trips.

Boating

Many visitors bring cartop boats or small trailered boats to San Felipe and Puertecitos for fishing. Others tow large trailered boats to begin an extended cruise of the Sea of Cortéz—at times with the planned destination being Cabo San Lucas or mainland Mexico ports such as Bahía Kino, San Carlos, Guaymas, or points even farther south. Starting from San Felipe or Puertecitos can save many miles of highway trailering farther into Baja or onto the mainland.

Boaters must learn to deal with the special conditions created by the area's extreme tidal ranges. They must coordinate launching and retrieving with high tides and avoid anchoring in shallow water at high tide. Boaters can launch using a special vehicle at Ruben's RV Park (see listing in this chapter). Four launch ramps are available in San Felipe at high tide—at Ruben's, El Cortéz Motel, Club de Pesca RV Park (see listing in this chapter), and at the marina, and the ramp in Puertecitos—for about $5 each. There are no longer any free launch ramps in the area.

Off-Roading

Running around the desert and on the beaches in various off-road vehicles (ORVs) is a major activity in these parts. People use all manner of vehicles, many of them homemade. A common denominator is that they are lightweight and have soft, fat tires. There are motor scooters, trail bikes, dune buggies, sand rails, all-terrain vehicles (ATVs), two-wheelers, three-wheelers, four-wheelers, and so on.

Tidepooling

The high tidal range of 20 feet or more exposes hundreds of yards of seafloor at low tide, inviting exploration. The incoming tide moves swiftly enough to warrant attentiveness and brisk walking to avoid being dunked, however.

Mountaineering

West of San Felipe and Puertecitos are the two northernmost ranges of the many mountains that form the high spine of the peninsula—the northern Sierra de Juárez and the southern Sierra San Pedro Mártir. The great eastern escarpment of Baja's highest peak, the 10,154-foot El Picacho del Diablo, looms behind San Felipe, offering a mountain climbing adventure, but one that only experts should attempt. It is an extremely grueling and dangerous ascent.

The eastern canyons of both ranges are steep and feature hidden pools and palm groves. Huge boulders and smooth water-worn rock faces are difficult and risky to surmount. Summer heat can turn these canyons into ovens. Exploring them for their hidden nooks is best done in the cool of winter. You might observe other intrepid mountaineers, desert bighorn sheep, in these canyons.

Excursions

If you don't have the equipment to get off the pavement or onto the water, you can have someone take you for a fee.

Dining

Two good dining choices in San Felipe are El Nido (348 Mar de Cortéz) and George's Restaurant and Bar (336 Mar de Cortéz Sur).

Campgrounds

1 GUADALUPE CANYON HOT SPRINGS AND CAMPGROUND

🚶 🏊 🐾 🏕️ ⛺

West of Mexicali
Northeast Baja Norte map, page 76

This is a very old location, possibly the oldest campground in all of Baja California. The hot springs and palm oasis were found by Don Jose Loya Murillo in 1940 while chasing cattle with his sons. In 1958 he retired from ranching and homesteaded in the canyon, building a few hot tubs. Over the years three campgrounds were operated communally by three brothers. At present campgrounds 1 and 2 are operated by Arturo and Angel Loya as Campo #1, and Campo #3 is operated by Javier Loya. It adjoins #1 on the uphill side and is less well developed, however we stayed there and liked it. The camps are open year-round and are busiest on weekends. You may be able to arrange for a guide to take you exploring in Indian caves and to view rock art. Other features include waterfalls, hiking, and rock climbing. Heavy rains can wash out the road. Winter is the time to come, as summer is hot.

Campsites, facilities: There are nine campsites in Arturo's Campo #1 and several others in Javier's Campo #3 accommodating from one to four vehicles each, all without hookups. Each site has picnic tables, barbecue pits, *palapas,* trees, and private concrete and rock hot tubs with valves to control the temperature of geo-thermal mineral water. Facilities include hot showers, flush and outhouse toilets, a pool with 80-degree Fahrenheit natural water, a restaurant (open on weekends), a small store, gas and oil sales, and cellular phone service. Tent camping is very popular, as access is most suitable for small vehicles. Potable water (all water here is mineral), food, ice, and firewood must be brought in by campers. Due to the remote location, security is not a problem.

Reservations, fees: Reservations are recommended on weekends. Fees are very high in Campo #1 units—$30 to $50 for one vehicle per night and $20 for each additional vehicle during peak season from October 15 to June 1. In peak season a two-night stay is required on weekends. In off-season from June 2 to October 14 rates start at $20 per night with no minimum stay. Rates for Campo #3 were not available at press time.

Directions: Take Highway 2 (the free road) east from Tecate approximately 66 miles or west from Mexicali about 28 miles, then head south on a graded dirt road at the "Cañon de Guadalupe" sign near Km 28. After about 27 miles, turn right (west) at a large sign and continue about six miles on a winding dirt road and the final two miles over a rough road with steep, narrow rocky spots and soft sand off the tracks. Passing can be tough and is not recommended for motor homes or trailers.

Contact: Make reservations for Campo #1 via email at mtalama@guadalupe-canyons.com. Drive in and contact Javier for Campo #3. Website: www.guadalupe-canyons.com.

2 CAMPO SONORA

🎣 🐾 🏕️ ⛺

South of Mexicali
Northeast Baja Norte map, page 76

The good news? The camp is set on the Río Hardy, where you can fish for carp and perch. There are also nearby hunting opportunities for waterfowl and white-winged doves. The bad news? This is a minimal facility and a poorly maintained one at that. Noise from the adjacent highway can be disturbing. A note of warning: It is difficult to find a place to purchase supplies without going back to Mexicali, so it's best to enter Mexico fully prepared for your entire trip if you'll be staying here. Visit in winter, as summer can be hot.

Campsites, facilities: There are seven campsites with *palapas,* very dirty toilets, and a small restaurant that is open in summer for drinks and snacks. Don't drink the water. The park is secured with a chain at the entrance to the parking lot. Tent campers are welcome. Obtain supplies in Mexicali.

Reservations, fees: All sites are first come, first served. The fee is low—$7 per night.

Directions: From the border just north of Mexicali head about 40 miles south on Highway 5. The park is at Km 58.

Contact: Drive in and talk to the owner.

🄳 CAMPO MOSQUEDA
🏃 🚴 🏊 🎣 ⛴ 🐴 🚐 ⛺

South of Mexicali
Northeast Baja Norte map, page 76

Being so close to the border makes this a very convenient destination. It is a large, attractive campground with lots of trees and palms. Some of the campsites border a small, pretty man-made lake. If you like freshwater fishing, you'll be happy: the lake is stocked with catfish and largemouth and smallmouth bass. Fees are $1 per rod and $3 per kilogram of fish caught. Waterskiing and hunting for waterfowl and white-winged doves are also excellent. A note of warning: It is difficult to find a place to purchase goods without going back to Mexicali, so it's best to enter Mexico fully supplied for your entire trip if you will be staying here. Visit in winter, as summer can be hot.

Campsites, facilities: There are 50 campsites, of which 20 have electricity. On the premises are clean restrooms with flush toilets and cold showers, a restaurant, and a lake. Don't drink the water. The owner lives on the premises, so security is good. Tent campers are welcome. Obtain supplies in Mexicali.

Reservations, fees: All sites are first come, first served. The fee is low—$7 per night.

Directions: From the border just north of Mexicali, head about 40 miles south on Highway 5. Turn off at Km 60, which is well marked with a large sign, and drive one mile.

Contact: Campo Mosqueda, Km 53.5 Carretera a San Felipe, Mexicali, Baja California, Mexico, Mex. tel. 686/666-1520.

🄴 CAMPO LOS AMIGOS
🏃 🚴 🏊 🐴 🚐 ⛺

North of San Felipe
Northeast Baja Norte map, page 77

This campground is at the northern end of the string of *campos* and *playas* along the Sea of Cortéz north of San Felipe. The shoreline to the north turns into extensive mudflats extending south from the mouth of the Colorado River. To the south there is a fine beach. Winter is the time to come, as summer is hot. For things to do here, see the San Felipe and Puertecitos Areas, earlier in this chapter.

Campsites, facilities: There's room for an indeterminate number of campers. Facilities include cold showers (available for $1), pit toilets, a few *palapas,* and tables. Don't drink the water. The manager lives on the premises, so security is good. Tent campers are welcome. Obtain supplies in San Felipe.

Reservations, fees: All sites are first come, first served. Fees are low—$2 for day use, $5 per night, and $150 per month.

Directions: From San Felipe drive about 10 miles north on Highway 5, then turn east at Km 173 and continue one mile on a wide, hard-packed dirt road.

Contact: Drive in and talk to the manager.

🄵 PLAYA GRANDE
🏃 🚴 🏊 🎣 🐴 🚐 ⛺

North of San Felipe
Northeast Baja Norte map, page 77

Playa Grande is worth a visit. The beach lives

up to its name, extending north and south in front of the camp. Camping here is an enjoyable experience, even though the facility is a bit run-down. Winter is the time to come, as summer is hot. For things to do here, see the San Felipe and Puertecitos Areas, earlier in this chapter.

Campsites, facilities: Pit toilets and 14 *palapas* are provided. Don't drink the water. The manager lives on the premises, so security is good. Tent campers are welcome. Obtain supplies in San Felipe.

Reservations, fees: All sites are first come, first served. Fees are $5–6.

Directions: From San Felipe drive about 10 miles north on Highway 5, turn east at Km 173, and continue one mile on a good dirt road.

Contact: Drive in and talk to the manager.

6 CAMPO JALISCO

North of San Felipe
Northeast Baja Norte map, page 77

Though this small RV park offers the bare minimum in services, it is smack-dab on a magnificent beach—wide and long with toe-tickling sand. When someone asks us for a beautiful, quiet, no-frills beach camp in the San Felipe area where they can get away from it all, we mention Campo Jalisco. Winter is the time to come, as summer is hot. For things to do here, see the San Felipe and Puertecitos Areas, earlier in this chapter.

Campsites, facilities: Of the 19 campsites, all with *palapas,* 14 are on the beach. Neither water nor electricity is provided, though there are flush toilets and cold showers. Don't drink the water. The owner lives on the premises, so security is good. Tent campers are welcome. Obtain supplies in San Felipe.

Reservations, fees: Camping is first come, first served. The fee is moderate—$10 per night.

Directions: From San Felipe drive about 10 miles north on Highway 5, turn east at Km 175, and continue one mile on a wide, hard-packed dirt road.

Contact: Drive in, and the owner will collect your fee.

7 CAMPO HACIENDA BEACH

North of San Felipe
Northeast Baja Norte map, page 77

Here you camp on the same great beach as at Campo Jalisco, but in a slightly different setting. Winter is the time to come, as summer is hot. For things to do here, see the San Felipe and Puertecitos Areas, earlier in this chapter.

Campsites, facilities: Set up your RV or tent wherever you please, as there are no marked campsites. Flush toilets and cold showers are sometimes available. For $1 you can shower at Campo Jalisco (see listing earlier in this chapter) next door. The owner lives on the premises and keeps a cable across the road, so security is good. Obtain supplies in San Felipe.

Reservations, fees: Camping is first come, first served. Fees are low—$6 per night and $35 per week.

Directions: From San Felipe drive about 10 miles north on Highway 5, turn east at Km 175, and continue one mile on a wide, hard-packed dirt road.

Contact: Drive in, and the owner will collect your fee.

8 EL DORADO RANCH RV PARK

North of San Felipe
Northeast Baja Norte map, page 77

Though campers may stay here, the primary goal of El Dorado Ranch is to sell memberships with permanent RV spaces or homesites. The park is on a beautiful beach and has more amenities than other RV facilities north of San Felipe. Winter is the time to come, as summer is hot. For things to do here, see the San Felipe and Puertecitos Areas, earlier in this chapter.

Campsites, facilities: There are 75

campsites (44 pull-through), all with full hookups and trees. The front row just above the beach has 15 campsites with tables. Tiled restrooms with flush toilets and hot showers, a laundry, a heated pool, a whirlpool tub, a store, two restaurants, nightly entertainment, rental horses, tennis courts, free shuttle daily to San Felipe, and dune buggy tours are available. Don't drink the water. Security is tight, as you must enter through a manned gate with a 24-hour guard. Tent camping is not provided for, though the brochures show a tent set up. Obtain supplies in San Felipe.

Reservations, fees: Reservations are accepted. The fee is very high—$28 per night, $165 per week, and $525 per month.

Directions: From San Felipe drive about eight miles north on Highway 5, then turn east at Km 176 and continue one mile on a wide, hard-packed dirt road.

Contact: El Dorado Ranch RV Park, P.O. Box 3809, Calexico, CA 92232, Mex. tel. 686/577-0010, fax 686/577-0009, email: email@eldoradoranch.com, website: eldoradoranch.com.

🄈 PETE'S CAMP EL PARAISO
🏃 🚲 🏊 🎣 🐴 🚐 🛖

North of San Felipe
Northeast Baja Norte map, page 77
An old campground, Pete's Camp El Paraiso has built up a substantial following over the years. It was crammed full on the weekend we visited, while the other campgrounds north of San Felipe were deserted. Don't come if you're in the mood for serenity; the place can be downright boisterous, as the clientele consists primarily of the beach-vehicle and partying crowd. Winter is the time to come, as summer is hot. For things to do here, see the San Felipe and Puertecitos Areas, earlier in this chapter.

Campsites, facilities: There are 82 campsites for RV and tent camping on the beach with *palapas*. Facilities include restrooms with hot showers (for $1) and flush toilets, a restaurant, a bar, and an RV dump station. Ask for drink-

ing water. A night watchman is on duty, as are police patrols, and the camp is well populated with permanent residents, so security is good. Obtain supplies in San Felipe.

Reservations, fees: Reservations are accepted. The fee is moderate—$10 per night, $70 per week, and $200 per month.

Directions: From San Felipe drive about eight miles north on Highway 5, then turn east at Km 178 and continue one mile on the good dirt road.

Contact: Pete's Camp, P.O. Box 516, Temecula, CA 92592, U.S. tel. 909/676-4224, fax 909/699-6673, email: rafael@petescamp.com, website: www.petescamp.com.

🔟 LA PLAYA ENCANTADA
🏃 🚲 🏊 🎣 🐴 🚐 🛖

North of San Felipe
Northeast Baja Norte map, page 77
This beach camp adjoins Pete's Camp El Paraiso (see listing earlier in this chapter) across a fence. The first time we were here, the place was new but not yet functioning. Two years later it appeared abandoned yet was still accessible. Before driving down to the beach, walk the last pitch of road to see if your vehicle can handle it. The camping area is so narrow it would be difficult for a truck and trailer to turn around. Winter is the time to come, as summer is hot. For things to do here, see San Felipe and Puertecitos Areas, earlier in this chapter.

Campsites, facilities: There are 30 *palapas,* along with showers and flush toilets that don't work. Water and security are not provided. Tent camping is appropriate. Obtain supplies in San Felipe.

Reservations, fees: All sites are first come, first served. When we visited, there was no one to ask about the fee, nor was it posted.

Directions: From San Felipe drive about eight miles north on Highway 5, turn east at Km 178, and continue one mile on the good dirt road.
Contact: Drive in and park.

11 EL CACHANILLA RV PARK

North of San Felipe

Northeast Baja Norte map, page 77

This park is part of the El Dorado Ranch operation. Some members stay here and drive over to El Dorado Ranch RV Park (see listing in this chapter) to take advantage of the amenities and play on the beach. For nonmembers there is little to recommend the place, as it is out in the desert with only a very distant view of the Sea of Cortéz. Winter is the time to come, as summer is hot. For things to do here, see the San Felipe and Puertecitos Areas, earlier in this chapter.

Campsites, facilities: There are 81 campsites, eight with full hookups, 11 with electric only, and 62 with no hookups. Facilities include a dump station ($2 fee), tiled restrooms with flush toilets and hot showers ($1 fee), laundry facilities, a pool, a small store, a restaurant, RV storage, a mechanical shop, air supply for tires, and a clubhouse with a pool table, a TV, darts, and a library. Don't drink the water. Security is provided by a watchman. Tent campers are welcome. Obtain supplies in San Felipe.

Reservations, fees: Reservations are accepted. Fees are high–$18 per night, $107 per week, and $345 per month.

Directions: From San Felipe drive about seven miles north on Highway 5, turn west at Km 179, and continue one mile on the good dirt road.

Contact: El Cachanilla RV Park, P.O. Box 3809, Calexico, CA 92232, Mex. tel. 686/576-0005, fax 686/577-0009.

12 CAMPO LOS COMPADRES

North of San Felipe

Northeast Baja Norte map, page 77

You camp on a gentle slope that leads down to a nice beach and has plenty of room for rigs or tents. The beach is wide and stretches far in both directions. We spent a pleasant night watching the tide come in and go out and enjoyed poking around in little tidepools among the boulders. We also admired the display of fireworks launched skyward from Pete's Camp El Paraíso (see listing in this chapter) to the north and marveled at the variety and number of beach vehicles coming and going. A little boy was sent down to collect the fee, which he stoutly insisted was $2 more than we had been told upon arrival. We didn't have the heart to complicate his life by arguing. Winter is the time to come, as summer is hot. For things to do here, see San Felipe and Puertecitos Areas, earlier in this chapter.

Campsites, facilities: Pit toilets and several *palapas* are provided for RVers and tenters. Don't drink the water. The manager lives on the premises, so security is good. Obtain supplies in San Felipe.

Reservations, fees: All sites are first come, first served. The fee is moderate–$10 per night.

Directions: From San Felipe drive about seven miles north on Highway 5, then turn east at Km 180 and continue one mile on the good dirt road.

Contact: Drive in and talk to the manager.

13 SAN DIEGO BEACH

North of San Felipe

Northeast Baja Norte map, page 77

You'll find little room to maneuver a vehicle on this tiny, pretty beach. It is suitable only for small rigs and tents—don't try it with a trailer. Winter is the time to come, as summer is hot. For things to do here, see the San Felipe and Puertecitos Areas, earlier in this chapter.

Campsites, facilities: Hot showers and *palapas* are provided. Don't drink the water. The manager lives on the premises, so security is good. Tent campers are welcome. Obtain supplies in San Felipe.

Reservations, fees: All sites are first come, first served. The fee is low— $7 per night.

Directions: From San Felipe drive about six miles north on Highway 5, turn east at Km 182, and continue one mile on the fair dirt road.
Contact: Drive in and talk to the manager.

14 PLAYA DEL SOL

🚶 🚴 ⛵ 🛶 🐕 🚐 ⛺

North of San Felipe
Northeast Baja Norte map, page 77
The campsites are set on several terraces rising above a beautiful beach—a long, wide strip of powdery sand. Winter is the time to come, as summer is hot. For things to do here, see the San Felipe and Puertecitos Areas, earlier in this chapter.
Campsites, facilities: There are 45 campsites with *palapas* for RVs and tents. Neither water nor electricity is provided, though there are flush toilets and hot showers ($1 fee). Don't drink the water. Security is provided by a resident owner. Obtain supplies in San Felipe.
Reservations, fees: Reservations are accepted. The fee is low—$5.50 per night.
Directions: From San Felipe drive about six miles north on Highway 5, turn east at Km 183, and continue one mile on the fair dirt road.
Contact: Playa del Sol, Apartado Postal 128, San Felipe, Baja California, Mexico, or P.O. Box 3635, Calexico, CA 92232. There is no phone.

15 PLAYA BLANCA

🚶 🚴 ⛵ 🛶 🐕 🚐 ⛺

North of San Felipe
Northeast Baja Norte map, page 77
Playa Blanca, a wide beach, extends far in both directions. It offers some trees and plenty of room for RV and tent camping. An abandoned one-story hotel sits on the dunes above a nice stretch of beach, attracting the occasional sightseer. The open camping area is astride a beach-vehicle route, so it can get loud. Winter is the time to come, as summer is hot. For things to do here, see the San Felipe and Puertecitos Areas, earlier in this chapter.

Campsites, facilities: Run-down toilets and some *palapas* are provided. Don't drink the water. There is no security. Obtain supplies in San Felipe.
Reservations, fees: All sites are first come, first served. The fee is moderate—$10 per night.
Directions: From San Felipe drive about five miles north on Highway 5, turn east at Km 184, and continue 1.5 miles to the Sea of Cortéz.
Contact: Drive in and talk to the manager.

16 CAMPO NUMERO UNO

🚶 🚴 ⛵ 🛶 🐕 🚐 ⛺

In San Felipe
Northeast Baja Norte map, page 77
The northernmost campground on the beach in San Felipe, Campo Numero Uno is a pleasant spot for folks who want to rough it in a tent or RV. Being off the beaten track, it is not well known. Winter is the time to come, as summer is hot. For things to do here, see the San Felipe and Puertecitos Areas, earlier in this chapter.
Campsites, facilities: Each of the 65 full-hookup campsites comes with *palapa,* table, and barbecue. On the premises you'll find tiled restrooms with flush toilets, cold showers, a dump station, and a restaurant, which is open only at busy times. Don't drink the water. The camp is secured by a resident manager, a guard, and a gated fence. Tent campers may use any of the sites. Obtain supplies in San Felipe.
Reservations, fees: All sites are first come, first served. Fees are moderate—$10 per night, $50 per week, or $150 per month.
Directions: Take Highway 5 into San Felipe, 124 miles south of Mexicali. The park is behind the hill on Avenida Mar de Cortéz Norte, on a narrow sand beach with rocks that are exposed at low tide. All the other northside beach parks are on the waterfront street east of Avenida Mar de Cortéz. Follow the signs.
Contact: Drive in and talk to the manager or phone Mex. tel. 686/577-1139.

17 MARCO'S RV PARK
🚶 🚴 🏊 🎣 ⛺ 🐕 🚐

In San Felipe

Northeast Baja Norte map, page 77

The properties on the other side of the street are set beside the Sea of Cortéz, so Marco's lacks the main attraction in this area—a beachfront location. It has built up a loyal clientele, however, with many people returning just for the privacy. Winter is the time to come, as summer is hot. For things to do here, see the San Felipe and Puertecitos Areas, earlier in this chapter.

Campsites, facilities: There are 15 campsites with full hookups, concrete pads, *palapas,* and tables. Flush toilets and hot showers are provided. Don't drink the water. The park is secured with a gate. Tent campers are prohibited. Obtain supplies in San Felipe.

Reservations, fees: All sites are first come, first served. Fees are moderate—$8 per night, $50 per week, or $200 per month.

Directions: Take Highway 5 into San Felipe, 124 miles south of Mexicali. The park is on the land side of the waterfront street, just north of Ruben's RV Park (see listing in this chapter), which is a landmark by virtue of being the largest RV park in that neighborhood.

Contact: Drive in and talk to the manager.

18 PLAYA BONITA RV PARK
🚶 🚴 🏊 🎣 ⛺ 🐕 🚐 ⛺

In San Felipe

Northeast Baja Norte map, page 77

Playa Bonita RV Park is a very nice little facility on a wide, extensive beach. It is quiet with a family atmosphere, and restrooms are very clean. Since it fills up in winter, early birds get to settle into the few choice campsites overlooking the water. Winter is the time to come, as summer is hot. For things to do here, see the San Felipe and Puertecitos Areas, earlier in this chapter.

Campsites, facilities: For RVs, there are 10 campsites with full hookups, concrete pads, *palapas,* barbecues, and tables under trees. For tents there are six campsites with trees, *palapas,* tables, some barbecues, electricity, and water. Flush toilets, tiled hot showers, and laundry facilities are provided. Don't drink the water. The park is secured with gates and a resident manager. Obtain supplies in San Felipe.

Reservations, fees: Reservations are accepted. Fees are high—they vary according to season and location of sites.

Directions: Take Highway 5 into San Felipe, 124 miles south of Mexicali. The park is on the waterfront street, Avenida Golfo de California, on the north side of town, north of Ruben's RV Park (see next campground listing).

Contact: Playa Bonita RV Park, 475 East Badillo Street, Covina, CA 91723. For reservations, U.S. tel. 626/967-8977, Mex. tel./fax 686/577-1215.

19 RUBEN'S RV PARK
🚶 🚴 🏊 🎣 ⛺ 🐕 🚐 ⛰

In San Felipe

Northeast Baja Norte map, page 77

In front of Ruben's there's a great beach, a huge parcel of bright white sand, making this a very popular spot. Tenters often pitch their tents on the balconies atop the shade structures to get a better ocean view. It is a large campground and at times is a beehive of activity. Boaters can launch their watercraft using an ancient four-wheel-drive army truck at just about any tide for $20 to $40, depending on the size of the boat; a launch ramp is also available. Winter is the time to come, as summer is hot. For things to do here, see the San Felipe and Puertecitos Areas, earlier in this chapter.

Campsites, facilities: There are 50 pull-through campsites with full hookups, tables, and shade structures topped with balconies that afford ocean views. On the premises are flush toilets, hot showers, a restaurant, and a special vehicle used for launching boats. Don't drink the water. The park is well populated and is secured with a gate. Tent campers are welcome. Obtain supplies in San Felipe.

Reservations, fees: Reservations are accepted. Fees are moderate—$12 per night, $70 per week, $225 per month, or $1,400 per year.

Directions: Take Highway 5 into San Felipe, 124 miles south of Mexicali. The park is on the beach, on the waterfront street on the north side of town.

Contact: Ruben's RV Park, Apartado Postal 196, San Felipe, Baja California, Mexico, Mex. tel. 686/577-1442.

20 JOSEFINA'S RV PARK

In San Felipe

Northeast Baja Norte map, page 77

This very pleasant little RV park is on the same big beach as Ruben's (see previous campground listing). The people staying here when we came urged us not to tell anyone about it, and no one knew what the name was. There is no sign, and the camp appears to be part of Ruben's, which is not the case. We've been here a couple of times and haven't been able to find anyone in charge. The manager at Ruben's told us the name was Josefina's RV Park, but another source came up with Campo La Palapa. We just love these little mysteries. Winter is the time to come, as summer can sizzle. For things to do here, see the San Felipe and Puertecitos Areas, earlier in this chapter.

Campsites, facilities: There are 21 campsites with full hookups, concrete pads, balconies, and tables. Flush toilets and hot showers are provided. Don't drink the water. A manager lives on the premises, and the park is secured with a gate. Tent campers are welcome. Obtain supplies in San Felipe.

Reservations, fees: All sites are first come, first served. Fees are moderate—$12 per night to camp on the beach or $10 for a site back from the beach.

Directions: Take Highway 5 into San Felipe,

124 miles south of Mexicali. The park is on the beach on the north waterfront street, adjoining Ruben's RV Park on the south.

Contact: Drive in and talk to the manager.

21 VISTA DEL MAR RV PARK

In San Felipe

Northeast Baja Norte map, page 77

This is a very clean park on a slope with a brick driveway and well-manicured grounds. Though it has an ocean view, it is not on the beach—which is the main attraction in San Felipe. Winter is the time to come, as summer is hot. For things to do here, see the San Felipe and Puertecitos Areas, earlier in this chapter.

Campsites, facilities: There are 20 campsites with full hookups, concrete pads, tables, barbecues, and palm trees. Flush toilets and hot showers are provided. Don't drink the water. A manager lives on the premises, and the park is secured with a gate. Tent campers are welcome. Obtain supplies in San Felipe.

Reservations, fees: Reservations are accepted. Fees are moderate—$12 per night or $10 without electricity.

Directions: Take Highway 5 into San Felipe, 124 miles south of Mexicali. The park is at the corner of Avenidas Mar de Cortéz and Puerto Vallarta.

Contact: Drive in and talk to the manager.

22 CAMPO POSADA DEL MAR

In San Felipe

Northeast Baja Norte map, page 77

Tucked among city streets away from the Sea of Cortéz, this campground holds little attraction for tourists. Winter is the time to come, as summer is hot. For things to do here, see the San Felipe and Puertecitos Areas, earlier in this chapter.

Campsites, facilities: There are 60 two-story *palapas* with full hookups, concrete pads, trees, tables, and barbecues. Both RVs and tents can be accommodated. Flush toilets, hot showers, and rooms are available. Don't drink the water. Security is provided by a gate and a residential manager. Obtain supplies in San Felipe.

Reservations, fees: Reservations are accepted. Fees are moderate to high—$10 to $20 per night.

Directions: Take Highway 5 into San Felipe, 124 miles south of Mexicali. The park is in town at the junction of Golfo de California and San Felipe.

Contact: Campo Posada del Mar, 555 Golfo de California, San Felipe, Baja California, Mexico, Mex. tel. 686/577-1543.

23 LA JOLLA RV PARK

In San Felipe

Northeast Baja Norte map, page 77

The park is situated in a quiet residential neighborhood. However, it is not on the beach, which is what most people who come to San Felipe want. Winter is the time to come, as summer is hot. For things to do here, see the San Felipe and Puertecitos Areas, earlier in this chapter.

Campsites, facilities: There are 55 pull-through campsites with full hookups and *palapas*. Both RVs and tents can be accommodated. Facilities include flush toilets, hot showers, laundry, a pool, and a whirlpool tub. Don't drink the water. A manager lives on the premises. Obtain supplies in San Felipe.

Reservations, fees: Reservations are accepted. The fee is high—$15 per night.

Directions: Take Highway 5 into San Felipe, 124 miles south of Mexicali. The park is in the middle of town at Avenidas Manzanillo and Mar Bermejo.

Contact: La Jolla RV Park, P.O. Box 9019, Calexico, CA 92232.

24 CAMPO SAN FELIPE

In San Felipe

Northeast Baja Norte map, page 77

This popular park, which adjoins Playa de Laura RV Park (see next campground listing) to the south, has been a haven for RVers and tent campers for many, many years. It's in the heart of town, within walking distance of shops, restaurants, and other attractions. Winter is the time to come, as summer is hot. For things to do here, see the San Felipe and Puertecitos Areas, earlier in this chapter.

Campsites, facilities: There are 39 campsites, of which 34 have full hookups. Of the 34, 25 are pull-through sites. There are concrete pads, *palapas*, tables, and a dump station. Five tent sites have *palapas*, electricity, and water. Tiled restrooms with flush toilets and hot showers and laundry facilities are available. Don't drink the water. A resident owner and a watchman provide security. Obtain supplies in San Felipe.

Reservations, fees: Reservations are accepted. Fees are moderate to high—$15 to $20 per night, $105 to $140 per week, and $365 to $500 per month for RVs, and $10 per night, $70 per week, and $230 per month for tents.

Directions: Take Highway 5 into San Felipe, 124 miles south of Mexicali. The park is on the beach in the southern part of town on Avenida Mar de Cortéz.

Contact: Campo San Felipe, P.O. Box 952, Calexico, CA 92232, Mex. tel. 686/577-1012, email: camposanfelipe@hotmail.com.

25 PLAYA DE LAURA RV PARK

In San Felipe

Northeast Baja Norte map, page 77

We have stayed in this popular park and appreciated the large beach and its proximity to restaurants. The place was a bit too congested for us, however, and things can get pretty raucous.

Winter is the time to come, as summer is hot. For things to do here, see the San Felipe and Puertecitos Areas, earlier in this chapter.

Campsites, facilities: There are 45 campsites (22 full-hookup pull-throughs and 23 other sites with electricity and water), all of which may be used by tent campers, with concrete pads, *palapas,* tables, barbecues, a dump station, and some shade structures topped with balconies. Tiled restrooms with flush toilets and hot showers are provided, and campers can launch boats over the sand. Sportfishing boats are available for charter. Don't drink the water. The park is well populated and patrolled by city police. Obtain supplies in San Felipe.

Reservations, fees: Camping is first come, first served. Fees are high—$17 per night, $100 per week, $400 per month, and $1,800 per year for RVs or tents.

Directions: Take Highway 5 into San Felipe, 124 miles south of Mexicali. The park is on the beach in the southern part of town on Avenida Mar de Cortéz.

Contact: Playa de Laura RV Park, P.O. Box 686, Calexico, CA 92232, Mex. tel. 686/577-1128, fax 686/554-4712.

26 BAJA MAR RV SPORT BEACH CLUB
🚶 🚴 🏊 🎣 🛶 🐕 🚐 ⛰️

In San Felipe

Northeast Baja Norte map, page 77

Recently opened, this modern, attractive, full-service park is right in the middle of town and fronts on the beach. Winter is the time to come, as summer is hot. For things to do here, see the San Felipe and Puertecitos Areas, earlier in this chapter.

Campsites, facilities: There are 70 campsites with full hookups, concrete pads, *palapas,* tables, and barbecues. All sites accommodate both RV and tent campers. Facilities include tiled restrooms with flush toilets and hot showers and a laundry facility. Don't drink the water.

Security is provided by a resident manager. Obtain supplies in San Felipe.

Reservations, fees: Camping is first come, first served. Fees are high—$14 to $19 per night, with tents and automobiles at the low end and RVs and beachfront sites at the high end. One day is free for weekly stays. The monthly rate is $300 to $375.

Directions: Take Highway 5 into San Felipe, 124 miles south of Mexicali. The park is on the beach in the southern part of town on Avenida Mar de Cortéz, on the south side of Playa de Laura RV Park.

Contact: Baja Mar RV Sport Beach Club, Mar de Cortéz Sur, San Felipe, Baja California, Mexico. There is no phone.

27 VICTOR'S RV PARK
🚶 🚴 🏊 🎣 🛶 🐕 🚐 ⛰️

In San Felipe

Northeast Baja Norte map, page 77

This is a very popular park with a number of permanents, which gives it a residential atmosphere. It fills up quickly and is a little tight for maneuvering. Winter is the time to come, as summer is hot. For things to do here, see the San Felipe and Puertecitos Areas, earlier in this chapter.

Campsites, facilities: There are 50 pull-through campsites with full hookups and concrete pads. Flush toilets and hot showers are provided. Don't drink the water. The park is secure. Tent campers are welcome. Obtain supplies in San Felipe.

Reservations, fees: Camping is first come, first served. Fees are high—$15 per night, $75 per week, $200 per month, and $2,000 per year.

Directions: Take Highway 5 into San Felipe, 124 miles south of Mexicali. The park is on the beach in the southern part of town on Avenida Mar de Cortéz.

Contact: Victor's RV Park, P.O. Box 1227, Calexico, CA 92232, Mex. tel. 686/577-1056, fax 686/577-1752, email: cortezho@telnor.net.

28 CLUB DE PESCA RV PARK

In San Felipe

Northeast Baja Norte map, page 77

This is primarily a residential park containing privately owned houses and mobile homes. Though there is room for travelers, the residential atmosphere seems a bit incompatible with the tourist experience. The wide beach is a playground for people with ATVs, trail bikes, sand rails, dune buggies, and other fat-tired, sand-floating vehicles. Strollers may even find it enjoyable—provided they're agile enough to get out of the way. Boat launching costs about $5. Winter is the time to come, as summer is hot. For things to do here, see the San Felipe and Puertecitos Areas, earlier in this chapter.

Campsites, facilities: There are 40 campsites with electricity, water, *palapas,* and concrete pads. Sites located away from the beach have sewer hookups. Flush toilets, hot showers, a dump station, a recreation room, a launch ramp, and a store are on the property. Don't drink the water. There is 24-hour security. Tent campers are welcome. Obtain supplies in San Felipe.

Reservations, fees: Reservations are accepted. Fees are high—$18 per night for a site on the beach and $13 in back. If you stay a week, you get one day free; stay a month and receive a 30 percent discount. Long-term rates are $1,560 per year.

Directions: Take Highway 5 into San Felipe, 124 miles south of Mexicali. The park is on the beach in the southern part of town at the south end of Avenida Mar de Cortéz.

Contact: Club de Pesca RV Park, P.O. Box 3090, Calexico, CA 92232, Mex. tel. 686/577-1180, fax 686/577-1888, email: clubdepesca @telnor.net.

29 SAN FELIPE MARINA RESORT AND RV PARK

South of San Felipe

Northeast Baja Norte map, page 77

The wide beach below the elevated camping area is Playa San Felipe, which extends southward for another 7.5 miles. Beach vehicles can run the entire 10-mile stretch between San Felipe and Punta Estrella. The owners of San Felipe Marina Resort and RV Park want to make this an exclusive members-only resort and will undoubtedly attain their goal. When they do, the park will no longer have spaces available for nonmembers. Winter is the time to come, as summer is hot. For things to do here, see the San Felipe and Puertecitos Areas, earlier in this chapter.

Campsites, facilities: There are 143 campsites with full hookups (30- and 50-amp electrical outlets), cable TV, concrete pads, *palapas,* barbecues, and trees. Facilities include flush toilets and hot showers in clean, tiled restrooms, a laundry facility, pools, a store, a restaurant, a health spa, and tennis courts. A marina is under construction. Don't drink the water unless they have begun treating it (there are plans to do so). Security is provided 24 hours daily. Tents are not allowed. Obtain supplies in San Felipe.

Reservations, fees: Reservations are accepted. Fees are high—$22 to $24 per night, $132 to $144 per week, and $375 per month.

Directions: From San Felipe take Highway 5 south about three miles. The park is adjacent to the paved airport road well above the beach.

Contact: Mex. tel. 686/577-1455, email: sf marina@telnor.net.

30 CAMPO SAN FERNANDO

South of San Felipe

Northeast Baja Norte map, page 77

The park is perched on a bluff above the Sea of Cortéz with a stupendous view in all directions. One special feature is the sulfur springs, which send hot water bubbling up among rocks at low tide, creating small pools. Some people like dunking their bodies into the smelly water. Winter is the time to come, as summer is hot. For things to do here, see the San Felipe and Puertecitos Areas, earlier in this chapter.

Campsites, facilities: There are 30 campsites with full hookups for both RVs and tents. Tiled restrooms with flush toilets and hot showers are provided, as well as a dump station. Don't drink the water. The camp is fenced and has a night guard. Obtain supplies in San Felipe.

Reservations, fees: Reservations are accepted. Fees are moderate—$12 per night, $60 per week, $190 per month, and $1,200 per year for RVs, and $3 per person per night for tents.

Directions: Drive south on Highway 5 from the San Felipe airport road (5.5 miles south of the center of San Felipe) about three miles and turn east on the dirt road into the park. Watch for the sign.

Contact: Campo San Fernando, P.O. Box 23, Calexico, CA 92232.

31 EL FARO RV PARK

South of San Felipe

Northeast Baja Norte map, page 77

One of the more upscale campgrounds in the San Felipe area, El Faro is, however, a bit removed from restaurants, fishing charters, and so forth. Below it lies the northern stretch of beautiful, wide Playa Punta Estrella. Winter is the time to come, as summer is hot. For things to do here, see the San Felipe and Puertecitos Areas, earlier in this chapter.

Campsites, facilities: There are 135 pull-through campsites with full hookups and concrete pads. On the premises are flush toilets, hot showers, and a pool. Don't drink the water. The park is secured with a gate. Tent campers are not welcome. Obtain supplies in San Felipe.

Reservations, fees: Reservations are accepted. The fee is very high—$25 per night.

Directions: Drive south on Highway 5 from the San Felipe airport road (5.5 miles south of the center of San Felipe) about four miles. Take the turnoff at Km 15 and continue a few hundred yards to the park. Watch for the sign.

Contact: El Faro RV Park, Apartado Postal 85, San Felipe, Baja California, Mexico.

32 VILLA MARINA RV PARK

South of San Felipe

Northeast Baja Norte map, page 77

This is a new RV park and is still under development. When electricity is brought in, the addition of facilities such as a pool, laundry facilities, a store, and a restaurant will be possible. Winter is the time to come, as summer is hot. For things to do here, see the San Felipe and Puertecitos Areas, earlier in this chapter.

Campsites, facilities: There are 36 campsites with concrete pads, young trees, tables, and barbecues, but no hookups. Facilities include a shaded pavilion on the beach, water for washing (do not drink it; bottled water is available), a dump station, and tiled restrooms with flush toilets and hot showers. Security is provided by a resident watchman and a gate. Tent campers are welcome. Obtain supplies in San Felipe.

Reservations, fees: Reservations are accepted. Fees are moderate—$10 per night, $60 per week, or $175 per month. Yearly rates are $1,500 for a site on the beach and $700 in back.

Directions: Drive south on Highway 5 from the San Felipe airport road (5.5 miles south of the center of San Felipe) about five miles.

Contact: Mex. tel./fax 686/577-1342.

33 RANCHO VISTA HERMOSA

🏃 🚴 🏊 🎣 🐕 🚐 ⛺

South of San Felipe
Northeast Baja Norte map, page 77
This is the northernmost in a string of beach *campos* and *playas* on the Sea of Cortéz between San Felipe and Puertecitos. Campers who regularly come to this area find the campground that best suits their tastes and stick with it faithfully. Many eventually bring in a trailer and leave it parked in a campsite leased on an annual basis and return to it, trip after trip, year after year, gradually adding improvements as it becomes a permanent fixture on the landscape. Winter is the time to come, as summer is hot. For things to do here, see the San Felipe and Puertecitos Areas, earlier in this chapter.

Campsites, facilities: Toilets are provided, but there is no drinking water and no security. Tent campers are welcome. Obtain supplies in San Felipe.

Reservations, fees: All sites are first come, first served. The fee is low—$5 per night.

Directions: Drive south on Highway 5 from the San Felipe airport road (5.5 miles south of the center of San Felipe) about five miles. The park is on the beach, a few hundred yards off the road. Watch for the sign.

Contact: Drive in and talk to the manager.

34 LAS CONCHAS RV PARK

🏃 🚴 🏊 🎣 🐕 🚐 ⛺

South of San Felipe
Northeast Baja Norte map, page 77
Some 300 feet of beautiful beachfront is the star attraction at this new park. As time goes on, improvements will undoubtedly be made, including the addition of electricity. Winter is the time to come, as summer is hot. For things to do here, see the San Felipe and Puertecitos Areas, earlier in this chapter.

Campsites, facilities: There are 20 pull-through or tent campsites, all without hookups. Facilities include concrete pads, *palapas,* tables, barbecues, lights, water for washing (do not drink it), a dump station, and tiled restrooms with flush toilets and hot showers. Security is provided by a resident watchman. Obtain supplies in San Felipe.

Reservations, fees: Reservations are accepted. Fees are moderate—$10 per night for RVs or tents, $50 per week, or $200 per month.

Directions: Drive south on Highway 5 from the San Felipe airport road (5.5 miles south of the center of San Felipe) about seven miles. The park is on the beach.

Contact: Las Conchas RV Park, P.O. Box 526, Calexico, CA 92232. There is no phone.

35 RANCHO PUNTA ESTRELLA BEACH

🏃 🚴 🏊 🎣 🐕 🚐 ⛺

South of San Felipe
Northeast Baja Norte map, page 77
A huge area between the highway and the RV park has been cleared of vegetation, indicating that ambitious plans for development are afoot. The beach is huge, sprawling north, south, and away from the Sea of Cortéz. Winter is the time to come, as summer is hot. For things to do here, see the San Felipe and Puertecitos Areas, earlier in this chapter.

Campsites, facilities: There are 48 campsites with water and electric hookups for both RVs and tents, *palapas,* barbecues, flush toilets, and cold showers. Don't drink the water. Security is provided by a resident manager. Obtain supplies in San Felipe.

Reservations, fees: Camping is first come, first served. Fees are high—$15 per night and $70 per week.

Directions: Drive south on Highway 5 from the San Felipe airport road (5.5 miles south of the center of San Felipe) about eight miles, then turn east and continue one mile to the beach. Watch for the sign.

Contact: Drive in and talk to the manager.

36 CAMPO GARCÍA
🚶 🚲 🏊 🎣 🐕 🚐 ⛺

North of Puertecitos

Northeast Baja Norte map, page 77

Campo García seems to attract a lot of families who return regularly to stay in annually leased sites. The entrance road is in good shape. Winter is the time to come, as summer is hot. For things to do here, see the San Felipe and Puertecitos Areas, earlier in this chapter.

Campsites, facilities: There's room for an indeterminate number of campers in vehicles or tents. Toilets are provided, but there are no other facilities. Don't drink the water. The manager lives on the premises. Obtain major supplies in San Felipe. Limited groceries and fuel can be purchased in Puertecitos, which has a Pemex station and a small store.

Reservations, fees: All sites are first come, first served. The fee is moderate—$10 per night.

Directions: The camping area is on the beach, about 27 miles south of the San Felipe airport road (5.5 miles south of the center of San Felipe) and one-half mile off Highway 5, the paved road to Puertecitos. Watch for the sign.

Contact: Drive in and talk to the manager.

37 PUNTA BAJA
🚶 🚲 🏊 🎣 🐕 🚐 ⛺

North of Puertecitos

Northeast Baja Norte map, page 77

Expect a primitive camping experience. There are no facilities, but you do get a beach that stretches far in both directions. Puertecitos is closer than San Felipe. Winter is the time to come, as summer is hot. For things to do here, see the San Felipe and Puertecitos Areas, earlier in this chapter.

Campsites, facilities: There's room for an indeterminate number of campers in vehicles or tents. No facilities are provided. No security is provided. Obtain major supplies in San Felipe. Limited groceries and fuel can be purchased in Puertecitos, which has a Pemex station and a small store.

Reservations, fees: All sites are first come, first served. Fees are $5–6.

Directions: Drive south on Highway 5 from the San Felipe airport road (5.5 miles south of the center of San Felipe) about 33 miles, then turn east and continue one mile to the beach. Watch for the sign.

Contact: Drive in and talk to the manager.

38 CAMPO TURISTICO VALLARTA
🚶 🚲 🏊 🎣 🐕 🚐 ⛺

North of Puertecitos

Northeast Baja Norte map, page 77

This camp fronts on sand dunes behind a rocky beach. The entrance road is a little longer than those leading to the campgrounds to the north, since the highway swings inland. Winter is the time to come, as summer is hot. For things to do here, see the San Felipe and Puertecitos Areas, earlier in this chapter.

Campsites, facilities: There are five *palapas* with concrete pads, plus some pit toilets. Tent campers are welcome. Obtain major supplies in San Felipe. Limited groceries and fuel can be purchased in Puertecitos, which has a Pemex station and a small store.

Reservations, fees: All sites are first come, first served. The fee is moderate—$8 per night.

Directions: Drive south on Highway 5 from the San Felipe airport road (5.5 miles south of the center of San Felipe) about 34 miles, then turn east and continue 1.5 miles to the beach. Watch for the sign.

Contact: Drive in and talk to the manager.

39 RANCHO EL ZIMARRÓN
🚶 🚲 🏊 🎣 🐕 🚐 ⛺

North of Puertecitos

Northeast Baja Norte map, page 77

Come here for truly primitive camping. Winter is the time to come, as summer is hot. For things to do here, see the San Felipe and Puertecitos Areas, earlier in this chapter.

Campsites, facilities: Tent campers are welcome.

Don't drink the water. There is no security. Obtain major supplies in San Felipe. Limited groceries and fuel can be purchased in Puertecitos, which has a Pemex station and a small store.

Reservations, fees: All sites are first come, first served. Although there was no one here to collect the fee when we visited, we expect the rate is low.

Directions: Drive south on Highway 5 from the San Felipe airport road (5.5 miles south of the center of San Felipe) about 44 miles, then turn east and continue one mile to the beach. Watch for the sign.

Contact: Drive in and talk to the manager.

40 CAMPO LA VIOLETA

North of Puertecitos
Northeast Baja Norte map, page 77

This place is set amid a cluster of *campos* and *playas* near Puertecitos. Winter is the time to come, as summer is hot. For things to do here, see the San Felipe and Puertecitos Areas, earlier in this chapter.

Campsites, facilities: Tent campers are welcome. Toilets, rental boats, and trailer storage are available. Don't drink the water. The manager lives on the premises. Limited groceries and fuel can be obtained in Puertecitos, which has a Pemex station and a small store.

Reservations, fees: All sites are first come, first served. Fees are $5-6.

Directions: Drive south on Highway 5 from the San Felipe airport road (5.5 miles south of the center of San Felipe) about 44 miles, then turn east and continue one mile to the beach. Watch for the sign.

Contact: Drive in and talk to the manager.

41 JACARANDA

North of Puertecitos
Northeast Baja Norte map, page 77

People in search of a primitive camping spot

might want to try this place. Talk to the locals about fishing techniques. Winter is the time to come, as summer is hot. For things to do here, see the San Felipe and Puertecitos Areas, earlier in this chapter.

Campsites, facilities: Tent campers are welcome. Don't drink the water. There is no security. Limited groceries and fuel can be obtained in Puertecitos, which has a Pemex station and a small store.

Reservations, fees: All sites are first come, first served. There is no fee.

Directions: Drive south on Highway 5 from the San Felipe airport road (5.5 miles south of the center of San Felipe) about 47 miles, then turn east and proceed to the beach. Watch for the sign.

Contact: Drive in and talk to the manager.

42 SPEEDY'S CAMPO

North of Puertecitos
Northeast Baja Norte map, page 77

This campground is set in a little cove, but it's just off the highway. There's not much in the way of privacy, as people seem to be constantly pulling in off the road. Speedy runs the store by the campground; we're not sure why there is no fee to camp here unless it's because he's more interested in selling goods to campers than in charging them for a space. Winter is the time to come, as summer is hot. For things to do here, see the San Felipe and Puertecitos Areas, earlier in this chapter.

Campsites, facilities: Tent campers are welcome. There are pit toilets and a little store. Don't drink the water. No security is provided. Limited groceries and fuel can be obtained in Puertecitos, which has a Pemex station and a small store.

Reservations, fees: Camping is first come, first served. There is no fee.

Directions: Drive south on Highway 5 from the San Felipe airport road (5.5 miles south of the center of San Felipe) about 48 miles, then turn east and proceed a short distance to the beach. Watch for the sign.

Contact: Drive in and talk to the manager.

43 OCTAVIO'S CAMPO PLAYA ESCONDIDA

🏃 🚴 🏊 ⛵ 🏕 🐕 🚐 ⛺

North of Puertecitos

Northeast Baja Norte map, page 77

A small cove with a nice beach is the setting for this campground. Anglers can rent *pangas* for fishing trips in the offshore waters. There is no set price for doing so; you pay whatever you can negotiate. Local commercial fishermen are often happier to take a tourist out for money than struggle with their nets. If a *pangero* is not catching much, he'll take you out for a reasonable fee. If he is catching a lot, though, he won't take you at all. Fishing charter businesses are different—they set prices but are always willing to negotiate. Winter is the time to come, as summer is hot. Puertecitos is a mere mile away. For things to do in the area, see the San Felipe and Puertecitos Areas, earlier in this chapter.

Campsites, facilities: Tent campers are welcome. Pit toilets and cold showers are provided. Don't drink the water. There is no security. Limited groceries and fuel can be obtained in Puertecitos, which has a Pemex station and a small store.

Reservations, fees: Camping is first come, first served. The fee is low—$5 per night.

Directions: Drive south on Highway 5 from the San Felipe airport road (5.5 miles south of the center of San Felipe) about 49 miles, then turn east and proceed one-half mile to the beach. Watch for the sign.

Contact: Drive in and talk to the manager.

44 PUERTECITOS CAMPGROUND

🏃 🚴 🏊 ⛵ 🏕 🌊 🐕 🚐 ⛺

In Puertecitos

Northeast Baja Norte map, page 77

Not only does this campground claim a great location on a sandy beach at the edge of a pretty inlet extending south to the Sea of Cortéz, it also has the only restaurant in town. Other facilities are being improved. Local commercial fishermen will charter their *pangas* for reasonable rates and guide you to fishing grounds around Islas de Las Encantadas, a group of five islands and exposed rocks about 15 miles south off the shores of Puertecitos. You'll find great fishing for white sea bass, bay bass, triggerfish, sierra, yellowtail, dorado, skipjack, and grouper.

If you're hauling your own boat, the steep, rough concrete and rock launch ramp at the point is suitable for large craft—it's also free. There is a hot sulfur spring near the ramp on the north side of the point, about one-quarter mile from the RV park. At low tide, it creates several hot pools in natural depressions in the rocky beach in which you can dunk yourself. These pools are best enjoyed during the maximum tidal action at full and new moons. Tides can have a range of 20 feet or more. Visit in winter, as summer is hot. For more information on things to do here, see the San Felipe and Puertecitos Areas, earlier in this chapter.

Campsites, facilities: There are 17 campsites with electricity (available from sundown to 10 P.M.), concrete pads, beach *palapas,* young palm trees, and tables. Toilets and a restaurant are on the property. Don't drink the water. The camp is secured with a watchman at the entrance to the town. Tent campers are welcome. Limited groceries and fuel can be obtained in Puertecitos, which has a Pemex station and a small store.

Reservations, fees: All sites are first come, first served. Fees are moderate—$6 per night for tents and $8 for RVs, with discounts for weekly stays.

Directions: Drive south on Highway 5 from the San Felipe airport road (5.5 miles south of the center of San Felipe) about 50 miles. The campground is in town.

Contact: Drive in and talk to the manager.

10 Best Beaches

① PLAYA LAS ALMEJAS
North of San Felipe

Northeast Baja Norte map, page 77

This is the extremely popular eight-mile-long beach north of San Felipe, roughly between Campo Los Amigos (see listing in this chapter) on the north and Playa Blanca (see listing in this chapter) on the south. Fishing is fair for corvina, croaker, and bass. You may find it difficult to secure privacy, due to all the off-road-vehicle traffic, however. The beach can be driven from one end to the other in beach vehicles. Pick up supplies in San Felipe. Winter is the time to come, as summer is hot.

Directions: Heading 10 miles north of San Felipe on Highway 5, you can access the beach in many places via dirt roads.

② PLAYA SAN FELIPE
In San Felipe

Northeast Baja Norte map, page 77

The mainstay of San Felipe's tourist business, this beach runs through town and beyond for about 10 miles to Punta Estrella. Beach vehicles can drive along most of the beach. Fishing is fair for corvina, croaker, and bass. Pick up supplies in San Felipe. Winter is the time to come, as summer is hot.

Directions: Take Highway 5 into the town of San Felipe. You can access the beach in a highway vehicle at several RV parks and numerous other places.

③ PLAYA PUNTA ESTRELLA
South of San Felipe

Northeast Baja Norte map, page 77

Extending some five miles south from Punta Estrella to Punta Diggs, this wide, sandy beach about 11 miles south of San Felipe is popular for camping and fishing. The Huatamote Wash enters the Sea of Cortéz about one-half mile north of Punta Diggs, creating a lagoon that

can block the beach. The slope of land is very shallow along this stretch of coast. At low tide the water can recede more than one-quarter mile, exposing a vast expanse of flats to explore. Fishing is fair for corvina, croaker, and bass. Pick up supplies in San Felipe. Winter is the time to come, as summer is hot.

Directions: Highway vehicles can access the beach via campgrounds between El Faro RV Park and Rancho Punta Estrella Beach (see listings in this chapter). Sand tracks allow access by four-wheel-drive vehicles, and beach vehicles can drive on the beach.

④ PLAYA EL PROVENIR
South of San Felipe

Northeast Baja Norte map, page 77

Extending south of Punta Diggs for about four miles, this is a wide sand beach with extensive low tidal flats. The Parra Wash may create a lagoon about two miles south of Punta Diggs that can interrupt vehicle traffic along the beach. Punta Diggs and other points in this area are low and not very prominent. Fishing is fair for corvina, croaker, and bass. Pick up supplies in San Felipe. Winter is the time to come, as summer is hot.

Directions: About 15 miles south of San Felipe, the beach is accessible by four-wheel-drive vehicles over sand tracks.

⑤ BEACHES BETWEEN BAHÍA SANTA MARÍA AND PUNTA SAN FERMIN
North of Puertecitos

Northeast Baja Norte map, page 77

An almost continuous stretch of wide sand beach with hundreds of yards of tidal flats extends from Bahía Santa María (about 25 miles south of San Felipe) for about 24 miles to Punta San Fermin. The land here is level, with few distinguishing features. The northern half has numerous camps along the beach that are easily accessible from the paved road one-half mile or less away, leading to congestion on popular weekends. The southern half is more remote and less populated as the highway is farther inland and there are only a couple of camps. Fishing is fair for corvina, croaker, and bass. Pick up supplies in San Felipe. Winter is the time to come, as summer is hot.

Directions: Highway vehicles can reach these beaches via campgrounds between Campo García and Rancho El Zimarrón (see listings in this chapter). Four-wheel-drive vehicles can use numerous sand tracks, and beach vehicles can navigate the beaches.

6 BEACHES BETWEEN PUNTA SAN FERMIN AND OCTAVIO'S CAMPO PLAYA ESCONDIDA

North of Puertecitos

Northeast Baja Norte map, page 77

Beaches are nearly continuous for about four miles between these two points. The wide, sandy swaths are backed by low-lying land and fronted by extensive tidal flats, as is common north to Punta Estrella. You can fish for corvina, bay bass, triggerfish, barracuda, sierra, pargo, and grouper in the vicinity. Limited groceries and fuel can be obtained in Puertecitos, which has a Pemex station and a small store. Winter is the time to come, as summer is hot.

Directions: Highway vehicles can use access roads between Rancho El Zimarrón and Octavio's Campo Playa Escondida (see listings in this chapter), which is one mile north of Puertecitos. Many sand tracks are suitable for four-wheel-drive vehicles.

7 PLAYA LA COSTILLA

South of Puertecitos

Northeast Baja Norte map, page 77

An offshore reef protects this beach, making it ideal for swimming. Shorefishing is good for bass, corvina, barracuda, and triggerfish. Security is provided by a resident manager. The only facilities are pit toilets. Pick up major sup-

plies in San Felipe; limited groceries and fuel can be obtained in Puertecitos. Winter is the time to come, as summer is hot. A word of warning: The road south of Puertecitos becomes very rough and requires high-clearance vehicles traveling dead slow. It's rough enough to damage motor homes and trailers.

Directions: This beach is six miles south of Puertecitos, on the graded road heading south to Bahía San Luis Gonzaga.

8 PLAYA BUFEO

South of Puertecitos

Northeast Baja Norte map, page 77

This very pretty, wide, white sand beach is tucked into a gently curving cove that extends about two miles north of the rocky outcrop of Punta Bufeo. The point provides protection from southerly and easterly winds. Fishing is good for bass, corvina, grouper, pargo, yellowtail, sierra, and triggerfish. The Punta Bufeo Resort, a restaurant, and an airstrip are near the beach. Come in fully supplied. Emergency necessities can be scrounged up at Bahía Gonzaga about eight miles south. Winter is the time to come, as summer is hot.

Directions: Drive south from Puertecitos for 38 miles on a very rough road or exit Highway 1 at Laguna Chapala and head 43 miles north on a somewhat better road. Turn east on a dirt road and continue three-quarters of a mile to the beach.

9 PLAYA EL FARO

South of Puertecitos

Northeast Baja Norte map, page 77

More than just beautiful to look at, this beach is very good for swimming. Fishing is good for bass, yellowtail, pompano, grouper, barracuda, and triggerfish. Come fully stocked, though emergency supplies can be scraped up around Bahía Gonzaga. Winter is the time to come, as summer is hot.

Directions: Drive south from Puertecitos for 42 miles on a very rough road or exit Highway 1 at Laguna Chapala and head 39 miles north on a somewhat better road. The beach is three miles north of Punta Willard (the Bahía Gonzaga area) on the Puertecitos–to–Bahía San Luis Gonzaga road.

🔟 BAHÍA CALAMAJUE

South of Puertecitos

Northeast Baja Norte map, page 77

A great sandy beach lies at the south end of the bay but is accessible only to adventurous souls with four-wheel-drive vehicles. Fishing is good for bass, yellowtail, grouper, and triggerfish. Come fully stocked, since you'll be a long way from anywhere. Winter is the time to come, as summer is hot.

Directions: Leave Highway 1 at Laguna Chapala and drive 12 miles north to the Calamajue road, then continue 27 miles northeast to Calamajue.

© FRED JONES

Chapter 3

Central Peninsula

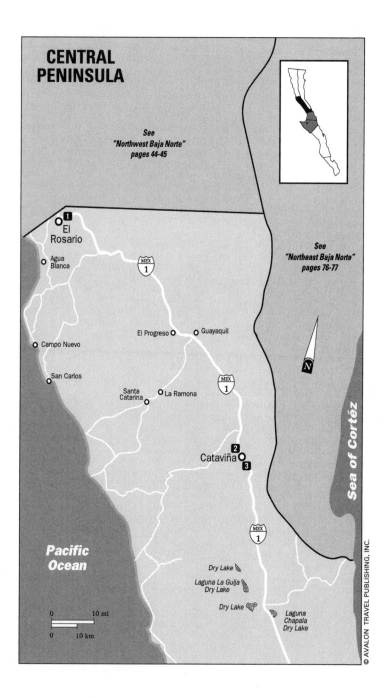

CENTRAL
PENINSULA

See
"Northwest Baja Norte"
pages 44-45

1
O❶
El
Rosario

O Agua
Blanca

MEX
1

See
"Northeast Baja Norte"
pages 76-77

El Progreso O   O Guayaquil

O Campo Nuevo

N

O San Carlos

Santa   O La Ramona
Catarina   O

MEX
1

Cataviña O ❷
❸

Sea of Cortéz

MEX
1

Pacific
Ocean

Dry Lake
Laguna La Guija
Dry Lake
Dry Lake
Laguna
Chapala
Dry Lake

0   10 mi
0   10 km

© AVALON TRAVEL PUBLISHING, INC.

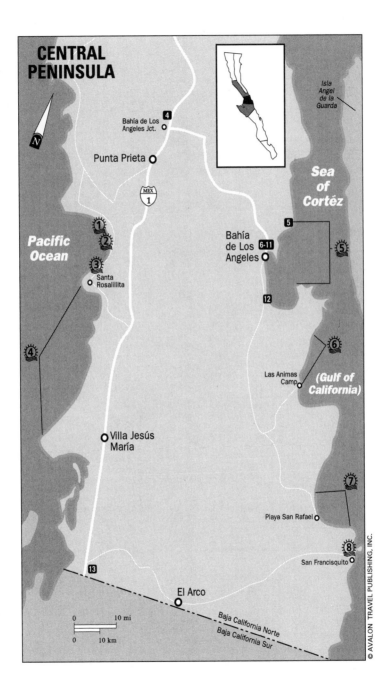

CENTRAL PENINSULA

Isla Angel de la Guarda

Bahía de Los Angeles Jct. ○ **4**

Punta Prieta ○

N

MEX 1

Sea of Cortéz

5

Pacific Ocean

1
2

3
○ Santa Rosalillita

Bahía de Los Angeles ○ **6-11**

5

4

12

Las Animas Camp ○ **(Gulf of California)**

6

○ Villa Jesús María

7

Playa San Rafael ○

8
San Francisquito ○

13

El Arco ○

Baja California Norte
Baja California Sur

0 ___ 10 mi
0 ___ 10 km

© AVALON TRAVEL PUBLISHING, INC.

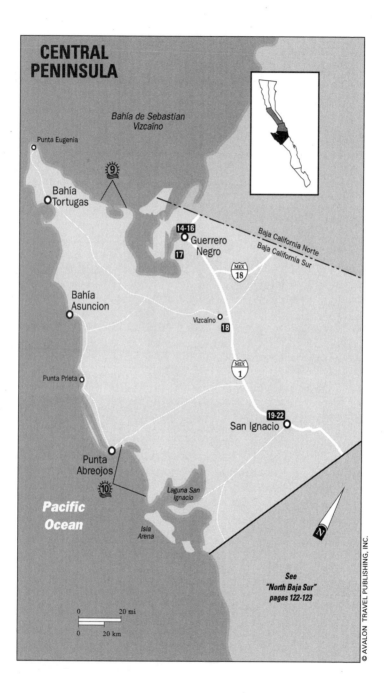

CENTRAL PENINSULA

Bahía de Sebastian Vizcaíno

Punta Eugenia

9

Bahía Tortugas

14-16
Guerrero Negro

17

Baja California Norte
Baja California Sur

MEX **18**

Bahía Asuncion

Vizcaíno
18

MEX **1**

Punta Prieta

19-22
San Ignacio

Punta Abreojos

10

Laguna San Ignacio

Pacific Ocean

Isla Arena

N

See "North Baja Sur" pages 122-123

© AVALON TRAVEL PUBLISHING, INC.

0   20 mi

0   20 km

Central Peninsula

The middle portion of the Baja California Peninsula has been least affected by tourist development. It is essentially wild, remote country traversed lengthwise by Highway 1. Bahía de Los Angeles boasts the greatest concentration of campgrounds and activities. Guerrero Negro and San Ignacio are rapidly becoming tourist centers in their own right, with many visitors focusing on watching gray whales and exploring caves decorated with ancient paintings of larger-than-life human and animal figures.

Some of the most unusual plants to be found anywhere can be seen while driving Highway 1 through this part of Baja. A few miles east of El Rosario, the first *cirios* come into view. These otherwordly plants are at the extreme northern edge of their range and seem stunted, though it is difficult to know just what constitutes normality with these oddballs. Tapering from a plump base to wispy, whiplike branches, their tan bark studded with tiny stubs of branchlets, they resemble nothing familiar. Following rains, small green leaves and delicate white flowers pop out, the plant sucks up all the water it can, then drops leaves and flowers and harbors its internal water supply until the next irrigation. The only other place in the world that *cirios* are found is in a small patch in Sonora—further proof that the Baja Peninsula was once firmly attached to mainland Mexico.

The first giant *cardón* cacti appear at about the same place. These in the fringe habitat are hardly giants, but farther inland they become so. Their appearance is much like that of the more familiar saguaro of Arizona, though they have multiple trunks. *Cardón* have strong internal hardwood rods that support their mass and serve as stout building material for ranch structures. In dry times, the flesh shrinks inward with pronounced ribbing. Following rain, they swell with water and appear almost round.

Farther south on Highway 1, the third of Central Baja's most prominent plants appears—the elephant tree. It actually looks like branched, spreading trees found the world over, except that the trunk and limbs are grossly round and fat. The plant may seem a bit shriveled in dry times. There are two large versions of these in Baja—one gray, the other pinkish.

Around Cataviña, midway between the Pacific Ocean and the Sea of Cortéz, is the Desert Natural Park. For miles Highway 1 threads its way between massive piles of enormous rounded boulders, among which are scattered magnificent specimens of *cirios, cardón,* and elephant trees, along with a full array of other Baja desert vegetation.

The scenery is on a grand scale, and bluish mountains across vast desert plains and Highway 1 are stretched far out in front of you. Many dirt side roads beckon off-road explorers, but crews of large RVs must continue on their pilgrimage to distant coastlines offering other things to do. The delights of Bahía de Los Angeles are known to many, and the lure of seeing gray whales and cave paintings out of Guerrero Negro and San Ignacio attracts more tourists each year.

There aren't a lot of places to get fuel along the roads between El Rosario, Villa Jesús María, and Bahía de Los Angeles, so top off all tanks at El Rosario. Magna Sin is available in five-gallon cans at both Cataviña and Bahía de Los Angeles Junction for $15 a can. If in doubt about your supply, ease your mind and toss in a can or two.

Highway 1 Area
(campgrounds 1–4 and 13–22)
For most people, the stretch of Highway 1 extending from El Rosario south past San Ignacio is little more than a corridor of travel en route to the enticing camping areas on the Sea of

Cortéz. There are a few scattered campgrounds along the 300-plus miles of essentially inland road to accommodate weary travelers for a night. Those with eyes that see more than the black ribbon rolling beneath their vehicle will be entranced by the odd plants and rock formations that grace this landscape and will find the long drive fascinating.

The dammed lake on the way into San Ignacio is fed by a powerful spring, a natural wonder that gives life to an enormous expanse of date palms. The many blessings visited on San Ignacio seem to have influenced its citizens, who are exceptionally gracious and hospitable. Stay a few days and absorb as much of it as you can. You will be better for the experience.

Sightseeing

San Ignacio is a lovely place for strolling. The town square is unique, dominated by huge, ancient Indian laurel trees that cast dense shade. Be sure to visit the magnificent Misión de San Ignacio Kadakaamán, across the street from the square, and the adjoining Cave Paintings Museum.

Whale-Watching and Cave Paintings

More and more local businesses conduct excursions to see whales and cave paintings. There are two good outfitters in Guerrero Negro: Malarrimo Motel and RV Park (see listing in this chapter) leads whale-watching and cave trips. Laguna Tours focuses on whales; you can reach them at Mex. tel. 615/157-0050.

You'll find several guide services for both whale-watching and cave paintings in San Ignacio. The best is Ecoturismo Kuyima, on the southeast corner of the town square. Call Mex. tel. 615/154-0070 for reservations. If you choose to drive yourself to Laguna San Ignacio and arrange there to have a guide take you out, be aware that the road is rough. Prior arrangements can be made with Kuyima to be transported in their vans, taken out on the lagoon in their *pangas,* and served a delicious lunch in their restaurant.

As for cave paintings, you can either arrange for a guide in town or drive up into the mountains and engage one there. Before heading out, everyone must obtain a free permit from the

With its eye showing at water level, a friendly gray whale scrutinizes a *panga* full of Vagabundos in San Ignacio Lagoon, Central Peninsula.

office of the National Institute for Archaeology and History (INAH), located next to the Cave Paintings Museum.

Numbering over a hundred so far, Baja's cave paintings have been found only in the mountains of the central peninsula from west of Bahía de Los Angeles in the north to west of the southern end of Bahía Concepción in the south. The best are here in the Sierra de San Francisco north of San Ignacio. The larger-than-life artworks depict individual figures of humans, animals, birds, and fish in black, red, yellow, and white. They cover the cave walls—actually shallow overhangs—with newer paintings overlaying older ones. Some caves provide greater protection than others and contain paintings that have retained their vibrant hues. In more exposed locations little is left except spots of paint. Recent research conducted by the Barcelona Group placed these magnificent works at somewhere between 3,500 and 5,000 years old, with the last ones being created around A.D. 350.

Bahía de Los Angeles Area
(campgrounds 5–12)

You can reach this area in one long day's drive from San Diego. At times, the 42-mile paved road in from Highway 1 deteriorates and can be slow going until you reach another repaired stretch. One of the most stunning views in Baja is the first sight of Bahía de Los Angeles from high in the hills. The reds and browns of the many islands in the bay contrast vividly with the bright blues of sky and water.

The small town has the basic necessities, including both Magna Sin gasoline and diesel at a premium price, due to having to be hauled in from Guerrero Negro. However, there are perennial problems with electricity and water, with very limited service. In other words, camping is somewhat more rustic than in other Baja locales. But for those of us who are captivated by the place, it is worth the extra effort. The most spectacular stand of *cirios, cardón,* and elephant trees we have seen is along the road in from Highway 1. And wildflower fans won't be disappointed; in spring there are profuse, colorful displays of flowers in every color imaginable. Some years the carpets of blooms extend as far as the eye can see. Even the *cirios* and *ocotillo* come out with showy flowers.

Fishing

This narrowed Midriff area on the Sea of Cortéz with its numerous islands creates upwellings of nutrient-rich water that supports a resident fin whale population (second in size only to the enormous blue whale), whale sharks, sport fish, and migratory game fish plus myriad seabirds. Fishing is the main activity for tourists. Most people bring their own boats and launch at one of three ramps, an unusually high concentration in launch-ramp-poor Baja.

Bahía de Los Angeles is famous for its feeding frenzies, with sharp-toothed game fish driving massive balls of bait to the surface, attracting hundreds of birds that dive madly into the maelstrom. Fishing is good for grouper, yellowtail, bass, barracuda, sierra, and triggerfish. At times, huge schools of yellowfin tuna enter the Midriff area and provide great fishing.

Dr. Abraham Vasquez, owner of Gecko Camp (see listing in this chapter) is probably the best guide for fishing with his 32-foot cruiser, as well as snorkeling, diving, kayaking, and nature tours. Guillermo's rents boats and guides. Boats leave at 7 A.M. and return at 3 P.M. (For more information, see Guillermo's campground in this chapter.) Diaz RV Park also rents *pangas* from 6 A.M. to 1 P.M. (For more information, see Diaz RV Park in this chapter.)

Off-Roading
Some interesting side roads will take you into the mountains behind the village and south toward San Francisquito—if you are prepared to handle the rugged and hazardous desert conditions.

Sightseeing
Guillermo's (see listing in this chapter) takes groups of up to six people sightseeing by boat.

In the village of Bahía de Los Angeles, there is a very interesting archaeological museum, a real must-see.

Campgrounds

1 SINAI RV PARK, MOTEL, AND RESTAURANT

In El Rosario

Central Peninsula map, page 102

El Rosario is not a prime tourist destination. Still, you should take a look at the ruins of one of two missions bearing the name Misión Nuestra Señora del Santísimo Rosario Viñadaco. The spot where the mission was founded in 1774 flooded out, and in 1802 the mission was relocated, only to be abandoned in 1832. The relocated mission has only a few remnants of adobe walls but is easily seen about a mile west of town on the south side of the stream. You'll find it beside the dirt road leading west, along with a sign that tells its history. (The ruins of the first mission have melted down and can't be seen at all.) In the fall, look for masses of red chilies drying on the south-facing hillsides south of town on the highway. It is a very colorful display. Top off your fuel tanks here. Winter is the best time to visit, as summers are hot.

Campsites, facilities: There are 24 campsites, of which 12 have full hookups. Flush toilets, hot showers, laundry facilities, and a restaurant are on the premises. Don't drink the water. The owner lives on site. Tent campers are welcome. Obtain supplies in El Rosario.

Reservations, fees: All sites are first come, first served. Fees are moderate—$13 per night or $50 per week.

Directions: As you head south on Highway 1, follow the road as it turns sharply left in El Rosario. Look for the park in about one mile on the left.

Contact: Sinai RV Park, Motel, and Restaurant, Mex. tel. 616/165-8818.

2 CENTRAL DESERT RV PARK *(EJIDO)*

In Cataviña

Central Peninsula map, page 102

There is no security at Central Desert RV Park, so camping alone here is not recommended. Instead, go a short distance south to Rancho Santa Ynéz, campground 3.

Campsites, facilities: There are 67 pull-through campsites, a few of which may have electricity. Flush toilets and hot showers are sometimes available. Don't drink the water. Tent campers are welcome. Obtain supplies in El Rosario.

Reservations, fees: All sites are first come, first served. The fee is low—$5 per night.

Directions: From El Rosario drive about 76 miles south on Highway 1. The park is in Cataviña, just north of La Pinta Hotel.

Contact: Drive in and talk to the manager.

3 RANCHO SANTA YNÉZ

South of Cataviña

Central Peninsula map, page 102

Long before the highway was paved, Rancho Santa Ynéz was one of the original stopping places for travelers. Nostalgic old-timers still enjoy dropping in to feast on the excellent tacos served in the restaurant flanking this campground. Winter is the time to visit, as summers are very hot. The campground is within the Desert Natural Park (Parque Natural del Desierto Central), a jumbled mass of enormous old, old granite boulders as big as houses. *Cirios,* giant *cardón* cacti, and elephant trees grow throughout the area. Other features include Indian rock art sites and running streams with tall palms. It is a fascinating place in which to poke around and explore, with exciting photo opportunities at every turn.

Campsites, facilities: You camp in a large, level parking area next to a small restaurant and motel. Flush toilets are on-site. The water is good to drink. Being at the ranch headquarters affords security. Tent campers are welcome. Obtain supplies in El Rosario.

Reservations, fees: Camping is first come, first served. The fee is very low—$5 per night.

Directions: From El Rosario drive about 76 miles south on Highway 1 to Cataviña. Continue one-half mile south on Highway 1, turn left at the sign, and go three-quarters of a mile east.

Contact: Drive in and park.

◢ PARADOR PUNTA PRIETA TRAILER PARK *(EJIDO)*

At the junction of Highway 1 and the road to Bahía de Los Angeles

Central Peninsula map, page 103

If darkness sneaks up on you as you're driving on Highway 1, this park provides a place to pull off the road and sleep for the night. Other than that, few tourists have reason to stop here. There is, however, an interesting cactus garden to examine among the RV spaces. Top off your fuel tanks if the Pemex station is operating. Winter is the time to visit, as summers are hot. There is no security, and camping alone is not recommended.

Campsites, facilities: There are 40 pull-through campsites with concrete pads and no hookups. Tent campers are welcome. Obtain supplies in El Rosario or Guerrero Negro.

Reservations, fees: All sites are first come, first served. The fee is low—$5 per night.

Directions: From El Rosario drive about 141 miles south on Highway 1. The park is at the junction of Highway 1 and the road to Bahía de Los Angeles, one-quarter mile north of the Pemex station.

Contact: Drive in and talk to the manager.

◢ PLAYA LA GRINGA

North of Bahía de Los Angeles

Central Peninsula map, page 103

Camping spots are all along the beach, and a fish camp is just short of a narrow spit of land going out to Punta La Gringa. (The beach was named for an American woman who tried to establish a camping operation here years ago. You can still see the ruins of a concrete restroom she built.) A narrow road leads on through a low saddle between hills and ends on a rocky beach facing Isla Smith. This is such a scenic location that it is pleasant just to be here. While kicking back, one of our friends saw a whale shark cruise by offshore. Fishermen in small boats that can be launched across the beach do well, since they are close to the prime fishing grounds around Isla Smith. Winter is the best time to visit, as it is very hot in summer. For things to do here, see the Bahía de Los Angeles Area, earlier in this chapter.

Campsites, facilities: There are no facilities. Obtain supplies in Bahía de Los Angeles.

Reservations, fees: All sites are first come, first served. There is no fee.

Directions: The beach is at the end of the dirt road north of the Bahía de Los Angeles village, which is about 183 miles south of El Rosario. Coming into town, make a sharp left turn at the first stop sign onto the dirt road, follow the signs to Daggett's, and continue north beyond it. The washboard dirt road takes you past numerous turnoffs to private beach camps within view. Some of the signs announce camping for a small fee—$2 or so. La Gringa is six miles north, at the end of the road.

Contact: Drive in and park.

◢ DAGGETT'S BEACH CAMPING

North of Bahía de Los Angeles

Central Peninsula map, page 103

This is a very clean camping area, from which

you can arrange to go fishing and scuba diving. It is also great for tidepool exploring, just watch out for sting rays. There are cave paintings nearby; ask Ruben for directions. This is on the north side of Camp Archelon (see next campground listing) and the turtle ponds. Donations are accepted; there is no fee to see the turtles. Winter is the best time to visit, as it is very hot in summer. For things to do here, see the Bahía de Los Angeles Area, earlier in this chapter.

Campsites, facilities: There are 16 beachfront campsites for RVs or tents with barbecues, purified water for $5 per drum, nice *palapas*, and several overflow sites with ocean view. Flush toilets, hot showers (by solar), a dump station, and a launch ramp for small boats are available. The owners live there and have an office on-site. Winter is the best time to visit, as it is very hot in summer. Obtain supplies in Bahía de Los Angeles.

Reservations, fees: Reservations are accepted. The fee is low—$8 per night.

Directions: Coming into town, make a sharp left turn at the first stop sign onto the dirt road and follow the signs to Daggett's on the wide washboard road. It is about two miles from the main road.

Contact: Daggett's Beach Camping, Apartado Postal 83, Guerrero Negro, Baja California Sur, Mexico, Mex. tel. 664/650-3206, fax 664/650-3206.

▟ CAMP ARCHELON

North of Bahía de Los Angeles
Central Peninsula map, page 103
This is beachfront camping adjoining the residence of Tony and Betty Resendiz, biologists who manage several above-ground pools holding sea turtles obtained from fishermen. The campsites are often used by volunteers working with the turtles but are open to the public. Winter is the best time to visit, as it is very hot in summer. For things to do here, see the Bahía de Los Angeles Area, earlier in this chapter.

Campsites, facilities: Beachfront parking is provided with six *palapas* on the beach and two in back for RVs or tents. A hot shower, flush toilet, and a dump station are on-site. Purified water is available in drums.

Reservations, fees: The fee is moderate—$8 per night.

Directions: Coming into town, make a sharp left turn at the first stop sign onto the dirt road, then right at the next intersection toward the waterfront. Camp Archelon is on the north side of the Brisa Marina RV Park (see next listing). It is about 1.5 miles from the main road.

Contact: Drive in and talk to the owners. There is no phone or mailing address.

▟ BRISA MARINA RV PARK *(EJIDO)*

North of Bahía de Los Angeles
Central Peninsula map, page 103
You can park here, but you'll be closer to the water if you go in front of the facility, to the side of the turtle ponds. Winter is the best time to visit, as it is very hot in summer. For things to do here, see the Bahía de Los Angeles Area, earlier in this chapter.

Campsites, facilities: There are 50 pull-through campsites with no hookups. You may pitch tents wherever you want. No security is provided. Obtain supplies in Bahía de Los Angeles.

Reservations, fees: All sites are first come, first served. There is no fee.

Directions: The park is north of Bahía de Los Angeles. Coming into town, make a sharp left turn at the first stop sign onto the dirt road, then right at the next intersection toward the waterfront. It is on the south side of Camp Archelon (see prior listing).

Contact: Drive in and park.

9 VILLA VITTA HOTEL, RESTAURANT, AND RV PARK

🚶 🚲 🏊 🎣 🛥 🐕 🚐 ⛰

In Bahía de Los Angeles
Central Peninsula map, page 103

The camping area is shadeless and unattractive. The restroom building was nonfunctional the last time we saw it, necessitating a hike across the road to use the facilities in the hotel—which was considerably inconvenient. Still, Villa Vitta has the best launch ramp in Bahía de Los Angeles. They charge $10 for launching, which includes both putting in and taking out. Winter is the best time to visit, as it is very hot in summer. For things to do here, see the Bahía de Los Angeles Area, earlier in this chapter.

Campsites, facilities: There are 100 pull-through campsites with electricity hookups and sewage disposal. Facilities include flush toilets and hot showers at the hotel (available to campers for a fee), a pool, a restaurant, a bar, a store, and a launch ramp. Don't drink the water. The park is secured with a gate. Tent campers are welcome. Obtain supplies in Bahía de Los Angeles.

Reservations, fees: All sites are first come, first served. The fee is moderate—$10 per night.
Directions: The RV park is on the beach, across the road from the Villa Vitta Hotel.
Contact: Drive into the Hotel and register.

10 GUILLERMO'S HOTEL, RV PARK, RESTAURANT, BAR, AND STORE

🚶 🚲 🏊 🎣 🛥 🐕 🚐 ⛰

In Bahía de Los Angeles
Central Peninsula map, page 103

We have stayed at Guillermo's several times over the years and find that it suits our needs. The owners are gracious and helpful, and the restaurant is very good. One bonus: Use of the launch ramp is free for guests of the hotel and RV park. Winter is the best time to visit, as summer is

very hot. For things to do here, see the Bahía de Los Angeles Area, earlier in this chapter.

Campsites, facilities: There are 40 pull-through campsites with full hookups. Flush toilets, hot showers, a restaurant, a bar, a store, and a launch ramp are on the premises. Don't drink the water, which is on only part of the day, as is electricity. There is no security. Tent campers are welcome. Obtain supplies in Bahía de Los Angeles.
Reservations, fees: Reservations are accepted. The fee is moderate—$6 per person per night.
Directions: The RV park is south of Villa Vitta on the beach.
Contact: Drive in and park. Mex. tel. 664/650-3209.

11 DIAZ RV PARK

🚶 🚲 🏊 🎣 🚐 🐕 🚐 ⛰

In Bahía de Los Angeles
Central Peninsula map, page 103

At this time Diaz RV Park is not being maintained very well and has fallen into a state of disrepair. Magna Sin gasoline and diesel are available at Diaz RV Park for a premium price, as fuel must be hauled in from Guerrero Negro (ask at the mechanic shop to obtain fuel). Winter is the best time to visit, as it is very hot in summer. For things to do here, see the Bahía de Los Angeles Area, earlier in this chapter.

Campsites, facilities: The five campsites have full hookups. Tenters are welcome. Facilities include poorly maintained flush toilets and cold showers, a restaurant, a store, and a launch ramp (the fee is $5, free for guests). Don't drink the water. The spigot near the gas station is supposed to have drinking water from the spring. Other water is piped in from elsewhere. There is no security. Obtain supplies in Bahía de Los Angeles.
Reservations, fees: All sites are first come, first served. The fee is low—$5 per night.
Directions: The RV park is in Bahía de Los Angeles, on the south side.
Contact: Drive in and register at the restaurant.

12 GECKO CAMP

South of Bahía de Los Angeles
Central Peninsula map, page 103

This secluded camp offers more privacy than you'll get right in town. Some people prefer the place for that very reason. It is a good choice for tent campers, being right on the water with a view of the mountains. The beaches here are very nice. We like the location and the owners are very helpful. Winter is the best time to visit, as summer is very hot. For things to do here, see the Bahía de Los Angeles Area, earlier in this chapter.

Campsites, facilities: There are four campsites with *palapas* on the beach but no hookups. Restrooms with flush toilets, cold showers, cabins, and a ramp for small boats are provided. A large boat is available to charter. Water for washing is available. Security is provided by its remoteness and resident owners, Dr. Abraham and Sylvia Vasquez. Tent campers are welcome. Winter is the best time to visit, as it is very hot in summer. Obtain supplies in Bahía de Los Angeles.

Reservations, fees: All sites are first come, first served. The fee is low—$6 per night.

Directions: Coming into the village of Bahía de Los Angeles, turn right when you see the rock wall dead ahead. Take the first left turn and proceed about six miles south on a rough dirt road to the camp on the beach.

Contact: Drive in and talk to the owners. Email: gecko@starband.net.

13 GUERRERO NEGRO RV PARK *(EJIDO)*

North of Guerrero Negro
Central Peninsula map, page 103

The local *ejido* makes an effort to keep facilities up and running, but the cost of electricity can exceed income. Over the years it has been hit or miss. Sometimes there are hookups and the restrooms are functioning properly, and at other times nothing works—or the park is closed altogether. Guerrero Negro is a convenient place to stop on pilgrimages south, and this park does the job when open. For things to do in Guerrero Negro, see the description of Malarrimo Motel, RV Park, Restaurant, and Bar (campground 16).

Campsites, facilities: There are 40 pull-through campsites with concrete pads. Some in the western and southern portions of the park have full hookups. Electricity varies from 80 to 150 volts, extremes that can cause damage. Modest restrooms with flush toilets and hot showers are on the premises. Don't drink the water. The park has a gate and a surrounding fence; a resident manager also provides security. Tent campers are welcome. Obtain supplies in Guerrero Negro.

Reservations, fees: All sites are first come, first served. The fee is moderate—$10 per night.

Directions: The RV park is on Highway 1 at the Baja Norte–Baja Sur state line, next to La Pinta Hotel. Guerrero Negro is about 222 miles south of El Rosario on Highway 1.

Contact: Drive in and talk to the manager.

14 MARIO'S RESTAURANT AND RV PARK

East of Guerrero Negro
Central Peninsula map, page 104

This may turn out to be a decent RV park, but we'll have to wait and see. For people on the fly looking for a respite it may be attractive. Mario also does whale-watching tours and has an attractive restaurant, though its *palapa* style leaves it open to the chilly local climate that prevails for most of the year.

Campsites, facilities: At the time of our visit construction had been started, but there was little to show for it. The owner planned to have 44 pull-through spaces with full hookups, two party *palapas,* tables, and restrooms with flush toilets and hot showers by the time of printing this book. A watchman is planned for security, since the park is on the highway.

Reservations, fees: Reservations can be made. Fees are moderate at $10 per night.

Directions: Drive through the check station south of the state line and look for the huge *palapa* restaurant on the west side of the highway before the turnoff into Guerrero Negro.

Contact: Mex. tel. 615/157-1940 or 615/159-4033.

15 DON VICENTE MOTEL AND RV PARK

[icons]

In Guerrero Negro

Central Peninsula map, page 104

There was no sign of RV use and there is little to recommend it, unless everywhere else is full—which is most unlikely. We would not recommend this site and only mention it because it is there.

Campsites, facilities: There are 12 40-foot spaces against a concrete block wall inside the grounds of the motel with electricity and water. Restrooms with flush toilets and hot showers are on-site, although they were locked at the time of our visit and looked run-down. There is an adjacent restaurant and a night watchman. The ground surface is fine sand.

Reservations, fees: Reservations can be made. Fees are moderate at $10 per night.

Directions: As you enter Guerrero Negro it is on the right.

Contact: Mex. tel. 615/157-0288.

16 MALARRIMO MOTEL, RV PARK, RESTAURANT, AND BAR

[icons]

In Guerrero Negro

Central Peninsula map, page 104

We have gravitated to this place over the years, as it's the most dependable campground in the area. The restaurant is renowned for its food—don't miss the Friday night fiesta. Another plus is that owner Enrique Achoy is very good about helping you find whatever you need in Guerrero Negro. Though this is a company town devoted to producing salt—and said to be the largest such operation in the world—tourism is becoming big business. In particular, winter whale-watching at nearby Scammon's Lagoon is attracting more and more tourists. Whale-watching trips in *pangas* can be booked at Malarrimo. (You can reach the lagoon by driving about eight miles south of Guerrero Negro on Highway 1 to a sign, then about 17 miles south on a graded dirt road.)

Many people also come for the winter bird-watching in the extensive marshes west of town, where you might see gulls, shorebirds, ducks, and ospreys. A word about the weather: The climate is better in summer, but getting to Guerrero Negro involves driving through hot desert. Winters, though, can be chilly. Many times during winter we have come north from the southern peninsula in shorts and T-shirts and been forced to bundle up in long pants and jackets once in Guerrero Negro. The change can be a shock.

A water purification plant (*Planta Purificada de Agua,* FRESK-PURA) is in town on the south side of the main street, one-half block west of the water tank. It has a hose that you can use to fill your RV tank, and it also sells water in five-gallon bottles (*garrafones*) and purified ice cubes.

Another asset in Guerrero Negro is Pescados y Mariscos, the seafood warehouse owned by Señora María del Socorro Espinoza. To get there from the main street in town, turn north on the next street west of the grocery store and just east of the water tower. Drive to the end of the road. It is on the left, across from the power-generating plant. You'll savor the largest and most tender scallops we have ever encountered, as well as fresh lobster and fish—at prices that are very reasonable.

Note: There is a permanent army base at the state line, and the soldiers stop everyone to check for drugs and firearms. They are uniformly polite and very professional. For information on what they will accept at the agricultural check station between the state line and town, see "Customs" in the Travel Tips section of the Introduction.

Campsites, facilities: There are 50 campsites with full hookups and concrete pads. Facilities include clean restrooms with flush toilets and hot showers, a pool table, and a restaurant. Don't drink the water. The park is behind the restaurant and motel. A guard provides security. Tent campers are welcome. Obtain supplies in Guerrero Negro, which has a wide selection of stores.

Reservations, fees: Reservations are accepted. The fee is moderate—$12 per night.

Directions: Guerrero Negro is about 222 miles south of El Rosario on Highway 1. As you enter town, you'll see the motel and RV park on the right side of the road.

Contact: Malarrimo Motel, RV Park, Restaurant, and Bar, Boulevard Emiliano Zapata s/n, Guerrero Negro, Baja California Sur, Mexico, Mex. tel. 615/157-0100, fax 615/157-0250; email: malarrimo@telnor.net, website: www.malarrimo.com.

17 LAGUNA OJO DE LIEBRE CAMPGROUND

On the north shore of Laguna Ojo de Liebre
Central Peninsula map, page 104

The charm here is camping within sight and sound of the whales during their winter stay in Scammon's Lagoon. It is a unique and memorable experience.

Campsites, facilities: Camp on the beach. The only facilities are outhouses. A restaurant is on-site, and *pangas* are available for hire to see the whales from 8 A.M. to 5 P.M. from December 15 to April 30 at a much lower cost than in Guerrero Negro. It is a safe area. Tent campers are welcome. Obtain supplies in Guerrero Negro.

Reservations, fees: Drive in and park. The fee is low—$3 per night.

Directions: From Guerrero Negro drive south on Highway 1 for about five miles to the "Parque Nacional de la Ballena Gris 25 Km" sign, then drive 15 miles on a broad, two-lane dirt road through the salt ponds, offering an interesting glimpse at this massive operation. The road is half washboard and half smooth gypsum.

Contact: Drive in and talk to the manager.

18 KADAKAAMÁN RV PARK

In Vizcaíno
Central Peninsula map, page 104

This would be a convenient place to pull off if you're caught on the road at nightfall. Other than that, there is nothing much to do unless you plan on leaving Highway 1 here and heading west for Malarrimo Beach—not a suitable trip for motor homes or trailers. For more on the beach, see the Highway 1 Area, earlier in this chapter.

Campsites, facilities: There are five campsites with electricity and water. Flush toilets and hot showers are on the premises. Don't drink the water. Meals can be taken in the owner's home, which adjoins the park. The park is secure, as the owner's home is so close. Tent campers are welcome. Obtain supplies in Guerrero Negro.

Reservations, fees: All sites are first come, first served. The fee is low—$5 per night.

Directions: From Guerrero Negro drive south on Highway 1 for about 45 miles to the park, which is on the east side of Vizcaíno.

Contact: Drive in and talk to the manager.

19 RICE AND BEANS OASIS RV PARK

In San Ignacio
Central Peninsula map, page 104

Since this park is alongside the highway, traffic noise is high as the big trucks go by in the night. The sharp turn off the highway can be negotiated easily by larger RVs by swinging wide through a parking area. However, if vehicles should be blocking it, it may be easier to turn around in the Pemex station beyond and come back.

Campsites, facilities: There are 28 campsites with full hookups, trees, flush toilets, hot showers, a laundry facility, and a restaurant. Don't drink the water. It is a safe area. Tent campers are welcome. Obtain supplies in San Ignacio.

Reservations, fees: Reservations are accepted. The fee is high—$15 per night.

Directions: Follow the signs on the west side of San Ignacio. The park is visible next to the highway on the south side.

Contact: Mex. tel./fax 615/154-0283.

20 LAKESIDE RV PARK

In San Ignacio

Central Peninsula map, page 104

With so many palm trees, this is not the place for big motor homes or trailers. Tenters, however, will be very happy. If you want to try it in your big rig anyway, park and walk it out first. The setting is pleasant, adjoining a permanent freshwater lake that is unique to San Ignacio. For things to do in town, see the Highway 1 Area, earlier in this chapter.

Campsites, facilities: You'll find numerous places to camp in a large date palm grove. No facilities are available. A fence and a resident family provide security. It is a great spot for tent camping. Obtain supplies in San Ignacio.

Reservations, fees: All sites are first come, first served. The fee is very low—$3 per night.

Directions: From Guerrero Negro drive south on Highway 1 for about 89 miles to San Ignacio. Heading into town, watch for the handmade sign on a car door to your left, about one-quarter mile from the highway.

Contact: Drive in and talk to the manager.

21 MARTIN QUEZADA RV PARK

On the outskirts of San Ignacio

Central Peninsula map, page 104

This is a pleasant spot, set in a date palm grove, and we have enjoyed our stays here. Tent campers in particular appreciate it, for they are likely to have the place all to themselves. For things to do in San Ignacio, see the Highway 1 Area, earlier in this chapter.

Campsites, facilities: There's plenty of room to park. Facilities include a water spigot and a pit toilet, but don't drink the water. A gate and a surrounding fence provide security. Tent campers are welcome. Obtain supplies in San Ignacio.

Reservations, fees: All sites are first come, first served. The fee is very low—$2 per night.

Directions: From Guerrero Negro drive south on Highway 1 for about 89 miles to San Ignacio. Heading into town, watch for the handmade sign on the left about three-quarters of a mile from the highway. Open the gate and drive in.

Contact: Drive in and park. Martin will come around to collect the fee.

22 EL PADRINO MOTEL, RV PARK, AND RESTAURANT

On the outskirts of San Ignacio

Central Peninsula map, page 104

El Padrino is slated to be expanded and will include an extensive date palm grove extending west to the lake. When the plans become reality, this should be a very special place to camp. Guides from El Padrino take small groups out on whale-watching excursions or to view cave paintings. The cost for whale trips is $45 per person, plus $3 for lunch; cave tours run $20 per person.

Campsites, facilities: There are about 100 campsites, 15 of which have electricity and water and five have no electricity; the rest have no hookups. Trees, four flush toilets, four hot showers, a restaurant, and a bar are on the premises. Don't drink the water. The park is secure, with a gate, a surrounding fence, and a resident caretaker. Tent campers are welcome. Obtain supplies in San Ignacio.

Reservations, fees: All sites are first come, first served. Fees are moderate—$10 per night without electricity and $15 with electricity.

Directions: From Guerrero Negro drive south on Highway 1 for about 89 miles to San Ignacio. The park is approximately 1.25 miles from town. Watch for the prominent sign on the right. **Contact:** El Padrino RV Park, Carretera Peninsular 0.5 Kilometro, San Ignacio, Baja California Sur, Mexico, Mex. tel. 615/154-0089, fax 615/154-0222.

10 Best Beaches

① BAHÍA FALSA BEACH
On the Pacific Ocean, north of Guerrero Negro

Central Peninsula map, page 103

Getting to this big beach requires quite a trip, but it's well worth the effort. Fishing for halibut, corvina, perch, and bass can be good. Surfers and sailboarders like to come here. Take only pickups, vans, or four-wheel-drive vehicles. The latter will give you greater peace of mind, for there can be bad stretches and the area is remote. Obtain supplies in El Rosario or Guerrero Negro. Summer is the best time to visit, as winter can be cool.

Directions: The beach stretches some four miles between Punta Cono on the north and Punta María on the south. Access is approximately 35 miles up the coast from the Santa Rosalillita road. Leave Highway 1 near Km 38 about 16 miles south of Punta Prieta at the Santa Rosalillita sign. It is about four miles on pavement and six miles on a good dirt road to Santa Rosalillita. A mile and a half short of the village, turn north on a good dirt road, which turns into a typical rough country road with many branches.

② PLAYA MARÍA
On the Pacific Ocean, north of Guerrero Negro

Central Peninsula map, page 103

Fishing for halibut, corvina, perch, and bass can be good at this big, pretty beach. Clammers won't be disappointed either. It is a very popular destination for surfers and sailboarders. Take only pickups, vans, or four-wheel-drive vehicles, since the road in can get rough. Obtain supplies in El Rosario or Guerrero Negro. Summer is the best season to visit, as winter can be cool.

Directions: The beach extends some seven miles between Punta María on the north and Punta Lobos on the south. Access is approximately 30 miles up the coast from the Santa Rosalillita road.

Leave Highway 1 near Km 38 about 16 miles south of Punta Prieta at the Santa Rosalillita sign. It is about four miles on pavement and six miles on a good dirt road to Santa Rosalillita. A mile and a half short of the village, turn north on a good dirt road, which turns into a typical rough country road with many branches.

③ PLAYA EL MARRON
On the Pacific Ocean, north of Guerrero Negro

Central Peninsula map, page 103

Surfers and sailboarders love this beautiful crescent-shaped beach that stretches about two miles. Fishing for halibut, corvina, perch, and bass can be good. Take only pickups, vans, or four-wheel-drive vehicles, since the road in can get rough. Obtain supplies in El Rosario or Guerrero Negro. Summer is the best season to visit, as winter can be cool.

Directions: The beach is on the south side of Punta Negra (or Punta Prieta). Access is approximately 17 miles up the coast from the Santa Rosalillita road. Leave Highway 1 near Km 38 about 16 miles south of Punta Prieta at the Santa Rosalillita sign. It is about four miles on pavement and six miles on a good dirt road to Santa Rosalillita. A mile and a half short of the village, turn north on a good dirt road, which turns into a typical rough country road with many branches.

④ ROSALILLITA BEACHES
On the Pacific Ocean, north of Guerrero Negro

Central Peninsula map, page 103

These beaches extend for about 30 miles south of Punta Santa Rosalillita (Santa Rosalía) to Morro Santo Domingo. All are especially popular with surfers and sailboarders and offer good fishing for halibut, croaker, corbina, bass, and corvina. If you're a digger, you'll find plenty of clams to keep you busy. Large motor homes and trailers are not recommended. Obtain supplies in El Rosario or Guerrero Negro. Summer is the best season to visit, as winter can be cool.

Directions: Access these beaches by the good side road at the Santa Rosalillita sign near Km 38 on Highway 1, about 16 miles south of Punta Prieta. The drive in is about 10 miles long, of which the first four are on pavement and the rest on dirt. Four-wheel-drive roads go south to Highway 1 between Km 62 and 63, about seven miles south of Rosarito. Coming in that way, the dirt road (pickups, vans, and four-wheel-drives only) goes three miles to a shingle beach, then north to the sand beaches around Punta Rosarito and farther north to Santa Rosalillita. You'll find a third access via dirt road from Highway 1 at Km 73, about 10 miles south of Rosarito. It goes three miles to El Tomatal (Miller's Landing), where there is a shingle beach. A fourth access is by paved road from the sign to Morro Santo Domingo at Km 96, Villa Jesús María, on Highway 1. After one mile, turn left on a gravel road and drive another 6.5 miles to Laguna Manuela. To reach the extensive beaches, drive north around Morro Santo Domingo over four-wheel-drive roads in soft sand to harder sand on the beaches.

⑤ BAHÍA DE LOS ANGELES BEACHES

On the Sea of Cortéz, around Bahía de Los Angeles

Central Peninsula map, page 103

These beaches extend from Playa La Gringa (see listing in this chapter) on the north all the way around the bay more than 10 miles to the south end. Fishing is good for grouper, bass, triggerfish, yellowtail, barracuda, and sierra. Obtain supplies in Bahía de Los Angeles. Winter is the best time to visit, as summer can be very hot.

Directions: From Cataviña drive 65 miles south on Highway 1 to the Bahía de Los Angeles junction. Turn east and head 40 miles to Bahía de Los Angeles.

⑥ PLAYA DE LAS ANIMAS

On the Sea of Cortéz, south of Bahía de Los Angeles

Central Peninsula map, page 103

Your vehicle must have four-wheel drive, due to the soft sand you'll encounter en route. There are about two miles of beach north of the old rancho. Obtain supplies in Bahía de Los Angeles.

Directions: From Bahía de Los Angeles drive about 28 miles south on a rough dirt road to the marked turnoff, then continue about seven miles to a fork. Take the north branch and go about another four miles to an old rancho on the shore, which is rocky and not good for camping. Drive one-half mile north to a wide sand beach. You can hike about one mile farther north to another wide sand beach.

⑦ PLAYA SAN RAFAEL

On the Sea of Cortéz, south of Bahía de Los Angeles

Central Peninsula map, page 103

There are three miles of white sand beach accessible by road north toward Punta San Rafael and another 15 miles of beach south of that toward Punta San Francisco, which is accessible by foot. Fishing is good for bass, grouper, halibut, and yellowtail. Four-wheel drive is advised from Bahía de Los Angeles, due to the soft sand en route. Obtain supplies in Bahía de Los Angeles. Winter is the best season to visit, as summer can be very hot.

Directions: From Bahía de Los Angeles drive about 45 miles south on a rough dirt road to the marked turnoff, then continue about one-quarter mile to the beach.

⑧ PLAYAS SAN FRANCISQUITO

On the Sea of Cortéz, south of Bahía de Los Angeles

Central Peninsula map, page 103

The *caleta* (cove) is small and well protected. Fishing is good for bass, barracuda, and grouper. Santa Teresa Beach, with its fine white sand, is more than a mile long. This is very remote country, and it is best to travel in a group for safety. You are completely on your own until you reach San Francisquito with its resort, restaurant, and private residences, where fuel, water, and assistance might be available. There are three *palapas* for camping for $5 per night, and restrooms with cold showers and flush toilets are available. Winter is the best time to visit, as it is very hot in summer. Obtain supplies in Bahía de Los Angeles or Guerrero Negro.

Directions: From Bahía de Los Angeles drive about 85 miles south on a rough dirt road suitable only for high-clearance or four-wheel-drive vehicles, keeping to the left near Rancho El Progreso about 12 miles from the small beach in Caleta San Francisquito and the larger one on Bahía Santa Teresa to the south, where the Punta San Francisco Resort is located. An easier route, recently improved, is about 80 miles from Highway 1 via El Arco, south of Guerrero Negro, again for high-clearance and four-wheel-drive vehicles.

9 MALARRIMO BEACH

Northwest of Guerrero Negro, on the south shore of Bahía de Sebastian Vizcaíno
Central Peninsula map, page 104

If you're a scavenger at heart, you'll love this beach. The peninsula on the south shore of Bahía de Sebastian Vizcaíno sticks out into the ocean like a hook, catching flotsam and jetsam from the North Pacific, burying it in sand, and adding more beach in front of it. Junk of the ages can be picked up on the beach and mined from the dunes well back from the present shore. You'll find anything that has ever floated: Japanese blown-glass net floats, ship wreckage, flotsam and jetsam (including plastic bottles by the thousands, alas), logs from Canada, you name it. Obtain supplies in Guerrero Negro. Summer is the best season to visit, as winter can be cool.

Directions: From Highway 1 about 43 miles south of Guerrero Negro, turn west at Viz-

caíno. The first 22 miles of the approximately 70-mile drive to the turnoff to Malarrimo is paved, and the next 48 miles have been graded in preparation for paving, so you may encounter severe washboarding. If you reach San José del Castro, you have gone a half mile too far. Turn north at the turnoff and continue for another 27 miles on a road best navigated by four-wheel-drive vehicles due to soft sand. Another access suitable for pickups is north and east by dirt road out of Bahía Tortugas, which reaches the north-facing coast about 10 miles west of Malarrimo proper.

10 ABREOJOS BEACHES

On the Pacific Ocean, south of Guerrero Negro and east of Punta Abreojos
Central Peninsula map, page 104

These beaches extend about 10 miles from Punta Abreojos south to Estero de Coyote, accessible by road, and for another 14 miles across the entrance to the *estero* on south to Laguna San Ignacio, accessible by boat. Large motor homes and trailers are not recommended. There is good fishing in the ocean for barracuda, mackerel, bass, bonito, yellowtail, dorado, corvina, and grouper and in the *esteros* for halibut, grouper, bass, corvina, triggerfish, and sierra. Pismo clams abound. A friend in the Baja Sur state government told us of sending two assistants on business to Abreojos, a small fishing village not geared to tourists. Finding no restaurant, they began knocking on doors to arrange for dinner. After several unsuccessful attempts, one lady tentatively offered to feed them but explained that she had only the simple fare they ate every day, which they might not find appealing. When asked what that simple fare was, she replied, "Just lobster and abalone." Obtain supplies in Guerrero Negro. Summer is the best time to visit, as winter can be cool.

Directions: Access is from Km 98 on Highway 1, 71 miles south of Guerrero Negro. You'll see a sign and a restaurant at the turnoff. Continue on a dirt road for about 50 miles.

© FRED JONES

Chapter 4

North Baja Sur

NORTH
BAJA SUR

Sea of Cortéz (Gulf of California)

See
"Central Peninsula"
pages 102-104

Caleta
Santa María

Santa Rosalía 〇
1

Arroyo Santa Agueda

2-3

San José de
Magdalena
〇

Isla San
Marcos
2

MEX 1

Punta
Chivato
4

Bahía de
Santa Inéz
3

Mulegé 〇
5-8

9-11
12-13
14-15
16
17
18-19
20

Bahía Concepción

4

Punta
Santo
Domingo

21
〇 San Juanico

Punta
Pequena
〇

Bahía San
Juanico
1

Bahía
San
Nicholas

Pacific
Ocean

La Purisima 〇 San Isidro
〇

Bahía
San Basilio

MEX 1

San José de Comondu
〇

0   10 mi

0   10 km

© AVALON TRAVEL PUBLISHING, INC.

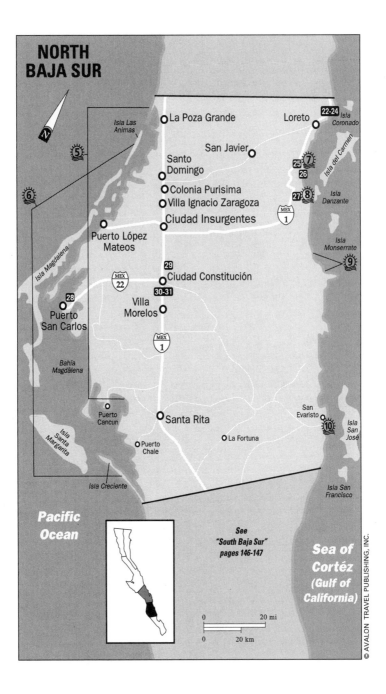

NORTH
BAJA SUR

N

Isla Las
Animas

La Poza Grande

Loreto

22-24 Isla
Coronado

San Javier

Santo
Domingo

25 7

26

Isla del Carmen

Colonia Purisima

Villa Ignacio Zaragoza

27 8

Isla
Danzante

Ciudad Insurgentes

MEX
1

Puerto López
Mateos

Isla Monserrate

9

Isla Magdalena

MEX
22

29

Ciudad Constitución

28

Puerto
San Carlos

30-31

Villa
Morelos

MEX
1

Bahía
Magdálena

Puerto
Cancun

Santa Rita

San
Evaristo

La Fortuna

10

Isla
San
José

Isla
Santa
Margarita

Puerto
Chale

Isla Creciente

Isla San
Francisco

Pacific
Ocean

See
"South Baja Sur"
pages 146-147

Sea of
Cortéz
(Gulf of
California)

0   20 mi

0   20 km

© AVALON TRAVEL PUBLISHING, INC.

North Baja Sur

This section of the Baja California Peninsula is very enticing for campers. Excitement builds while travelers descend the Santa Rosalía Grade, now known as Cuesta del Infierno, and reaches a crescendo as the Sea of Cortéz comes into view with Isla San Marcos prominent in the scene. There is an irresistible certainty that the best part of the trip is about to begin—balmy air, warm water, white sand beaches, great fishing, and relaxation.

Numerous RV parks and campsites for both tents and RVs are found on beaches off Highway 1 on the Sea of Cortéz. Punta Chivato and Bahía Concepción offer some of the most stunning scenery in Baja. The Pacific Ocean side of this portion of the peninsula has some outstanding beaches, but access to most of them is a bit difficult. There are persistent rumors of developing a better road from La Purisima north to San Ignacio, which would improve access to a long stretch of coastline.

Santa Rosalía–Mulegé Area
(campgrounds 1–8)

One of the most popular destinations in Baja, this section of the Sea of Cortéz coast contains two vastly different cities—Santa Rosalía and Mulegé—and some exceptional beaches around Punta Chivato. Campers have a variety of camping areas and activities from which to choose.

A company town without a company, Santa Rosalía has been reorienting its focus toward tourism by preserving the small-town atmosphere and protecting its marina. While not a prime travel destination, it does have narrow, shaded streets that are pleasant for strolling. The town also offers many goods and services.

Mulegé has a lot to offer, which is why so many foreigners have selected it for their winter quarters. Among the many charms are a vast number of date palms and a spring-fed river, the Río Mulegé, which give the town an exotic tropical appearance.

Fishing

Fishing is particularly good around Isla San Marcos, eight miles east of San Lucas Cove and nine miles north of Punta Chivato. Most anglers launch small boats over packed sand at San Lucas Cove RV Park or Punta Chivato Beach (see listings in this chapter). Others hire a local *panga* fisherman. You can catch grouper, bass, triggerfish, yellowtail, dorado, barracuda, sierra, and skipjack, and the *panga* fishermen know better than anyone else what is biting where at any given time.

Punta Chivato Beach is a popular camping area for people who fish nearby around Islas Santa Inéz, as well as around Isla San Marcos. A good concrete launch ramp west of the Punta Chivato Hotel is available for larger boats, if you are able to tow one in over the usually difficult road from Highway 1.

From Mulegé the waters north to Islas Santa Inéz and south along the shore and off Punta Concepción can be good for grouper, yellowtail, sierra, and bass. A good concrete launch ramp is near the mouth of the Río Mulegé across the airstrip from the Serenidad Hotel. Commercial *panga* fishermen are always willing to be engaged for a day of fishing, if they are not otherwise occupied.

Boating

Small boats can be launched into the river, which is quite shallow but does give access to the Sea of Cortéz for those who know the channel. Those with large boats can launch at high tide on the ramp, just east of the airstrip in Mulegé. You must thread your way around the Serenidad Hotel to get there, however, taking special care at the sharp right turn on the northwest corner of the hotel to avoid a power pole and cable.

Diving and Snorkeling

Cortez Explorers at 75a Calle Moctezuma in Mulegé offers boats, guides, and rental equipment for scuba diving and snorkeling. A certification card is required for diving. They lead snorkeling excursions outside Punta Concepción or to Islas Santa Inéz. Contact them by phone or fax at Mex. tel. 615/153-0500, email: info@cortez-explorer.com, website: www.cortez-explorer.com. They also rent bicycles and ATVs.

Sightseeing

Santa Rosalía was founded in 1885 by Compañia del Boleo to allow the exploitation of rich copper deposits. Remains of the smelter, an old steam engine, and other mining equipment that was used for a hundred years are still present. The unique preconstructed metal Church of Santa Bárbara, designed by Alexandre-Gustave Eiffel, was installed in 1897 on the main street, several blocks west of the waterfront. A few blocks east of it is a renowned bakery, El Boleo, which produces marvelous bread. The French Hotel on the northern mesa above the main street is worth a visit. It is in restored French colonial style and reflects French tastes introduced to Santa Rosalía when the mining company moved in during the 19th century.

Mulegé is a charming village crammed tightly between the river and steep hills to the north. Don't drive in with a trailer or large motor home—you won't believe how narrow the streets are. They are pleasant to explore on foot, however.

The restored Misión Santa Rosalía de Mulegé, located on a hill west of town, and the museum in the old territorial prison on the north side are well worth visiting. You can also arrange excursions out of Mulegé with Baja Adventure Tours to see Indian rock art, go bird-watching, or visit Bahía Concepción. You can contact owner Ciro A. Cuesta Romero at Mex. tel./fax 615/153-0021, email: cirocuesta@yahoo.com.mx. He is located in Hotel Vieja Hacienda, Madero #3 Centro, Mulegé.

Dining

Mulegé boasts some very fine restaurants, including Serenidad, Las Casitas, and Los Equipales.

Bahía Concepción Area
(campgrounds 9–20)

Bahía Concepción is one of the most beautiful spots in all of Baja California. From the north the first view of this gem is absolutely stunning. Many people decide this is just what they have been looking for and park on the first stretch of beach they can find, then luxuriate in the delights of tranquil water and opulent colors: the tans and reds of rocky shores and islands set against the bright blues of sea and sky with fringes of glistening white sand beaches.

Fishing

At times you can find sierra, barracuda, bass, triggerfish, and others, but the netters have pretty much cleaned out the baitfish that the bigger ones need for food. If you want to hire a *panga* fisherman, ask the management at one of the RV parks for assistance.

Boating
Small boats can be launched over the firm sand and anchored close to shore.

Diving and Snorkeling
The water can be quite clear and filled with colorful fish. Try the eastern shore of the bay. You should have no trouble finding butter and chocolate clams, pen shells (the adductor muscle makes great "scallops"), and big rock scallops. If you have your own tanks, Cortez Explorer in Mulegé can refill them.

Kayaking
Spend an interesting day on Bahía Concepción with Baja Tropicales Island Kayak Adventures, which includes clam digging, refreshments, and a clam feast. For reservations, call them at Mex. tel. 615/153-0409 or fax 615/153-0190. They are located at EcoMundo at Km 119 about 15 miles south of Mulegé at the Playa Escondida (see listing in this chapter) turnoff.

Other Activities
Windsurfing and waterskiing are popular in these protected waters.

Loreto Area
(campgrounds 22–27)
This slice of Baja is nearly as attractive as Bahía Concepción. Isla Carmen lies off Loreto and heads a whole string of islands that continue all the way south to La Paz and beyond. The vista from the highway overlook north of Puerto Escondido is every bit as good as that of Bahía Concepción from the high point on the highway north of Santispac (see listing in this chapter).

Fishing can be exceptional around the islands, cruising is great, and the beaches attract many campers. Puerto Escondido, with its excellent harbor, first-class launch ramp, and the Tripui RV Park (see listing in this chapter) is a focal point of activity.

Fishing
With your own boat in tow, opportunities are unlimited. Anglers will find good fishing offshore for striped marlin, sailfish, dorado, yellowtail, grouper, bass, barracuda, sierra, jack crevalle, and bonito. Get to know some of the resident experts at Tripui RV Park. If you don't have a boat, you can charter one in Loreto.

Arturo's Sportfishing Fleet has an office on Miguel Hidalgo, one block from the *malecón* (waterfront). Reach them at Apartado Postal 5, Loreto, Baja California Sur, Mexico, Mex. tel. 613/135-0409, fax 613/135-0022.

Diving and Snorkeling
Both diving and snorkeling are great activities around the islands. Deportes Blazer on Miguel Hidalgo near the *malecón* rents equipment. The owner also fills your tanks upon presentation of a diving certification card. You can reach him at Miguel Hidalgo 23, Colonia Centro, Loreto, Baja California Sur, Mexico, Mex. tel. 613/135-0911, fax 613/135-0788.

Arturo's Sportfishing also offers guided diving and snorkeling trips and rents equipment.

Golf

An 18-hole golf course is located at Nopoló, south of Loreto. It is open from 6 A.M. to 9 P.M. For more information, contact Campo de Golf, Boulevard Misión de San Ignacio, Loreto, Baja California Sur, Mexico.

Tennis

The Centro Turistico de Loreto at Nopoló south of Loreto has tournament facilities and lights.

Other Activities and Excursions

Arturo's Sportfishing also takes people on trips to surrounding islands and mountains, or on sailing and waterskiing excursions.

Las Parras Tours does these types of excursions and whale watching at Puerto Lopez Mateos on Bahía Magdalena. Call them at Mex. tel. 613/135-1010 or fax 613/135-0900.

C&C Ground Services & Tours takes people to Puerto Lopez Mateos for whale watching, using an air-conditioned bus with a restroom. Call Mex. tel. 613/133-0151.

Sightseeing

Loreto's downtown area is very attractive, and the mall is very pleasant for strolling, as is the *malecón*. Misión de Nuestra Señora de Loreto is well worth visiting. Founded in 1697, it was the first mission in the Californias—the mother of them all. Still in operation, it remains lovely.

Nopoló is worth driving around to see the golf course, hotel, wide streets, and the planned subdivisions.

If you have a high-clearance vehicle, you will enjoy the 22-mile drive up to San Javier and a visit to the Misión de San Francisco Javier, founded in 1699. It is another well-kept, functioning church with some old vestments carefully preserved from the days of the padres. The road is steep and a bit rough, so only people in pickups, vans, and four-wheel-drive vehicles should attempt the drive.

Dining

A number of very good restaurants are in Loreto—La Terraza, Chile Willie's, El Nido, and Carmen Restaurant among them.

Pacific Coast Area
(campgrounds 21, 28–31)

The Pacific Coast area of North Baja Sur is dominated by Bahía Magdalena, a huge mangrove-lined bay that few people know much about. One of those rare experts, Dwight (Chino) Suitter, a fellow Vagabundo who spent many winters on the bay, shared some of his hard-won information with us. The two towns—Puerto San Carlos and Puerto López Mateos—are commercial ports and not particularly oriented to tourism, though whale watching is becoming more of an industry in López Mateos. There are few places for people in highway vehicles to camp. Off-roaders, however, have a wide choice of sandy roads to run on and remote beaches on which to camp, both north and south of Bahía Magdalena.

Fishing

Fishing is the main lure in Bahía Magdalena. An unusual opportunity presents itself to people with small boats that can be maneuvered up the small channels, though doing so takes local knowledge. Expect to catch grouper, halibut, bass, snapper, corvina, mackerel, snook, and pompano. Puerto San Carlos is the launching point for adventurous fishing trips 50 miles offshore to Thetis Banks, a target for the long-range boats out of San Diego in search of striped marlin and wahoo. You can find butter and chocolate clams easily at low tide.

Other Activities
Gray whales are in the area from January through April, and Puerto López Mateos and Puerto San Carlos on Bahía Magdalena are developing tourist businesses for whale watching. Once people learn that whales can be approached as closely here as anywhere and that a good paved road leads to both towns, this may turn into as popular a destination as Scammon's Lagoon or Laguna San Ignacio.

Campgrounds

1 LAS PALMAS RV PARK

South of Santa Rosalía

North Baja Sur map, page 122

This is a good place to spend the night, or to stay longer if you are drawn to Santa Rosalía or are waiting for the ferry to Guaymas. Keep in mind that you cannot depend upon obtaining the Temporary Vehicle Importation Permit required to enter the mainland of Mexico in Santa Rosalía. Plan ahead and get one in Tijuana at the customs office just inside the border. Otherwise, you may have to go on to La Paz for it. (For details see the Travel Tips section of the Introduction.) Winter is the time to visit here, as summer is hot. For things to do here, see Santa Rosalía–Mulegé Area, earlier in this chapter.

Campsites, facilities: There are 30 full-hookup campsites with grass, palms, and other trees. Facilities include well-maintained tiled flush toilets, hot showers, laundry facilities, a dump station, and a restaurant/bar that is open from mid-November through mid-March. The water is good to drink. The park is secured with a gate in a chain-link fence, and the manager lives on the premises. Tent campers are welcome. Obtain supplies in Santa Rosalía.

Reservations, fees: Reservations are accepted. Fees are moderate—$13 per night, $84 per week, $300 per month, and $3,000 per year.

Directions: From Santa Rosalía drive two miles south on Highway 1 to the park.

Contact: Las Palmas RV Park, Apartado Postal 123, Santa Rosalía, Baja California Sur, Mexico, Mex. fax 615/152-2270, email: jramiro_contreras@hotmail.com.

2 CAMACHO RV PARK

South of Santa Rosalía

North Baja Sur map, page 122

This park adjoins San Lucas Cove RV Park on its north side. There is a fish camp on the premises. See further details in the description of San Lucas Cove, the next listing.

Campsites, facilities: There are 10 campsites for RVs or tents without hookups. There are *palapas,* a few palms and mesquite trees, and restrooms with flush toilets and hot showers. Don't drink the water. A 24-hour guard is on-site. Obtain supplies in Santa Rosalía.

Reservations, fees: All sites are first come, first served. The fee is low—$6 per night, $40 per week, and $140 per month.

Directions: Head nine miles south of Santa Rosalía on Highway 1. The access road is at Km 182. Watch for the sign on the left. The park is one-half mile east.

Contact: Drive in and park.

3 SAN LUCAS COVE RV PARK

South of Santa Rosalía

North Baja Sur map, page 122

Set on the water in a protected cove with a few palms and mesquite trees, this park is very popular with visitors who come for the pleasant ambience. Swimming in the cove is comfortable. Small boats can be launched over the firm beach and safely anchored just offshore. If you want to fish, Isla San Marcos, six miles away, can be very good for grouper, bass, triggerfish, yellowtail, dorado, barracuda, sierra, and skipjack. Diving is also good. You'll find plenty of other fishing opportunities along the coast, both north and south. Arrange to hire a guide and a *panga* through the park or by asking around. There are clams in the cove. Mostly this is a good spot for kicking back. On one hot, muggy July night, we were entertained by a marvelous sound-and-light show over the Sea of Cortéz. Sunrise colors seem to be exceptionally intense and varied here. Winter is the time to visit—avoid the summer heat. For other things to do in and around here, see the Santa Rosalía Area, earlier in this chapter.

Campsites, facilities: There are 22 campsites on the water and 50 pull-through sites behind them in a large open area, all without hookups. A few *palapas* and palms are near the water, while a few of the other sites have trees. The concrete and slate restrooms have flush toilets and hot showers. Don't drink the water. Security is provided by a resident manager. Tent campers are welcome. Obtain supplies in Santa Rosalía.

Reservations, fees: All sites are first come, first served. The fee is low—$6 per night, $35 per week, $120 per month, and $1,000 per year.

Directions: Head nine miles south of Santa Rosalía on Highway 1. The access road is at Km 182. Watch for the sign on the left. The exit off Highway 1 is steep and sharp at the sign, but there is a gentler exit on a short frontage road just to the north. Go slow as you approach Km 182 so you can get off gently. The park is one-half mile east.

Contact: Drive in and park.

❹ PUNTA CHIVATO BEACH
🚶 🚴 🏊 🛶 🚤 🐕 🚐 ⛰

South of Santa Rosalía
North Baja Sur map, page 122

The view toward the peninsula is delightful. This is considered by many tourists to be one of the prettiest locations in Baja. A launch ramp west of the hotel is suitable at high tide for large boats, if you can get them there over the difficult road. Small boats can be launched across the beach. Fishing can be quite good nearby around Islas Santa Inéz for yellowfin tuna, yellowtail, dorado, skip-

jack, grouper, sierra, pargo, and barracuda, though a trip north to Isla San Marcos often produces better results. Winter is the time to visit, as summer is hot. For more on things to do here, see the Mulegé Area, earlier in this chapter.

Campsites, facilities: You'll find pit toilets, cold showers, and some *palapas*. Buy drinking water in one-liter plastic jugs at the little store near the Punta Chivato Hotel. There is no security. This is a great spot for tent camping. Obtain major supplies in Santa Rosalía.

Reservations, fees: All sites are first come, first served. The fee is moderate—$10 per night on the beach east of the hotel.

Directions: From Santa Rosalía drive 25 miles south on Highway 1 to Km 156. Turn east onto the washboard road and continue about 10 miles to the beach.

Contact: Drive in and pay there.

❺ VISTA PARADISO
🚶 🚴 🐕 🚐 ⛰

In Mulegé
North Baja Sur map, page 122

The Río Mulegé runs alongside this park and makes for a pleasant setting. Only pickups with campers and smaller vehicles can reach it, for access is through the middle of Mulegé, and the streets are too narrow for anything larger. The campground is about as minimal as they come.

Campsites, facilities: This is a primitive campground with a cleared area that can accommodate a few campers. Water is available, but you should drink bottled water. An outhouse and trees are on the property. Security is provided by a resident family. Tent campers are welcome. Obtain supplies in Mulegé.

Reservations, fees: Camping is first come, first served. The fee is low—$7 per night.

Directions: The park is on the north side of the river, 0.4 mile east of the end of the pavement at the eastern edge of Mulegé.

Contact: Drive in and talk to the manager.

6 ORCHARD (HUERTA SAUCEDO) RV PARK

🚶 🚴 🛶 🚤 🎣 🚙 ⛺

In Mulegé

North Baja Sur map, page 122

This is a very pleasant and well-kept park with lots of space, though the riverfront is completely taken up with permanent residences. Many trees provide abundant shade. Winter is the time to visit, as summer is hot. For things to do here, see the Mulegé Area, earlier in this chapter.

Campsites, facilities: There are 43 campsites, of which 25 are pull-through. A few have concrete pads, and all come with full hookups. On the premises are *palapas* and clean restrooms with flush toilets and hot showers. The water is safe to drink. A resident guard provides security. Tent campers are welcome. Obtain supplies in Mulegé.

Reservations, fees: Reservations are accepted. Fees are high—$16 per night with full hookups or $6 for a tent with two people. Long-term rates are $98 per week and $245 to $265 per month with full hookups, with one free day per week for tents.

Directions: The park is on the south side of the river off Highway 1, about one mile south of the turnoff into Mulegé. Watch for the sign.

Contact: Orchard (Huerta Saucedo) RV Park, Apartado Postal 24, Mulegé, Baja California Sur, Mexico, Mex. tel./fax 615/153-0109.

7 VILLA MARÍA RV PARK

🚶 🚴 🛶 🚤 🎣 🚙 ⛺

In Mulegé

North Baja Sur map, page 122

The clientele consists primarily of year-round residents, but a designated area is reserved for travelers. There is a common *palapa* for tent campers to use for cooking, eating, and lounging. Another perk is the bakery, which makes the kinds of treats tourists like—breakfast pastries, rolls, and bread. Some of the regulars

are standing at the door each morning when it opens. Winter is the time to visit, as summer is hot. For things to do here, see the Mulegé Area, earlier in this chapter.

Campsites, facilities: There are 24 pull-through campsites on grass, all with full hookups, plus some tent sites in a separate area with a central *palapa*. Facilities include clean restrooms with flush toilets and hot showers, a laundry facility, a dump station, a great swimming pool, and a well-regarded bakery. Don't drink the water. The owner lives on the premises. Tent camping is encouraged. Obtain supplies in Mulegé.

Reservations, fees: Reservations are accepted. Fees are moderate—$13 per night for two people at sites with full hookups. Lower fees for tent camping can be arranged. Long-term rates are $72 per week and $275 per month.

Directions: The park is on the south side of the river off Highway 1, about 1.5 miles south of the turnoff into Mulegé. Watch for the sign.

Contact: Villa María RV Park, Apartado Postal 5, Mulegé, Baja California Sur, Mexico, Mex. tel./fax 615/153-0246.

8 SERENIDAD HOTEL AND RV PARK

🚶 🚴 🛶 🚤 🎣 🚙

In Mulegé

North Baja Sur map, page 122

For a special treat, head to the hotel's restaurant for the Wednesday night Mexican buffet or the Saturday night pig roast (complete with dancing), two affairs that are renowned among locals. When you arrive, turn into the walled compound on the southern side of the hotel and back your vehicle against the south wall. Winter is the time to visit, as summer is hot. For things to do here, see the Mulegé Area, earlier in this chapter.

Campsites, facilities: There are nine campsites in a concrete-walled compound with full hookups. A laundry facility and a dump station are on-site. The tiled restrooms have flush toilets and hot showers. A launch ramp is nearby on the Río

Mulegé. In the hotel are a pool, a restaurant, and a bar. The water is safe to drink. A 24-hour guard provides security. Tent campers are not welcome. Obtain supplies in Mulegé.

Reservations, fees: Reservations are accepted. Fees are moderate—$12 per night, $70 per week, and $275 per month. Pay at the hotel.

Directions: From Highway 1 drive past the turnoff into Mulegé, cross the bridge over the river, and continue south about 2.5 miles. Watch for the sign on the east side marking the turnoff to Serenidad. The dirt access road leads about one-half mile north along the western edge of the airstrip.

Contact: Serenidad Hotel and RV Park, Apartado Postal 9, Mulegé, Baja California Sur, Mexico, Mex. tel. 615/153-0530, fax 615/153-0311.

9 LOS NARANJOS BEACH
🏃 🚴 ≋ ⚓ 🚐 🐕 🚙 ⛰

On Bahía Concepción
North Baja Sur map, page 122

This campground adjoins the next park, Campo Playa Punta Arena, on the east side. We were quite taken with the location on the shore of Bahía Concepción and plan to return often.

Campsites, facilities: There is room for an indeterminate number of campers. Ten campsites have water. Restrooms with flush toilets and hot showers and a dump station are available. You must pay $1 to have the hot water turned on. A restaurant is also on-site. Small boats can be launched across the beach. Don't drink the water. There is no security as such, but the owners live there and it is in a remote location. Tent campers are welcome. Obtain supplies in Mulegé.

Reservations, fees: All sites are first come, first served. Fees are low—$4 per night without one of the nine *palapas* on the water, $6 with; $28 per week without *palapas*, $42 with; one day free per month. Five *cabañas* are available for $7 per night, $10 with beds.

Directions: From Mulegé drive about 10 miles south on Highway 1. At Km 119, near the north

end of the bay, look for the sign and turn left onto a fairly rough dirt road. Continue for about two miles, taking right turns where there are signs. Don't be concerned if you don't see the beach on your approach—it is out of sight to the south.

Contact: Drive in and talk to the owner.

10 CAMPO PLAYA PUNTA ARENA
🏃 🚴 ≋ ⚓ 🚐 🐕 🚙 ⛰

On Bahía Concepción
North Baja Sur map, page 122

This is a very pretty beach, a wide sweep of clean white sand stretching several hundred yards and facing south with an expansive view down beautiful Bahía Concepción. Several permanent residences are lined up along the water's edge, but there is plenty of room for transients in RVs or tents. Winter is the favored season to visit here, as summer is hot. For things to do, see the Bahía Concepción Area, earlier in this chapter.

Campsites, facilities: There's room for an indeterminate number of campers. Marginal toilets and six *palapas* are provided. Don't drink the water. There is no security as such, but the owners live there and it is in a remote location. Tent campers are welcome. Obtain supplies in Mulegé.

Reservations, fees: All sites are first come, first served. Fees are low—$4 to park for the night without a *palapa* or $6 per night for a *palapa* on the water.

Directions: From Mulegé drive about 10 miles south on Highway 1. At Km 119, near the north end of the bay, look for the sign and turn left onto a fairly rough dirt road. Continue for about two miles, taking right turns where there are signs. Don't be concerned if you don't see the beach on your approach—it is out of sight to the south.

Contact: Drive in and talk to the manager.

Playa Santispac on Bahía Concepción is very popular.

11 PLAYA SANTISPAC

On Bahía Concepción
North Baja Sur map, page 122

A great number of people spend the entire winter here, attracted to the well-protected location and the pleasant view. Early birds get their choice of spots. RVers must have a great tolerance for elbow-to-elbow living, but tent campers will find plenty of room. Two more perks: Anna's Restaurant, Bar, and Bakery and Maru Restaurant. Winter is the best time to visit, as summer is hot. For things to do here, see the Bahía Concepción Area, earlier in this chapter.

Campsites, facilities: Two restaurants, pit toilets, cold showers, and a dump station are on the premises. Don't drink the water. There is no security. Tent campers are welcome. Obtain supplies in Mulegé.

Reservations, fees: All sites are first come, first served. Fees are low—$6 per night for a small *palapa* on the water and $7 for a large one. Use of the pit toilets and showers costs $1 each.

Directions: From Mulegé drive about 13 miles south on Highway 1 to the beach, at Km 114.
Contact: Drive in and talk to the manager.

12 POSADA CONCEPCIÓN RV PARK

On Bahía Concepción
North Baja Sur map, page 122

Occupied mostly by permanent residents, this RV park will serve in a pinch should you need to get off the highway when overtaken by dark and have nowhere else to go. It's all right as long as you don't mind camping in the middle of a residential community well back from the one attraction—the beach. For things to do here, see the Bahía Concepción Area, earlier in this chapter.

Campsites, facilities: There are eight spaces near the highway for overnighters, all of which have full hookups. *Palapas,* flush toilets, hot showers, and sulfur hot springs are available on-site. Don't drink the water, which is hauled in and not treated. The owner lives on the premises. Tent campers are prohibited. Obtain supplies in Mulegé.

Reservations, fees: All sites are first come, first served. The fee is moderate—$10 per night. A 10 percent discount applies if you stay a month.

Directions: From Mulegé drive about 14 miles south on Highway 1. The park is at Km 112.

Contact: Posada Concepción, Apartado Postal 14, Mulegé, Baja California Sur, Mexico.

13 PLAYA ESCONDIDA

On Bahía Concepción
North Baja Sur map, page 122

Here is a very attractive site. The beach is tucked between hills with islands nearby, affording some protection from the wind. This is an ideal choice for those who want to camp in a tent right on the edge of the placid waters of Bahía Concepción in much less congested conditions than nearby Playa Santispac (campground 11). With a kayak or small inflatable boat, campers can enjoy great snorkeling and clamming around the offshore islands and can drift close to roosting seabirds that are not afraid of humans.

Campsites, facilities: Several *palapas* on the water's edge, pit toilets, and trash barrels are provided, though cleanliness leaves a lot to be desired. There is no water. Security is provided by a resident manager. Obtain supplies in Mulegé.

Reservations, fees: Camping is first come, first served. The fee is low—$6 per night.

Directions: From Mulegé drive about 14 miles south on Highway 1 to Posada Concepción and continue south for another half mile. Watch for the sign near Km 112 at a dirt road going three-quarters of a mile east of the highway.

Contact: Drive in and pay.

14 PLAYA LOS COCOS

On Bahía Concepción
North Baja Sur map, page 122

Photos of Playa Los Cocos would make a great promo for a South Sea Islands vacation. The glistening, soft-sand beach is lapped by crystal-clear water that rarely displays a ripple and has a gorgeous light green hue from the white sands a few inches beneath the surface. Tent camping is delightful here, with camps pitched inches from the water's edge, enabling one to take a few steps from the shade of a palm tree, cool off with a quick dip, and return to deep contemplation. Small boats can be launched over the sand and anchored just offshore. Many people come early and spend the winter. That makes perfect sense, for summer is just too hot. For things to do here, see the Bahía Concepción Area, earlier in this chapter.

Campsites, facilities: Pit toilets and a dump station are provided, but there is no water and no security. Obtain supplies in Mulegé.

Reservations, fees: All sites are first come, first served. Fees are low—$4 per night or a long-term rate of $105 per month.

Directions: From Mulegé drive about 15 miles south on Highway 1. The beach access is at Km 111. Go slow and watch for the dirt road to the left, then proceed a few hundred yards east.

Contact: Drive in and park. Someone will come around to collect the fee.

15 PLAYA EL BURRO

On Bahía Concepción
North Baja Sur map, page 122

As you round the hill to the north on the highway, check out the beach below you. It is a popular spot in a protected cove. You can launch small boats over the sand and anchor them in front of your rig. A group of regulars spend their winters at El Burro, and caravaners led by the Vagabundos del Mar uniformly like to stay here. However, the waterfront sites are being offered to people on an annual lease, relegating the temporarys to a second row of campsites. We have heard that years ago a lame burro colt lived near the beach—perhaps this is the source of the name. Tent camping

Playa El Coyote on Bahía Concepción is a very scenic spot that's perfect for tent campers.

here is delightful. Winter is the favored season to visit, as summer is hot. For things to do here, see the Bahía Concepción Area, earlier in this chapter.

Campsites, facilities: *Palapas,* toilets, and a dump site are provided. There is no water and no security. Obtain supplies in Mulegé.

Reservations, fees: All sites are first come, first served. Fees are very low—$3 per night or a long-term rate of $60 per month. The south end is under different management and there is usually no charge there.

Directions: From Mulegé drive about 16 miles south on Highway 1. The beach is at Km 109.

Contact: Drive in and park. Someone will come around to collect the fee.

16 PLAYA EL COYOTE

On Bahía Concepción
North Baja Sur map, page 122
This protected cove is a good spot for tent campers, especially those looking for a little

solitude, since it's not as popular as the other beaches on Bahía Concepción. Winter is the favored season to visit, as summer is hot. For things to do here, see the Bahía Concepción Area, earlier in this chapter.

Campsites, facilities: A few *palapas* are set right off the highway. An outhouse and a cold shower with water heated from the sun are available, but there is no drinkable water and no security. Obtain supplies in Mulegé.

Reservations, fees: All sites are first come, first served. The fee is low—$5 per night with a *palapa* and $4 without.

Directions: From Mulegé drive about 17 miles south on Highway 1. The beach is at Km 108, at the south end of Bahía Coyote. A rough road takes off to the south along the water's edge against a rocky slope and leads to a larger, more open area with some trees.

Contact: Drive in and park. Someone will come around to collect the fee.

17 BUENAVENTURA RESORT HOTEL, RESTAURANT, AND RV PARK

🚶 🚲 🏊 🛶 ⛴ 🐕 🚐 ⛺

On Bahía Concepción
North Baja Sur map, page 122

You camp amid a cluster of resort buildings that creates a congested atmosphere. The nearby bar and restaurant can be crowded and noisy—not very conducive to tranquillity, nor is the racket from trucks decelerating down the hills into the arroyo. Winter is the best season to visit. For things to do here, see the Bahía Concepción Area, earlier in this chapter.

Campsites, facilities: There are pit toilets, *palapas,* hot showers, a restaurant, a bar, a mini-market, and a concrete ramp for launching boats into the surf. Don't drink the water. Security is provided by gates that are closed at night. Tent campers are welcome. Obtain major supplies in Mulegé.

Reservations, fees: All sites are first come, first served. The fee is moderate—$10 per night. Showers cost $1.50 for eight minutes.

Directions: From Mulegé drive about 25 miles south on Highway 1. The beach is at Km 94.

Contact: Buenaventura Resort Hotel, Restaurant, and RV Park. Mex. tel. 613/104-4064, Mex. tel./fax 615/153-0408, website: www.hotelsanbuenaventura.com.

18 PLAYA EL REQUESÓN

🚶 🚲 🏊 🛶 ⛴ 🐕 🚐 ⛺

On Bahía Concepción
North Baja Sur map, page 122

If you're a beach lover, what could be better than two beaches together? At Playa El Requesón you camp on a beautiful sand spit flanked on each side by a beach and water. Don't drive out on the really narrow part—it goes under at high tide. This is one of the old-time campsites, popular with locals as well as tourists. The cove on the north side is great for playing around and clamming. Small vehicles can drive around

the hill at the northwest corner of the spit on a portion of the old Baja road to a small cove that's great for tent camping. Winter is the favored season to visit, as summer is hot. For things to do here, see the Bahía Concepción Area, earlier in this chapter.

Campsites, facilities: Pit toilets are provided, but there is no water and no security. Obtain supplies in Mulegé.

Reservations, fees: All sites are first come, first served. The fee is very low—$2 per night.

Directions: From Mulegé drive about 26 miles south on Highway 1. The beach access is at Km 92. Go slow and watch for the dirt road leading off to the left. Though a little rough, the road is only a few hundred yards long, and everyone makes it easily.

Contact: Drive in and park. Someone will come around to collect the fee.

19 PLAYA LA PERLA

🚶 🚲 🏊 🛶 ⛴ 🐕 🚐 ⛺

On Bahía Concepción
North Baja Sur map, page 122

This is just around the corner from El Requesón, above, and is on a small inlet with a nice beach.

Campsites, facilities: There are 10 *palapas* scattered around the shoreline, pit toilets, and cold showers. There is no water. A resident manager provides security. Obtain supplies in Mulegé.

Reservations, fees: All sites are first come, first served. The fee is low—$5 per night.

Directions: From Mulegé drive about 27 miles south on Highway 1. The access road is near Km 91. Go slow and watch for the dirt road leading off to the left.

Contact: Drive in and camp.

20 PLAYA ARMENTA

🚶 🚲 🏊 🛶 ⛴ 🐕 🚐 ⛺

On Bahía Concepción
North Baja Sur map, page 122

Though not one of the better beaches in the

area, Playa Armenta will do in a pinch. It's best for tent camping. Winter is the favored season to visit here, as summer is hot. For things to do here, see the Bahía Concepción Area, earlier in this chapter.

Campsites, facilities: Some small *palapas* and a pit toilet are provided. There is no water and no security. Obtain supplies in Mulegé.

Reservations, fees: All sites are first come, first served. The fee is very low—$3 per night with a *palapa* and $2 without.

Directions: From Mulegé drive about 28 miles south on Highway 1. The beach access is near Km 90. Turn off the highway at the sign and follow the dirt road around a bluff to a small beach.

Contact: Drive in and camp.

21 SCORPION BAY

At San Juanico

North Baja Sur map, page 122

This is almost exclusively a surfing location. The wind usually blows, and tarps and windbreaks are necessary, as well as insect barriers.

Campsites, facilities: Campers select their own campsites on a bluff along the water's edge. There are pathways to the beach, and a restaurant and cantina are on-site. Plans are in the works for a bathhouse and full hookups. There are also some *cabañas* for noncampers. Basic provisions are available in San Juanico.

Reservations, fees: No reservations are accepted. Fees are low—sites rent for $5 per night or $50 per month, plus camp fees when occupied—$4 per person per night.

Directions: Drive north of Ciudad Insurgentes on the Pacific Coast for 110 miles, the last 30 miles on dirt. Two other uncertain and rough routes are south from San Ignacio and directly west over the mountains to La Purisima from Highway 1 south of Bahía Concepción.

Contact: U.S. tel. 619/239-1335, fax 619/235-6018, Mex. fax 613/138-2850, email: ruben@

scorpionbay.net. Make camping arrangements on-site with the manager.

22 RIVERA DEL MAR TRAILER RV PARK

In Loreto

North Baja Sur map, page 123

This is the newest RV park in Loreto, and all facilities are in pristine condition. Campers have access to a launch ramp five blocks away in the boat harbor. The park is convenient to everything in town. Winter is the favored season to visit here, as summer is hot. For things to do here, see the Loreto Area, earlier in this chapter.

Campsites, facilities: Each of the 25 campsites has full hookups. There is some shade. Flush toilets and hot showers in a tiled bathroom are on-site. Internet service, a launderette, and snacks are available. There is also a central area with barbecue facilities. Don't drink the water. There is good security with the owners living on the property and homes surrounding the central RV park area, all inside a surrounding fence. A tent camping area is available. Obtain supplies in Loreto.

Reservations, fees: Reservations are accepted. Fees are moderate—$14 for RVs with full hookups and $12 without hookups; tents are $5 per person.

Directions: From Mulegé drive about 84 miles south on Highway 1 to Loreto. Enter town on Salvatierra to El Pescador Market, turn left one block to Benito Juarez, then right several blocks to Francisco Madero and left five blocks to the park on the left.

Contact: Rivera del Mar Trailer RV Park, Francisco Madero #100, Loreto, Baja California Sur, Mexico, Mex. tel. 613/135-0718, email: lanyvall@yahoo.com.mx.

23 EL MORO RV PARK

🚶 🚲 🏊 🚣 ⛴ 🐕 🚐 ⛺

In Loreto

North Baja Sur map, page 123

Campers have access to a launch ramp five blocks away in the boat harbor. The park is convenient to everything in town. Dogs and chickens making noise next door can disturb your sleep, however. Most of the spaces are occupied by annual lessees. The last time we were there only five spots were available. Winter is the favored season to visit here, as summer is hot. For things to do here, see the Loreto Area, earlier in this chapter.

Campsites, facilities: Each of the 12 campsites has full hookups, a table, and a barbecue. Flush toilets and hot showers are provided, as is a dump station. Don't drink the water. The park is secured with a gate and a watchman. Tent campers are welcome. Obtain supplies in Loreto.

Reservations, fees: Reservations are accepted. Fees are moderate—$12 per night for RVs, $72 per week, $220 per month; and $4 per night in tents or $100 per month.

Directions: From Mulegé drive about 84 miles south on Highway 1 to Loreto. The park is in town, one-half block from the *malecón* on Salvatierra. Go through town to the waterfront and turn left at the sign.

Contact: El Moro RV Park, Rosendo Robles #8, Loreto, Baja California Sur, Mexico, Mex. tel./fax 613/135-0542.

24 LORETO SHORES VILLAS AND RV PARK

🚶 🚲 🏊 🚣 ⛴ 🐕 🚐 ⛺

In Loreto

North Baja Sur map, page 123

All RV spaces, where tenters are also welcome to set up camp, are behind a large multiple-dwelling building that blocks views of the Sea of Cortéz. Winter is the favored season to visit here, as summer is hot. For things to do here, see the Loreto Area, earlier in this chapter.

Campsites, facilities: There are 33 pull-through campsites with full hookups and trees, plus five separate tent camping sites. Facilities include clean, tiled restrooms with flush toilets and hot showers, a recreation hall, a dump station, and laundry facilities. Don't drink the water. Security is provided 24 hours a day by a roving guard inside the gate, which closes at 11 P.M. and opens at 5 A.M. Tent campers are welcome. Obtain supplies in Loreto.

Reservations, fees: Reservations are accepted. Fees are moderate—$16.50 per night for RVs, $99 per week, $300 per month, and $3,500 per year. Fees for tents are $5 per night, $30 per week, and $120 per month.

Directions: From Mulegé drive about 84 miles south on Highway 1 to Loreto. The park is on the south side of town on the beach. Go through town on Salvatierra and turn right on Francisco Madero, continuing across the big arroyo until you see the sign.

Contact: Loreto Shores Villas and RV Park, Apartado Postal 219, Loreto, Baja California Sur, Mexico, Mex. tel. 613/135-1513, fax 613/135-0711, email: loretoshores@yahoo.com.

25 JUNCALITO BEACH

🚶 🚲 🏊 🚣 ⛴ 🐕 🚐 ⛺

South of Loreto

North Baja Sur map, page 123

This is a favorite beach with the primitive camping set. Why is it so popular? Because not only is it free, but it's located in a very attractive setting. Tripui RV Park—where you'll find a restaurant, a store, and laundry facilities—is just 2.5 miles south of here. The scenery is great, the beach is in a somewhat protected cove, fishing is fantastic around several islands offshore, and boaters can anchor their craft close to the beach. Whereas tent campers will be very pleased, RVers most likely won't. Before going in with a large motor home or trailer, walk it out to see if you'll fit. Odds are this isn't the place for you. Winter is the favored season to visit, as summer is hot. For things to do here, see the Loreto Area, earlier in this chapter.

Campsites, facilities: The only facilities are trash barrels. There is no water and no security. Obtain supplies at the store in Tripui RV Park.

Reservations, fees: All sites are first come, first served. There is no fee.

Directions: From Loreto drive about 14 miles south on Highway 1 (approximately one mile north of the turnoff to Tripui RV Park and Puerto Escondido), then head one-half mile down a rough dirt road to the beach on the southern end of Bahía Juncalito. The village of Juncalito occupies the northern waterfront. Look for the sign on the east side of the highway.

Contact: Drive in and park.

26 TRIPUI RV PARK

South of Loreto at Puerto Escondido
North Baja Sur map, page 123

We have spent many happy weeks playing at Tripui, one of the better parks in Baja California Sur. The islands offshore are great for cruising, sailing a dinghy to pretty sand beaches, and fishing for dorado and yellowtail. Skipjack are abundant and provide great sport but are not good to eat. Live mackerel can be caught early in the morning off the entrance to Puerto Escondido. The excellent launch ramp at Puerto Escondido about one mile down the road is one of the best in Baja. Any size boat can be launched on this fine concrete ramp into the protected waters of the harbor. Winter is the favored season to visit here, as summer is hot. For more information on things to do here, see the Loreto Area, earlier in this chapter.

Campsites, facilities: There are 30 campsites with full hookups along a paved road in an area with its own entrance, just before the main entrance to Tripui. There are also 10 tent spaces. Go in the main entrance and register at the office, then return. On the premises are tiled restrooms with flush toilets and hot showers, a dump station, satellite TV, laundry facilities, a pool, a restaurant, a gift store, and motel rooms. They also have telephone, fax, and Internet services. Down at the harbor there's a launch ramp operated by the Marina de Puerto Escondido, which charges a $3 daily fee. Don't drink the water. The park is secured by a gate and three watchmen. Obtain supplies in the park store.

Reservations, fees: Reservations are accepted. Fees are high—$15 per night for RVs, $94.50 per week, $382.50 per month, and $2,900 per year. Tents are $7 per night.

Directions: From Loreto drive 15 miles south on Highway 1. Watch for the signed turnoff. Turn and continue 1.5 miles east on pavement to the park.

Contact: Tripui RV Park, Apartado Postal 100, Loreto, Baja California Sur, Mexico, Mex. tel. 613/133-0814, fax 613/133-0828.

27 PLAYA LIGUI

South of Loreto
North Baja Sur map, page 123

This is not for trailers or larger rigs. There is thorny brush to scratch against, soft sand, and a small beach—but it is pretty. Additional beaches about two miles north and two miles south to Ensenada Blanca can be reached by sand roads suitable only for pickups, vans, or four-wheel-drive vehicles. Inflatable or cartop boats can be carried or dragged across the beach for fun fishing and snorkeling around the many little islands. The small ones that stick straight up are called Los Candeleros (the Candles). Some very nice, cozy little coves await exploration down the coast, well within the range of such small boats. Diving and snorkeling around the islands are delightful, with lots of colorful reef fish to look at. We spent a week doing that out of a tent and loved it. Winter is the favored season to visit here, as summer is hot. For things to do here, see the Loreto Area, earlier in this chapter.

Campsites, facilities: A pit toilet and trash barrels are provided. There is no water and no security. Obtain supplies from the store at Tripui RV Park.

Reservations, fees: All sites are first come, first served. There is no fee.

Directions: From Loreto drive about 22 miles south on Highway 1 (six miles south of Tripui RV Park and Puerto Escondido). At the fence ignore the *Propriedad Privada* (Private Property) sign, but look closely at the small "Trailer Park E. Blanca" sign. It has a rough map showing the turn to take to the low ridge at the south end of the beach and the most accessible camping area. Drive down the dirt road straight east of Highway 1 about three-quarters of a mile to the beach and take the last right turn and follow the signs marked *"Playa"* for another three-quarters of a mile. The rest of the beach immediately to the north is used by local fishermen for their *pangas.*

Contact: Drive in and park.

28 RV PARK NANCY

In San Carlos

North Baja Sur map, page 123

This is the only campground in the San Carlos area, and it is run by Americans.

Campsites, facilities: There are eight small campsites with full hookups. Big rigs would have a problem getting situated. There is a clean restroom with a flush toilet and a hot shower and a locked gate for security. Pull-through sites are said to be in the works.

Reservations, fees: Fees are $8–10.

Directions: Watch for the sign in San Carlos, 37 miles west of Ciudad Constitución on Highway 22.

Contact: Drive in and talk to the owners.

29 MANFRED'S RV TRAILER PARK

In Ciudad Constitución

North Baja Sur map, page 123

Manfred's is a good choice for campers who want to become acquainted with the vast Bahía Magdalena area. It is a convenient overnight stopping place with an excellent array of stores and services in Ciudad Constitución that support a large agricultural community. Be sure to read the billboard with the rules enumerated. For more information, see the Pacific Coast Area, earlier in this chapter.

Campsites, facilities: There are 86 campsites, of which 38 are pull-throughs with full hookups and 48 have electricity and water but no sewage lines. On the property are tiled restrooms with flush toilets and hot showers, a pool, a whirlpool tub, and trees. Don't drink the water. Gates, which close at 9:30 P.M., and the resident manager provide security. Tent campers are welcome. Obtain supplies in Ciudad Constitución.

Reservations, fees: Reservations are accepted. Fees are high—$17 per night for RVs and $6 to $10 for tents.

Directions: From the center of Ciudad Constitución drive over half a mile north on Highway 1 to the park on the east side of the road at Km 213.

Contact: Manfred's RV Trailer Park, Apartado Postal 120, Ciudad Constitución, Baja California Sur, Mexico, Mex. tel./fax 613/132-1103.

30 CAMPESTRE LA PILA

South of Ciudad Constitución

North Baja Sur map, page 123

The ground is bare and dusty, and only a few small trees provide landscaping. In other words, there is not a lot to recommend Campestre La Pila, except as a port of refuge if you're on the road when it's getting dark. This is a recreation area for the local people and is not geared to tourism. If you find yourself here, however, Ciudad Constitución is a good place to shop for those hard-to-find items like camera batteries and hardware. It is a farming community, and you can purchase many items there that are difficult to obtain south of Ensenada. If you need any major vehicle repairs, this is the place to stop and take care of the problem. Winter is the time to go, as summer is hot. For more information, see the Pacific Coast Area, earlier in this chapter.

Campsites, facilities: There are 32 pull-through campsites with electricity and water hookups. Flush toilets, hot showers, pools, and a dump station are available. Don't drink the water. The park is secured with a chain, and the manager lives on the premises. Tent campers are welcome. Obtain supplies in Ciudad Constitución.

Reservations, fees: All sites are first come, first served. The fee is moderate—$8 per night.

Directions: From the northern outskirts of Ciudad Constitución at the junction of Highway 22 (going west to Puerto San Carlos) and Highway 1, drive south through the city on Highway 1 for about 1.5 miles to the big "Campestre La Pila" sign; turn west and continue about one-half mile to the campground.

Contact: Drive in and go to the office.

31 MIKE AND BERTHA'S RV PARK—PALAPA 206

In Ciudad Constitución

North Baja Sur map, page 123

This park is in a huge flat field with structures around, but no one was available to talk to when we were there. They advertise long-term storage for vehicles, trailers, and boats.

Campsites, facilities: There were six pull-through sites ready for full hookups, but not connected, when we visited. A recent flyer states that six more pull-throughs have electricity and sewer. There are said to be clean flush toilets and showers, which may be in a large *palapa* that appears to be a party area set up for the sale of refreshments. Barbecues are on the property.

Reservations, fees: Fees are moderate—$11 per night with full hookups, $7.50 with partial hookups, and $5.50 for dry camping on two acres.

Directions: The park is two miles south of Ciudad Constitución on the west side of Highway 1.

Contact: Mike and Bertha's RV Park—Palapa 206, Apartado Postal 186, Ciudad Constitución, Baja California Sur, Mexico, Mex. tel. 613/132-3463.

10 Best Beaches

① SAN JUANICO BEACH
On the Pacific coast, north of Puerto López Mateos

North Baja Sur map, page 122

Well known to surfers for years, San Juanico has one of the most beautiful beaches in Baja Sur, running about eight miles south. Most of it is along high sand bluffs and is drivable only at low tide. Fishing is good for halibut, grouper, pargo, snook, sierra, corvina, and corbina. All-terrain vehicles and four-wheel drives can do a loop south and back to San Juanico (see Scorpion Bay campground in this chapter).

Directions: From Ciudad Insurgentes drive about 80 miles north on the paved road ending near La Purisima and continue for 30 miles on the washboard dirt road to San Juanico. People with large motor homes and trailers will have to decide how much shake, rattle, and roll they can handle. You can also come south from San Ignacio on an even worse road, which is suitable only for pickups, vans, and four-wheel drives.

② SAN BRUNO BEACHES
On the Sea of Cortéz, south of Santa Rosalía

North Baja Sur map, page 122

These white sand beaches are accessible to people with off-road vehicles. Several rocky areas between the beaches offer good fishing from the shore. Winter is the time to go, as summer is hot. For more information, see the Santa Rosalía Area, earlier in this chapter.

Directions: The beaches extend for five miles south of San Bruno, which is one mile east of Highway 1 at Km 173, about 14 miles south of Santa Rosalía.

③ PUNTA CHIVATO BEACHES
On the Sea of Cortéz, south of Santa Rosalía

North Baja Sur map, page 122

Playa La Palmita is readily accessible by pickups and vans on several dirt roads down small gullies. It takes four-wheel-drive vehicles to work farther south from La Palmita or to access the southern beaches off Highway 1 north of Mulegé. Fishing off the beach might net you a roosterfish. It is a great place for seeking out seashells. We spent four delightful days on Playa La Palmita following the shade around the camper, reading books, enjoying the sweeping view, and heading a hop away from our camp to cool down with a dip in the placid bay waters. Winter is the time to go, as summer is hot. For more information, see the Santa Rosalía–Mulegé Area, earlier in this chapter.

Directions: The beaches are most easily reached about 12 miles east of Highway 1 at Km 156, approximately 25 miles south of Santa Rosalía, off the washboard road to the Punta Chivato Hotel. Starting with the northernmost beach, Playa La Palmita west of the airstrip, Playas Mapachito and El Chivato extend about 10 miles south along the western shore of Bahía de Santa Inéz. See the listing for Punta Chivato Beach campground in this chapter.

④ BAHÍA CONCEPCIÓN BEACHES
On the Sea of Cortéz, south of Mulegé

North Baja Sur map, page 122

This is the greatest aggregation of uniformly lovely beaches—all with stunning views and fronting on placid waters—to be found in Baja, the whole of Mexico, or, for that matter, anywhere else in the world we have been, heard of, or read about. In other words, go. If fishing's your thing, you may be disappointed, but the clamming is great. Winter is the best time to visit, as summer gets scorching hot. For more on things to do here, see the Bahía Concepción Area, earlier in this chapter.

Directions: The northernmost beach, at Campo Playa Punta Arena (see listing in this chapter), is about 10 miles south of Mulegé. It is about 20 miles from there to the southernmost beach,

Playa Armenta (see listing in this chapter). In between are seven other campgrounds.

⑤ BAHÍA MAGDALENA BAY BEACHES

On the Pacific coast, in the Bahía Magdalena complex

North Baja Sur map, page 123

Shellfish are abundant everywhere along these beaches, and fishing is good for grouper, corvina, bass, snapper, halibut, mackerel, and pompano. It is an all-terrain-vehicle enthusiast's paradise with tidal flats and sand roads. One note of caution: The hard sand turns to mud at low tide. Visit in winter, as summer is hot. For more on the Bahía Magdalena area, see the following listing.

Directions: These beaches are accessible on sand roads with pickups, vans, or four-wheel drives. Beaches north of Puerto López Mateos include Playa Santa Elenita, which is about four miles north of the Mateos-Insurgentes paved road, and Playas Las Vacas and Los Prados, which are about eight miles north. Others north to La Poza Grande can be reached off the paved road north to La Purisima and the main dirt road north to La Poza Grande. You'll also find beaches south of Puerto López Mateos, such as the one at Curva del Diablo, about 10 miles south of the Mateos-Insurgentes paved road, then about 15 miles west. This is where the tides from north and south meet. La Curva Beach is also south of Puerto López Mateos. The beach at Puerto Cancun on Bahía Almeja can be reached from Km 173 on Highway 1 about 25 miles south of Ciudad Constitución, then about 16 miles west on a dirt road. Again, don't try these roads with big rigs.

⑥ BAHÍA MAGDALENA BARRIER ISLAND BEACHES

On the Pacific coast, in the Bahía Magdalena complex

North Baja Sur map, page 123

Most of the barrier islands of the Bahía Magdalena complex have exciting, pristine beach-es, particularly on the ocean side. They are Islas Las Animas, Santo Domingo, Magdalena, and Creciente. In total, the islands extend about 100 miles from north to south. They don't just offer tiny sand coves—Isla Magdalena has two long Pacific beaches, 45 miles from the northern tip of the island at Boca Soledad south to Cabo San Lázaro and 22 miles south of Cabo San Lázaro to Cabo Corso. Isla Santo Domingo has 11 miles of beach. Once you arrive by small boat, you can explore these marvelous ocean beaches by foot, all-terrain vehicle, or motorcycle. Adventurous explorers have a rare opportunity here to go where few have trod.

Directions: The beach on Isla Las Animas can be reached by a small boat from a graded sand road west of La Poza Grande, which is 36 miles north of Ciudad Insurgentes on the paved highway. Small boats can go from both La Banqueta (17 miles north of Ciudad Insurgentes, then 1.5 miles west of the highway through Santo Domingo on good hard sand) and Puerto López Mateos to Isla Santo Domingo. Both Puerto López Mateos and Puerto San Carlos offer small-boat access to Isla Magdalena. Small boats can also go from Puerto Chale (about 15 miles from Highway 1 at Santa Rita, which is about 32 miles south of Ciudad Constitución) to Isla Creciente.

⑦ JUNCALITO BEACH

On the Sea of Cortéz, south of Loreto

North Baja Sur map, page 123

This beach is in a somewhat protected cove, the fishing is fantastic around several islands offshore, and boaters can anchor their craft close to the beach. Winter is the favored season to visit, as summer is hot.

Directions: From Loreto drive about 14 miles south on Highway 1 (approximately one mile north of the turnoff to Tripui RV Park and Puerto Escondido), then head one-half mile down a rough dirt road to the beach on the southern end of Bahía Juncalito. The village of Juncalito occupies the northern waterfront. Look for the sign on the east side of the highway.

8 LIGUI BEACHES

On the Sea of Cortéz, south of Loreto

North Baja Sur map, page 123

Off the coast of these pretty beaches are many little islands. The small ones that stick straight up are called Los Candeleros (the Candles). Some very nice, cozy little coves await exploration down the coast, well within the range of small boats. Diving and snorkeling around the islands are delightful, with lots of colorful reef fish to look at. Winter is the favored season to visit here, as summer is hot.

Directions: From Loreto drive about 22 miles south on Highway 1 (six miles south of Tripui RV Park and Puerto Escondido). At the fence ignore the *Propriedad Privada* (Private Property) sign, but look closely at the small "Trailer Park E. Blanca" sign. It has a rough map showing the turn to take to the low ridge at the south end of the beach and the most accessible camping area. Drive down the dirt road straight east of Highway 1 about three-quarters of a mile to the beach and take the last right turn and follow the signs marked *"Playa"* for another three-quarters of a mile. The rest of the beach immediately to the north is used by local fishermen for their *pangas*.

9 AGUA VERDE BEACHES

On the Sea of Cortéz, south of Loreto

North Baja Sur map, page 123

On the drive in remember that you have to come back up. Playa San Cosme is at the bottom of the grade. There are low sandy beaches between rock outcrops for about 1.5 miles on the north side of Punta San Cosme. Campsites can also be found elsewhere along the eight miles of road to Agua Verde village. Fishing is fair for grouper and barracuda near the shore. The view of Agua Verde Cove is worth the trip. It has long been a favored anchorage for cruising boats. Now you can enjoy it, too. We anchored

there overnight with a group of Vagabundo boaters and were delighted. Winter is when you should visit.

Directions: From Km 63 on Highway 1 about 35 miles south of Loreto, head southeast on a dirt road for about 25 miles. The final pitch is steep with sharp switchbacks and is suitable only for pickups, vans, or four-wheel-drive vehicles—not motor homes or trailers.

10 SAN EVARISTO BEACHES

On the Sea of Cortéz, north of La Paz

North Baja Sur map, page 123

You will need a four-wheel-drive vehicle to reach San Evaristo via either route mentioned below. Pickups and vans can get to El Mechudo, about 10 miles south of San Evaristo on the San Juan de la Costa route, but four-wheel drive is necessary from El Mechudo on. We went in some years ago, shortly after this road was completed, with a friend who owns the saltworks at San Evaristo and Isla San José. It was a fascinating trip, but going up and back from La Paz in one day was too much. The cove at San Evaristo is a favored anchorage for cruisers who want to land their dinghies and stretch their legs. It has a very nice little beach that provides a protected place to sunbathe and wade. Other beaches are between San Evaristo and El Mechudo. Fishing can be good for bass, grouper, snapper, pargo, roosterfish, dorado, and sierra, improving the farther north you go.

Directions: The village of San Evaristo is about 45 miles north of San Juan de la Costa on a rough dirt road (about 80 miles north of La Paz). A paved road leads 24 miles into San Juan de la Costa from Km 17 on Highway 1, about 10 miles north of La Paz. Another, but worse, route is approximately 50 miles in from Highway 1 at Las Pocitas, which is about 27 miles south of Santa Rita and 62 miles south of Ciudad Constitución.

© FRED JONES

Chapter 5

South Baja Sur

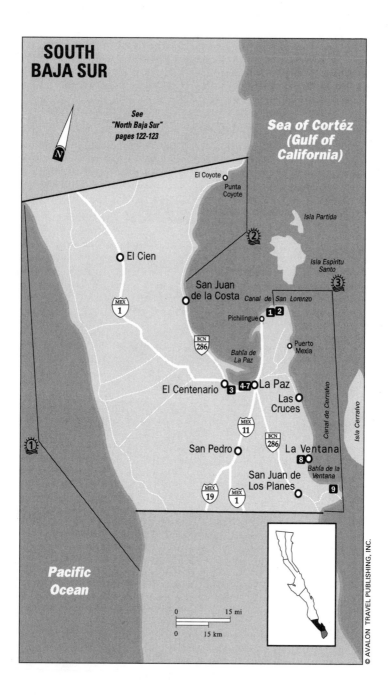

SOUTH
BAJA SUR

See
"North Baja Sur"
pages 122-123

Sea of Cortéz
(Gulf of
California)

El Coyote
Punta
Coyote

Isla Partida

El Cien

Isla Espiritu
Santo

San Juan
de la Costa

Canal de San Lorenzo

Pichilingue

MEX 1

BCN 286

Bahía de
La Paz

Puerto
Mexia

El Centenario

La Paz

Las
Cruces

Canal de Cerralvo

Isla Cerralvo

MEX 11

BCN 286

San Pedro

La Ventana

San Juan de
Los Planes

Bahía de la
Ventana

MEX 19

MEX 1

Pacific
Ocean

© AVALON TRAVEL PUBLISHING, INC.

0   15 mi

0   15 km

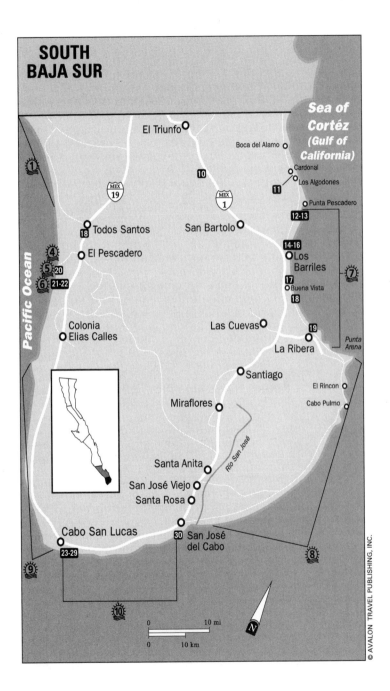

SOUTH
BAJA SUR

El Triunfo

**Sea of
Cortéz
(Gulf of
California)**

Boca del Alamo

Cardonal
Los Algodones

Punta Pescadero

Todos Santos

San Bartolo

Los
Barriles

El Pescadero

Buena Vista

Pacific Ocean

Colonia
Elias Calles

Las Cuevas

La Ribera

Punta
Arena

Santiago

El Rincon

Cabo Pulmo

Miraflores

Rio San José

Santa Anita

San José Viejo

Santa Rosa

Cabo San Lucas

San José
del Cabo

0   10 mi

0   10 km

N

© AVALON TRAVEL PUBLISHING, INC.

South Baja Sur

The southern part of the Baja California Peninsula has a special allure. For one thing, the tip of the peninsula is officially in the tropics—south of the Tropic of Cancer. It is a long enough drive (1,000 miles from the border to Land's End) to constitute a major trip with a substantial commitment of time—five days the way we do it. Anything less than a month leaves precious little time for savoring all the delightful experiences that await. We find something of interest wherever we are, and the time just melts away.

La Paz Area
(campgrounds 1–9)

La Paz enjoys a unique standing in Baja's history, for this is where Hernán Cortéz first landed over 460 years ago (in 1535). The romantic image of divers endangering their lives searching for riches among beds of pearl oysters, spurred on by legends of black pearls, permeates the atmosphere. This is a cosmopolitan city, the seat of the state government and the commercial center for the state of Baja California Sur. With a mix of antiquity and modernity, the city has a laid-back lifestyle that natives cherish. It will never succumb to the breakneck frenzy of Mexico City or its U.S. counterpart, New York City. Though tourist dollars are important, there is a conscious effort to avoid turning La Paz into another Cabo San Lucas. As one friend, a young businessman, once observed, "La Paz is a sedate matron, but we would like her to lift her skirts a little." We enjoy being there.

Fishing

While fishing can be good out of La Paz, it is not as consistent as in the Cape or East Cape areas. North toward Isla Espiritu Santo you'll find yellowfin tuna, pargo, dorado, sierra, barracuda, skipjack, snapper, and grouper. South toward Isla Cerralvo, roosterfish, jack crevalle, sailfish, and marlin can be found.

The fishing charter we favor is Fisherman's Fleet, which fishes primarily out of Bahía de Los Muertos. Contact them at 170 Oakdell Drive, Menlo Park, CA 94025, Mex. tel. 612/122-1313, fax 612/122-7334, email: david@lapaz.cromwell.com.mx.

Another is Jonathan Roldan's Sportfishing Services at La Concha Resort on the Pichilingue road northeast of La Paz, U.S. tel. 800/999-BAJA (800/999-2252) or Mex. tel. 612/121-6120, fax 612/121-6123, email: atomba@cortezclub.com.

Boating

Trailered boats may be launched at several places. We prefer the ramp at Marina de La Paz at the foot of Legaspy, though the Palmira Marina on the east side of town is also good and is closer to the Sea of Cortéz.

Cruising and camping by boat around Islas Espiritu Santo, Partida, and other islands farther north is a great experience.

Diving and Snorkeling

Baja Diving Service can be reached at Alvaro Obregón 1665-2, La Paz, Baja California Sur, Mexico, Mex. tel. 612/122-1826. This outfitter takes divers on day trips to the famous El Bajo seamount, where huge manta rays and schools of scalloped hammerhead sharks may be seen in summer and fall. Closer day trips can be made to Los Islotes, home to a sea lion colony, or the sunken wreck of the *Salvatierra,* a modern-day ferry, south of Isla Espiritu Santo. Baja Diving Service provides tanks, weight belts, lunch, and sodas on all trips. Snorkeling excursions include gear, lunch, and refreshments. They offer diving gear rentals and lessons and also operate a decompression chamber at Pichilingue. Also available are kayaking tours and bicycle and ATV rentals.

The Cortez Club offers a full-service diving operation. It is located at La Concha Resort northeast of La Paz on the Pichilingue road. It also has kayaks, wave runners, sailboats, and windsurfing gear, as well as snorkeling and beach-combing trips. Contact the Cortez Club at 7860 Mission Centre Court #202, San Diego, CA 92108, U.S. tel. 800/999-BAJA (800/999-2252), fax 619/294-7366, Mex. tel. 612/121-6121, fax 612/121-6123, email: atomba@cortezclub.com.

Shopping

La Paz is a free port with numerous shops in the downtown area selling a wide selection of merchandise from around the world at reasonable prices. There are also two large department stores where we tend to restock on clothing: Dorian's, on 16 de Septiembre and 21 de Agosto, and La Perla, a block away on Martínez between Esquerro Mutualismo and Mijares.

The Weaver on Abasolo between Jalisco and Nyarít sells handwoven rugs and native fabrics created by the owner.

Sightseeing

You'll find plenty to see and do in La Paz. An often-overlooked spot worth visiting is the Anthropological Museum at Altamirano and Cinco de Mayo. Strolling along the *malecón* in the evening is very pleasant, as is watching a sunset from Los Pelicanos Bar in Los Arcos Hotel on the *malecón* at Rosales. The municipal market at Revolución and Degollado is a browser's delight, with attractive displays of fruits, vegetables, fresh fish and meats, baked goods, clothing, and hardware sold from stalls by vendors who specialize in certain items. And if you don't camp at Playa Balandra (see campground in this chapter) or Playa Tecolote (see campground in this chapter), you should at least drive out to these beautiful spots to have a picnic and enjoy the scenery.

Dining
La Paz has a large selection of good restaurants. We like Bismark on Degollado and Altamirano, and El Moro, east on the *malecón.*

Nightlife
Scorpio's Nightclub is on Boulevard Forjadores and Tabachines. El Taste Restaurant and Nightclub is on the *malecón* and Avenida Juarez.

Ferries
Many people take the ferry from La Paz to Topolobampo (Los Mochis) or Mazatlán. For details, see the Travel Tips section of the Introduction.

East Cape Area
(campgrounds 10–19)
After Cabo San Lucas, this has to be Baja's prime fishing area. Deep water comes into Bahía de Palmas, bringing marlin and other migratory game fish close to shore and earning the Buena Vista fishing resorts a fine reputation among anglers. The East Cape also bills itself as the windsurfing capital of the world—perhaps a little grand, but still reflective of the dependable occurrence of stout winter winds. Whereas conditions are great for sail devices, it is less than ideal for boating. Surfers will discover some great beaches between Los Frailes and San José del Cabo.

Fishing
Just about every type of fish in the Sea of Cortéz can be taken here: marlin (striped, blue, and black), sailfish, roosterfish, wahoo, dorado, yellowfin tuna, amberjack, grouper, pargo, sea bass, jack crevalle, pompano, snapper, sierra, ladyfish, giant needlefish, and others. Deep, deep water comes close to shore in Bahía de Palmas, bringing in the big migratory game fish.

Boaters can launch their craft across the beach in Los Barriles near Playa de Oro RV Park (which no longer accepts travelers) or, if they're guests, by using a tractor or truck at Martín Verdugo's RV Park (see campground in this chapter).

Several hotels have their own fleets of sportfishing boats:

Hotels Playa del Sol and Palmas de Cortéz in Los Barriles, P.O. Box 9016, Calabasas, CA 91372, U.S. tel. 818/591-9463 or 800/368-4334, fax 818/591-1077.

Hotel Rancho Buena Vista, P.O. Box 1408, Santa Maria, CA 93456, U.S. tel. 805/928-1719 or 800/258-8200, fax 805/925-2990.

Cabo Pulmo Divers on the beach at Cabo Pulmo rents *pangas* for fishing.

Diving and Snorkeling
Cabo Pulmo has super diving on what is considered to be the only coral reef in the Sea of Cortéz. At least one expert claims that others exist, and we know that coral does appear widely. Perhaps it all depends upon the definition of a reef, which seems to require a great expanse of corals and solid limestone from their consolidation.

Vista Sea Sport conducts dive trips to all the local spots, offers classes, and rents scuba gear. Certification cards are required. Contact them at Apartado Postal 42, Buena Vista, Baja California Sur, Mexico, Mex. tel./fax 614/141-0031.

Windsurfing

This sport has become a mainstay of the local economy. The dependable winter winds attract windsurfers from all over the world. International tournaments are held with high attendance. During the height of the season, Bahía de Palmas is sprinkled with myriad colorful sails whipping back and forth at high speeds.

Sightseeing

The only zoo in Baja Sur is in Santiago, reached by driving about 17 miles west of Los Barriles on Highway 1, then continuing 1.5 miles north of the highway. To find the zoo, drive around the town square, go out the south side, and continue for about one-half mile south, then one-half mile west, and another half mile south. Follow the enamel signs depicting an elephant and an arrow. The zoo houses several Mexican species (coyotes, raccoons, bobcats, deer, etc.) and some domestic animals (including house cats and dogs), as well as a display of fossils discovered in the area. It is worth a visit.

Another eight miles south on Highway 1, the town of Miraflores specializes in leather. A tannery and a shop selling various leather goods is on the left as you enter town.

Dining

Tio Pablo in Los Barriles has good food at reasonable prices.

Pacific Coast Area
(campgrounds 20–22)

The vast beaches along the Pacific coast south of Todos Santos were unknown to the great majority of Baja travelers until the rough dirt road through here was paved in 1984. Dedicated surfers, though, had staked out their favorite spots long before then—Playa San Pedro, Playa Pescadero, and Playa Los Cerritos (see campgrounds in this chapter). Campers taking the shortest route between La Paz and Cabo San Lucas have discovered these spots, too. The inevitable is now happening: fences have been erected, blocking access to many beaches.

Todos Santos remains a tranquil piece of colonial Mexico, however, with wide shaded streets and restored old buildings. We spent a pleasant hour one afternoon listening to two boys just out of school playing guitars and singing in front of the church across from the town square.

Todos Santos sits on the Tropic of Cancer and is blessed with a dependable water supply. The fortuitous combination of climate and water led to development of a thriving sugarcane industry in the 19th century. This industry faded when the big spring that fed the crops failed around 1950, then disappeared completely when the price of sugar fell in the mid-1960s. Ruins of several old sugarcane mills still exist. The local spring ultimately recovered and today sustains mango, papaya, and palm trees in the lush arroyo below town.

Fishing

Pangas can be rented out of Punta Lobos (where there's a lighthouse) from individual *pangeros*. The sandy access road is 1.5 miles south of town on Highway 19. At about 2 P.M., the *pangeros* return from fishing and put their boats up on the beach. Check out their catch, which is mostly rock cod but also might include some large sharks. Don't expect any frills, such as lifejackets, VHF radios, tackle, lunch, or drinks, when you ship out with these fellows. It's up to you to be fully equipped.

Surfing
The beaches south of Todos Santos are popular with surfers. There are numerous points that create the right conditions for good runs.

Sightseeing
Walking around Todos Santos is interesting, and there are a few nice shops, including art galleries and clothing boutiques. We enjoy going through the Cultural Museum on the main street.

For a unique experience, go to the oceanfront at Punta Lobos to watch the *pangas* shoot the beach. The technique is to circle behind the breaker line until a big wave is spotted, then straighten out in line with it and open the motor full throttle, timing the approach so as to shoot out of the top of the wave as it breaks, continuing up the abrupt slope of the beach. If they don't make it to the top, a pickup hauls them up with a long rope.

If you want help identifying all the desert plants you have been seeing and wondering about on your journeys, a botanical garden is located three miles south of town on Highway 19.

Dining
We make the renowned Santa Fe Restaurant a regular stop when near Todos Santos. It is closed from about August 1 through October. Reservations are a good idea, as people come from all around for a genuine gourmet dining experience; from other towns in Mexico call 91-612/125-0340. The salads are made fresh from the locally grown varieties of lettuce, herbs, and vegetables. The lobster ravioli in cream sauce and the shrimp fettuccine are simply great.

On the highway south of Todos Santos at Pescadero there's a different sort of restaurant built around a huge old mango tree—Los Arboles. The food, mostly grown on the spot, is delightful, as is the setting.

Cape Area
(campgrounds 23–30)
San José del Cabo and Cabo San Lucas are rapidly joining together in one long strip of hotels and condominiums. Developers and others in the tourist business have coined the term "Los Cabos" to describe the strip, but this fails to capture the special allure the towns have held since Ray Cannon first began enticing crowds of big game fishermen here with his Baja fishing stories in the early 1960s. The fishing was fantastic then and still is world-class.

Beaches that used to harbor campers through the winter months are now restricted to day use only.

Today, campers must use RV parks. Although camping opportunities are diminished, the Cape will always be very popular and high on everyone's must-see list. Even when the last campground has been converted to something else, campers will commute from Todos Santos to experience the beaches—as some are doing now.

Fishing
Whatever the time of year, there are always game fish to seek, including marlin (striped, blue, and black), sailfish, yellowfin tuna, dorado, wahoo, and roosterfish. People with seaworthy boats

can venture out on their own. The Cabo Island Marina ramp in town charges a stiff fee. Parking is available on nearby streets. The public ramp on the south side of the harbor is used to dress out the sportfish catch every afternoon. Parking is a problem around here, but there is no fee. You can catch your own bait in the outer harbor, saving the high price per piece that the local fishermen charge.

Many sportfishing fleets serve the area, some better than others. Here are a few we can recommend:

La Playa, just north of San José del Cabo on the coast road, is the place to hire *panga* captains who fish Gordo Banks for wahoo and dorado and whatever else may be around. Boats leave at 6 A.M. and return at noon, and head out again from 6 P.M. to 8 P.M. Reservations can be made on the beach from 11 A.M. to 6 P.M.

A reservation office for Victor's Aquatics in San José del Cabo is located in the Hotel Stouffer Presidente (Mex. tel. 624/142-2250). Contact Jig Stop Tours in Dana Point, California, U.S. tel. 714/496-3555, fax 714/496-1384.

In Cabo San Lucas Gaviota's Fleet can be contacted at Condo Hotel Bahía, Suite 526, Apartado Postal 144, Cabo San Lucas, Baja California Sur, Mexico, Mex. tel. 624/143-0430, fax 624/143-0497.

The Pisces Fleet office is located one block from the Giggling Marlin. Contact them at Apartado Postal 137, Cabo San Lucas, Baja California Sur, Mexico, Mex. tel. 624/143-1288, fax 624/143-0588.

Solmar Sportfishing Fleet is located across from the vendors' stands on the south side of the harbor. Contact them at P.O. Box 383, Pacific Palisades, CA 90272, U.S. tel. 310/459-9861 or 800/344-3349, fax 310/454-1686.

Diving and Snorkeling

You'll find sand falls off *El Arco* (the Arch, a hole eroded in a rock) at Land's End and several other interesting dive sites, including Santa María Cove, Japanese Shipwreck, Cabeza Ballena, Pelican Rock, Lover's Beach, and Sunken Ship at the tip of the cape. There are many dive shops and a state-of-the-art hyperbaric medical facility in Cabo San Lucas. We list those facilities with which we and our friends are familiar:

Amigos del Mar is located across from the vendors' stands on the south side of the harbor in Cabo San Lucas. They rent all gear by the piece, fill tanks for those who show a certification card, and offer instruction. They also offer a variety of boat cruises that don't involve diving or snorkeling. Contact them at Apartado Postal 43, Cabo San Lucas, Baja California Sur, Mexico, Mex. tel. 624/143-0505, fax 624/143-0887 in Cabo, U.S. tel. 800/344-3349, fax 310/454-1686.

Club Acuadeportes is located at Chileno Beach at Km 14 on Highway 1 and Hacienda Beach, in front of the Hacienda Hotel in Cabo. They rent dive gear by the piece, fill tanks if you show a certification card, and offer instruction. They also rent Sunfish, catamarans, pedal boats, canoes, kayaks, personal watercraft, and other beach and water sports equipment, and offer boat cruises that don't involve diving. Contact them at Apartado Postal 136, Cabo San Lucas, Baja California Sur, Mexico, Mex. tel./fax 624/143-0117.

Beach Bumming

Heading to the beach for the day isn't always as easy as it sounds. There are so many here you can spend a lot of time deciding just which one to hit. Here are the beaches between San José del Cabo and Cabo San Lucas. All are dedicated for day use only and allow no camping:

- **La Playa:** just north of San José del Cabo, where the *pangas* leave for fishing trips
- **Playa Hotelera:** in front of the hotels in San José del Cabo
- **Playa Costa Azul:** access off Highway 1 between Km 28 and 29
- **Playa Palmilla:** at the Hotel Palmilla
- **Playa Costa Brava:** access off Highway 1 between Km 18 and 19
- **Playa El Tule:** access off Highway 1 between Km 16 and 17
- **Playa Chileno:** access off Highway 1 between Km 14 and 15
- **Bahía Santa María:** access off Highway 1 between Km 12 and 13
- **Playa Médano:** the big beach in Cabo San Lucas, between Las Cascadas and the Hotel Hacienda
- **Playa del Amor:** access by water taxi, heading toward the Arch
- **Playa Solmar:** in front of the Hotel Solmar

Golf

Several highly touted courses give golfers plenty of playing options at very high fees. The website www.golfinmexico.com lists courses in the area.

Other Activities

There are all sorts of other things to do, including glass-bottomed boat trips, catamaran cruises, parasailing, horseback riding, zipping around in all-terrain vehicles or scooters, and whale watching. The Cape area is designed to keep visitors occupied.

Shopping

The many enticing shops in town offer good prices and wide selections for anything you might expect to find in Mexico. On the south side of the harbor, there's an open-air vendor area, the Handicrafts Plaza, where launches from the cruise ships dock. Here the prices are higher, quality is questionable, and shoppers find themselves in a pressure-cooker environment because the cruise ship passengers have little time to compare, think, and come to a reasoned decision.

The municipal market in San José del Cabo is special. It is on Mauricio Castro one block south of Doblada, the one-way street that gets you back to Highway 1 from Boulevard Mijares in the middle of town. Wandering around in here makes shopping for veggies, meat, and fish enjoyable.

Dining

You'll have plenty of restaurants from which to choose. At the simple end of the spectrum, Asadero Fiesta Grill, a barbecue place next door to Squid Roe, serves the best ribs and chicken you can hope to find anywhere. Eat there or take it out.

At the other end of the spectrum is Da Giorgio's, on Highway 1 three miles north of Cabo. Diners feast in such a truly beautiful setting with a spectacular view of Land's End and Cabo San Lucas that lunch or dinner is always a special treat. The open-air restaurant features a series of pools and waterfalls cascading down a cliff. Be there at sunset for the grandest view.

Nightlife

If you're looking for a night of carousing in Cabo and can't find satisfaction at the Giggling Marlin, Cabo Wabo, Studio 94, or Squid Roe, you aren't really trying. For a two-handed margarita and a block and tackle that hoists you into the air feet first, go for the Giggling Marlin. Gloria tried both and survived, but the second marg' got her. All of the clubs have big crowds and loud music.

Campgrounds

1 PLAYA BALANDRA

🚶 🚴 🏊 🐕 🚐 ⛺

Northeast of La Paz

South Baja Sur map, page 146

This secluded cove cradles a pretty beach with glistening white sand and azure waters. It's great for swimming and lounging about. However, because the cove is sheltered by a ridge from cooling sea breezes it can get hot. Although overnighting is acceptable, the beach is not suitable for longer stays, nor can it accommodate many rigs or tents. Local people come here for picnics, and use can be heavy, especially on weekends. The beach has a much-photographed balancing rock, which fell over some years ago, only to be recently resurrected. Winter is the preferred season, as summer is hot. For things to do here, see the La Paz Area, earlier in this chapter.

Campsites, facilities: About 12 vehicles can park overnight in a small paved lot. Tenters can set up camp off to the side on packed desert soil. Beach *palapas,* trash barrels, and pit toilets are provided. There is no water or security. Obtain supplies in La Paz.

Reservations, fees: All sites are first come, first served. There is no fee.

Directions: From Ciudad Constitución drive 133 miles south on Highway 1 to La Paz. The beach is on the paved road 4.2 miles east of Pichilingue, the La Paz ferry terminal north of town on the east side of Bahía de La Paz.

Contact: Drive in and park.

2 PLAYA TECOLOTE

🚶 🚴 🏊 🚣 🛥 🐕 🚐 ⛺

Northeast of La Paz

South Baja Sur map, page 146

The beach here is about 1.5 miles long, facing north to Isla Espiritu Santo across the four-mile-wide Canal de San Lorenzo. This wide swath of soft sand is backed with dunes and, behind that, a broad, level plain. It is exposed to northerly winds, which can make for heavy surf; otherwise surf is minimal. Camp away from the restaurants in either direction behind the dunes in RVs or tents. The hill on the west end provides afternoon shade and an unobstructed view of Isla Espiritu Santo. The larger restaurant rents boats and personal watercraft and can arrange fishing trips. Winter is the preferred season, as summer is hot. For things to do here, see the La Paz Area, earlier in this chapter.

Campsites, facilities: There are two restaurant *palapas.* The small one on the west end of this long beach is not always open. The larger restaurant has restrooms, available only to diners. Trash barrels are provided, but there is no water or security. Obtain supplies in La Paz.

Reservations, fees: Camping is first come, first served. There is no fee.

Directions: From Ciudad Constitución drive 133 miles south on Highway 1 to La Paz. The beach is on a paved road 4.8 miles east of Pichilingue, the La Paz ferry terminal north of town on the east side of Bahía de La Paz. Go past the turnoff to Balandra.

Contact: Drive in and park.

3 LOS OASIS RV PARK

🏊 🐕 🚐 ⛺

North of La Paz

South Baja Sur map, page 146

This end of Bahía de La Paz is so shallow that mudflats are exposed at low tide. Another drawback: It is far from the city, which somewhat hinders campers who want easy access to sightseeing, shopping, dining, nightlife, and the La Paz ambience. Winter is the preferred season, as summer is hot. For things to do here, see the La Paz Area, earlier in this chapter.

Campsites, facilities: There are 24 campsites with full hookups. Clean restrooms with flush toilets and hot showers, laundry facilities, a pool, and a restaurant are on the premises. Don't drink the water. A gate provides security. Tent campers are welcome. Obtain supplies in La Paz.

Reservations, fees: Reservations are accepted. Fees are moderate—$12 per night for two people and $2 for each additional person, $60 per week, and $240 per month.

Directions: The park is on Highway 1 as it meets Bahía de La Paz at El Centenario, nine miles north of La Paz.

Contact: Los Oasis RV Park, Kilometro 15 Carretera al Norte, El Centenario, La Paz, Baja California Sur, Mexico, Mex. tel. 612/124-6090, fax 612/125-1142.

▣ CASA BLANCA RV PARK

▣ ▣ ▣ ▣

In La Paz

South Baja Sur map, page 146

Young trees grace this very pleasant, somewhat new park. However, the high walls of the facility are made of concrete blocks painted white, and the reflected glare and heat struck us as too strong for comfort. Winter is the best season to visit, as summer is hot. Although tent campers are allowed, this is primarily an RV park and the sites aren't really suitable for tents. For things to do here, see the La Paz Area, earlier in this chapter.

Campsites, facilities: There are 43 campsites with full hookups. Facilities include *palapas,* tables, barbecues, clean, tiled restrooms with flush toilets and hot showers, a laundry facility, a pool, a tennis court, and a store. Don't drink the water. A gate in the walled compound and a guard provide security. Obtain supplies in La Paz.

Reservations, fees: Reservations are accepted. Fees are high—$17 per night, one day free per week, and $350 per month.

Directions: From Ciudad Constitución drive

133 miles south on Highway 1 to La Paz. The park is on the west side of town near the Fidepaz development, at Avenida Delfines. The sign on the right is prominent.

Contact: Casa Blanca RV Park, Delphines y Carretera al Norte, Fracc. Fidepaz, La Paz, Baja California Sur, Mexico, Mex. tel. 612/124-0009, fax 612/125-1142.

▣ EL CARDÓN TRAILER PARK

▣ ▣ ▣ ▣

In La Paz

South Baja Sur map, page 146

The oldest park in La Paz, this family-run operation has served campers well for decades. Within the park you'll find many old shade trees. Winter is the preferred season, as summer is hot. For things to do here, see the La Paz Area, earlier in this chapter.

Campsites, facilities: There are 80 RV sites (36 pull-through) with full hookups, *palapas,* and concrete pads. Ten additional tent sites have *palapas.* Several tiled restrooms—each with a sink, flush toilet, and hot shower—are in a common building. Other facilities include laundry and a pool. Don't drink the water at the campsites; it is brackish well water. Security is good, as the park is in a walled compound with a gate and a 24-hour guard. Obtain supplies in La Paz.

Reservations, fees: Reservations are accepted. Fees are moderate—$8 per night for tents and $12 for RVs. Stay a week and get one day free. Fees for monthly stays are $7 per day. There is an extra charge for use of air conditioners.

Directions: From Ciudad Constitución drive 133 miles south on Highway 1 to La Paz. The park is on the west side of town on the highway into La Paz. The sign on the right is prominent.

Contact: El Cardón Trailer Park, Apartado Postal 104, La Paz, Baja California Sur, Mexico, Mex. tel. 612/124-0078.

The Aquamarina RV Park in La Paz has exceptionally beautiful landscaping.

6 LA PAZ RV PARK

In La Paz
South Baja Sur map, page 146

The palm trees, gravel driveways, and concrete pads in this clean park prevent the place from getting too dusty or dirty. Though the park is not directly on the beachfront, you only have to walk a couple blocks to get there. Winter is the preferred season, as summer is hot. For things to do here, see the La Paz Area, earlier in this chapter.

Campsites, facilities: There are 38 campsites (eight pull-through) with full hookups, concrete pads, *palapas,* trees, and barbecues. Facilities include flush toilets, hot showers, a laundry facility, satellite TV access, a pool, and a spa. Don't drink the water. Security is good, as the park is in a walled compound with a gate and a guard. Obtain supplies in La Paz.

Reservations, fees: Reservations are accepted. Fees are high—$18 per night. Long-term rates are $90 per week, $300 per month, and $3,000 per year for RVs, and $10 per day, $60 per week, $200 per month, and $2,000 per year for tents.

Directions: From Ciudad Constitución drive 133 miles south on Highway 1 to La Paz. Just past El Cardon turn left at the stoplight and sign to Avenida Telephonica (this street is named Colosio to the right) to the 8th street on the right (opposite the northern end of the schoolyard on the left). Turn right on it to the end, then swing wide to the left and turn a sharp 180° into the park.

Contact: La Paz RV Park, Apartado Postal 482, La Paz, Baja California Sur, Mexico, Mex. tel. 612/124-0830, fax 612/124-0837.

7 AQUAMARINA RV PARK

In La Paz
South Baja Sur map, page 146

Spaces are designed for travel trailers and motor homes. Slideouts can be difficult. Huge motor homes pay extra for electricity. Lush palms and flowering shrubs give this park a more tropical appearance than any other in Baja. Aquamarina has been a labor of love for owners and La Paz pioneers Richard and Maria Luisa Adcock. (Maria is Mexico's first and only female licensed ship captain.) The park is now open from mid-October through mid-March. It is locked to new arrivals from noon until the following morning on weekends and holidays, but if you make some noise or bang on one or both of the gates, the owners will let you in. Winter is the preferred season, as summer is hot. For things to do here, see the La Paz Area, earlier in this chapter.

Campsites, facilities: There are 19 RV campsites, with full hookups, trees, and asphalt or concrete pads. Facilities include clean, tiled restrooms with flush toilets and hot showers, concrete pads, a laundry facility, a pool, a concrete launch ramp, and berthing for boats. Don't drink the water. Security is good; the park is in a walled compound with gates and resident owners. Tent campers are welcome in open space. Obtain supplies in La Paz.

Reservations, fees: Reservations are accepted. Fees are high—$19 per night, $122 per week, and $485 per month.

Directions: From Ciudad Constitución drive 133 miles south on Highway 1 to La Paz. Continue east toward the center of La Paz on Abasolo three blocks past the CCC Supermarket to the stop sign at Nyarít. Turn left and continue to the waterfront. This road has deteriorated and low tree branches can break roof antennas.

Contact: Aquamarina RV Park, Apartado Postal 133, La Paz, Baja California Sur, Mexico, Mex. tel. 612/122-3761, fax 612/125-6228, email: marisla@balandra.uabcs.mx.

8 LA VENTANA CAMPGROUND
🏃 🚴 ⛱ 🎣 🛶 🐕 🚐 ⛺

Southeast of La Paz
South Baja Sur map, page 146

Campsites are set among sparse palms and mesquite trees, providing limited shade. The campground is on a sheltered sand beach with a view of Isla Cerralvo 10 miles away across Canal de Cerralvo. Small, lightweight boats can be launched over the sand. Windsurfers frequent the beach during the winter when winds are strong and dependable. Nearby fishing is fair. Motor homes up to 34 feet long can make it here, though the gravel road in may be rough. Winter is the preferred season, as summer is hot. For more on fishing in and around La Paz, see the La Paz Area, earlier in this chapter.

Campsites, facilities: Between 50 and 70 vehicles can park here. Several water spigots, flush toilets, and cold showers are provided. Don't drink the water. There is no security. Tent campers are welcome. Obtain your main supplies in La Paz; limited supplies can be purchased in San Juan de Los Planes.

Reservations, fees: All sites are first come, first served. The fee is very low—$3 per night.

Directions: From Highway 1 on the southern outskirts of La Paz, take State Highway 286 south for 24 miles until you reach a paved road leading north. Turn left and head five miles to La Ventana. The campground is on the north side of the village.

Contact: Drive in and park.

9 PUNTA ARENA DE LA VENTANA BEACH
🏃 🚴 ⛱ 🎣 🛶 🐕 🚐 ⛺

Southeast of La Paz
South Baja Sur map, page 146

With Isla Cerralvo in sight directly across the channel, this is a delightful spot for RVers and tenters alike. As it is remote, you may feel more comfortable having others along for company. The beach extends about 10 miles north toward La Ventana and offers good fishing. At daybreak schools of jack crevalle often work the surf in feeding frenzies. Try casting into them for great sport. Roosterfish may be in the area as well. Fishermen put their *pangas* in here and can be helpful in dispensing fishing information. Sometimes they're even willing to hire themselves out as guides. For a pleasant hike, stroll a couple miles to the west and you'll find a beached modern, rusty steel ship, the *Cedros,* broadsided right at the surf line. Winter is the preferred season, as summer is hot. For things to do here, see the La Paz Area, earlier in this chapter.

Campsites, facilities: The beach is ideal for tent camping. There are no facilities or security. Obtain your main supplies in La Paz; limited supplies can be purchased in San Juan de Los Planes.

Reservations, fees: Camping is first come, first served. There is no fee.

Directions: From Highway 1 on the southern outskirts of La Paz, take State Highway 286 south for about 29 miles to San Juan de Los Planes, then continue three miles on pavement and eight miles on a washboard dirt road to the Punta Arena access road, which bears left. Follow this road about four miles to the beach. The lighthouse is in view to the east.

Contact: Drive in and park.

10 RANCHO VERDE RV PARK

North of San Bartolo
South Baja Sur map, page 147

Part of a 3,000-acre ranch, this RV park is in a hilly inland area with brush and trees that provide a different kind of landscape from that found at the more common beach campgrounds. Winter is the preferred season, as summer is hot. For more information, see the East Cape Area, earlier in this chapter.

Campsites, facilities: There are 29 campsites with water and sewer hookups, tables, barbecues, and trees. Also available are tiled restrooms with flush toilets and hot showers, nature trails, hiking trails, horseback rides, and a citrus orchard with a variety of fresh fruit. Don't drink the water. The park is totally fenced, and security is provided by resident owners. Tent campers are welcome. Obtain supplies in La Paz.

Reservations, fees: Reservations are accepted. Fees are moderate—$11 per night for RVs and $7 for tents, $66 per week for RVs and $42 for tents, $264 per month for RVs and $168 for tents. Horses rent for $10 per hour.

Directions: From San Bartolo drive about eight miles north on Highway 1 to the park at Km 141 or about the same distance south of San Antonio.

Contact: Rancho Verde RV Park, P.O. Box 1050, Eureka, MT 59917, U.S. tel. 406/889-3030 or 888/516-9462, fax 406/889-3033, email: info@rancho-verde.com, website: www.rancho-verde.com.

11 EL CARDONAL HIDE-A-WAY

North of Los Barriles
South Baja Sur map, page 147

Here is an off-the-beaten-path find on a remote stretch of beautiful coastline. It's a lovely location for tent camping on the shore of the Sea of Cortéz, with a sandy beach and great recreational potential. You can explore the rocky shore north and south of El Cardonal, swim, snorkel, or fish from shore. Winter is the preferred season, as summer is hot. For more information, see the East Cape Area, earlier in this chapter.

Campsites, facilities: Each of the four full-hookup RV campsites, five with electricity and water, and the 20 tent sites with no hookups have trees, tables, and barbecues. Facilities include tiled restrooms with flush toilets and hot showers, laundry service, a restaurant, stores, a dump station, and launching for small boats over the beach. For recreation, there's badminton, volleyball, horseshoes, condo golf, and snorkeling. Motel rooms and tents are available. The water is good to drink. Resident owners and remoteness provide security. Obtain supplies in Los Barriles.

Reservations, fees: Reservations are accepted. Fees are moderate—$11 per night, $54 per week, and $220 per month for RVs with full hookups; $10 per night, $66 per week, and $275 per month for partial hookups; and $8 per night, $73 per week, and $300 per month for tents.

Directions: From La Paz drive about 65 miles south on Highway 1 to Los Barriles. Then proceed north along the coast for 14 miles on gravel road.

Contact: El Cardonal Hide-a-Way, La Paz, Baja California Sur, Mexico, Mex. tel./fax 612/100-3382, email: elcardonaleddy@hotmail.com, website: www.elcardonal.net.

12 QUINTA MARIA

North of Los Barriles

South Baja Sur map, page 147

The main business here is renting very nice bungalows with ocean views. Several hotels in Los Barriles charter *pangas* and cruisers to fish the deep waters of the Sea of Cortéz. Winter is the preferred season, as summer is hot. For more information, see the East Cape Area, earlier in this chapter.

Campsites, facilities: There are many dry camping spots on sand adjacent to the water. Features include palms, water, tiled restrooms with flush toilets and hot showers, a laundry facility, and a pool. There is no security. Obtain supplies in Los Barriles.

Reservations, fees: Fees are low—$5 per person per night.

Directions: From La Paz drive about 65 miles south on Highway 1 to Los Barriles and then head north along the coast 2.75 miles from the center of town. Quinta Maria is 0.75 mile beyond the end of pavement.

Contact: Quinta Maria, Km 5.5 Carretera Los Barriles-El Cardonal, Municipio de La Paz, Baja California Sur, Mexico, Mex. tel./fax 612/126-0821 or Mex. tel. 612/125-3316.

13 PLAYA NORTE

North of Los Barriles

South Baja Sur map, page 147

Playa Norte is on the beach and is a popular windsurfing spot. Several hotels in Los Barriles charter *pangas* and cruisers to fish the deep waters of the Sea of Cortéz. Winter is the preferred season, as summer is hot. For more information, see the East Cape Area, earlier in this chapter.

Campsites, facilities: There are 25 spaces with no hookups. There are trees around the campground, water taps, tiled restrooms with flush toilets and hot showers, and a dump station. Don't drink the water. There is expected to be a caretaker, but there is no security. Obtain supplies in Los Barriles.

Reservations, fees: Reservations are taken. Fees are low—$7 per night.

Directions: From La Paz drive about 65 miles south on Highway 1 to Los Barriles and then head north along the coast 1.5 miles upcoast from the center of town.

Contact: U.S. tel. 425/355-4343, fax 425/347-5699.

14 EAST CAPE RESORT

North of Los Barriles

South Baja Sur map, page 147

This is a new park and was not quite finished when we were there. A negative is an adjacent swampy pond that develops in the rainy season and harbors mosquitoes. It's a short walk across the street to the beach. Several hotels in Los Barriles charter *pangas* and cruisers to fish the deep waters of the Sea of Cortéz. Winter is the preferred season, as summer is hot. For more information, see the East Cape Area, earlier in this chapter.

Campsites, facilities: There are 51 spaces with full hookups, of which six are pull-throughs. There are trees around the park and tiled restrooms with flush toilets and hot showers. Obtain supplies in Los Barriles.

Reservations, fees: Reservations are taken. Fees are high—$18 per night, $100 per week, and $325 per month for RVs, and $8 per night, $50 per week, and $175 per month for tents.

Directions: From La Paz drive about 65 miles south on Highway 1 to Los Barriles and then head north along the coast a half mile upcoast from the center of town.

Contact: U.S. tel. 208/726-1955, fax 208/726-1801, Mex. tel. 612/141-0231, email: tc@thelucasmarketinggroup.com, website: www.thelucasmarketinggroup.com.

15 JUANITO'S GARDEN RV PARK

🚶 🚲 🏊 🛶 🎣 🐕 �RV 🏕

In Los Barriles

South Baja Sur map, page 147

Though not right on the beach, this RV park is within walking distance, just a quarter mile away. In the park, which is set on a slight slope, dust is kept down by a layer of imported beach sand. Features include clean, private restrooms with locking doors, a coin-operated washing machine, and well-kept landscaping. Winter is the favored season, as summer is hot. For things to do here, see the East Cape Area, earlier in this chapter.

Campsites, facilities: There are 30 RV campsites, 20 with full hookups and 10 with partial hookups, but most are filled with permanent lessees. Some have *palapas* and trees. Facilities include tiled restrooms with flush toilets and hot showers, a laundry facility, a pool, a store, and a restaurant. Long-term storage is available. The water is safe to drink. The park is fenced with a gate and has a resident manager. Obtain supplies in Los Barriles.

Reservations, fees: Reservations are accepted. Fees are moderate—$11 per night, $66 per week, $250 per month, and $2,500 per year without a *palapa* or $3,600 with a *palapa*.

Directions: From La Paz drive about 65 miles south on Highway 1 to Los Barriles. The park

is on the north end of town, on the inland side of the road.

Contact: Juanito's Garden RV Park, Apartado Postal 50, Los Barriles, Baja California Sur, Mexico, Mex. tel./fax 612/141-0024, email: losbarrileshotel@prodigy.net.mx, website: www.losbarrileshotel.com.

16 MARTÍN VERDUGO'S RV PARK AND MOTEL

🚶 🚲 🏊 🛶 🎣 🐕 �RV 🏕

In Los Barriles

South Baja Sur map, page 147

Martín is always busy around the park, working hard to make sure everything is clean and functioning properly. Rock and mortar walls define the exterior boundaries of the property and contain grading where there is a slight slope. This is a very popular place, and long-term reservations for winter stays in front near the water must be made a year or more in advance. Winter is the favored season, as summer is hot. For things to do here, see the East Cape Area, earlier in this chapter.

Campsites, facilities: There are 72 RV campsites with full hookups (two pull-through) and 25 sites for tents, a few of which have electricity and water. On the premises are trees, clean tiled restrooms with flush toilets and hot showers, a laundry facility, a pool, motel rooms, and steel mats for launching boats over the sand. The water is safe to drink. The park is secured with a guard and a perimeter fence. Obtain supplies in Los Barriles.

Reservations, fees: Reservations are accepted. Fees are moderate—$12 per night for RVs in front, $11 in back, and $10 for tents. Long-term rates are $80 per week for RVs in front, $74 in back, and $66 for tents; $260 per month for RVs in front, $245 in back, and $225 for tents.

Directions: From La Paz drive about 65 miles south on Highway 1 to Los Barriles. The park is on the north side of town on the beach.

Contact: Martín Verdugo's RV Park

and Motel, Apartado Postal 17, Los Barriles, Baja California Sur, Mexico, Mex. tel./fax 612/141-0054, email: martin@cromwell.lapaz.com.mx.

17 SPA RV PARK

🥾 🚲 🏊 🛶 🐾 🚐

South of Los Barriles

South Baja Sur map, page 147

The campsites are small with limited room to maneuver rigs. Winter is the favored season, as summer is hot. For more information on things to do here, see the East Cape Area, earlier in this chapter.

Campsites, facilities: There are eight campsites with full hookups. You'll find trees, hot showers, a toilet in a trailer, laundry facilities, a pool, a hot tub, a party *palapa,* a store, a restaurant, and an area for launching light boats across the sand. The water is safe to drink. Security is provided by resident owners. Tent campers and children are forbidden. Obtain supplies in Los Barriles.

Reservations, fees: All sites are first come, first served. The fee is high—$15 per night, $39 for three nights, $85 per week, and $290 per month.

Directions: From La Paz drive about 65 miles south on Highway 1 to Los Barriles. Continue three miles south, then turn left at the Hotel Buena Vista entrance.

Contact: Drive in and talk to the owner.

18 LA CAPILLA RV PARK

🥾 🚲 🏊 🛶 🎣 🐾 🚐 ⛰

South of Los Barriles

South Baja Sur map, page 147

You could say the facilities are rustic, but this is a pretty good choice for tent campers—no asphalt or concrete to contend with, just desert soil in which to pound tent stakes on a beach with an ocean view. The campsites are open to cooling breezes in a somewhat remote area with no other development around. The beach is clean white sand with normally mild surf, great for strolling and shelling. It's also fine for putting in cartop boats and inflatables. Winter is the favored season, as summer is hot. For more information on things to do here, see the East Cape Area, earlier in this chapter.

Campsites, facilities: There are 20 campsites with full hookups and *palapas.* Flush toilets and hot showers are provided. The water is safe to drink. There is no security on the premises, but the owners live nearby. Tent campers are welcome. Obtain supplies in Los Barriles.

Reservations, fees: All sites are first come, first served. The fee is low—$7 per night.

Directions: From La Paz drive about 65 miles south on Highway 1 to the Los Barriles turnoff. Continue 3.6 miles south, turn left at the signed road to Rancho Leonero, and drive 1.7 miles to the park (one-half mile beyond the sign indicating the turnoff to Rancho Leonero).

Contact: Drive in and talk to the manager.

19 CORRECAMINOS RV PARK

🥾 🚲 🏊 🛶 🐾 🚐 ⛰

In La Ribera

South Baja Sur map, page 147

Old mango trees provide generous shade for RVers at this park. Guests with tents or pickups may set up camp on the fenced and gated beach a quarter mile away. Ask park management to open the beach gate for you. Winter is the favored season, as summer is hot. For things to do here, see the East Cape Area, earlier in this chapter.

Campsites, facilities: There are 13 pull-through campsites with full hookups and some *palapas.* Flush toilets, hot showers, and laundry facilities are available. The water is safe to drink. A gate secures the park. Tent campers are welcome. Obtain supplies in La Ribera.

Reservations, fees: Reservations are accepted. Fees are moderate—$10 per night with full hookups and $7 for tents.

Directions: From Highway 1 at Las Cuevas, turn onto the paved road to La Ribera. Go about 6.5 miles, through La Ribera, then turn left at the sign for the park and continue another half mile.

Contact: La Ribera RV Park, c/o Lee Bray, Apartado Postal 27, Buena Vista, Baja California Sur, Mexico. There is no phone.

20 EL LITRO TRAILER PARK

On the south side of Todos Santos
South Baja Sur map, page 147

This new park provides ready access to Todos Santos, an interesting town to explore on foot. The plan is to expand to 25 sites. Winter is the best time to come, as summer is hot. For things to do here, see the Pacific Coast Area, earlier in this chapter.

Campsites, facilities: There are eight campsites with full hookups and space for about 30 RVs with some *palapas,* in addition to a tenting area with lots of trees. A restroom with flush toilets and hot showers is available. Don't drink the water. Guards provide security 24 hours daily. Obtain supplies in Todos Santos.

Reservations, fees: Camping is first come, first served. The fees are moderate—$10 per night or $63 per week for RVs and $4 per night for tents.

Directions: In Todos Santos drive two blocks south of the Pemex station. Look for the sign, turn, and go four blocks west to the park.

Contact: Drive in and talk to the manager.

21 SAN PEDRITO RV PARK

South of Todos Santos
South Baja Sur map, page 147

A longtime favorite among surfers, this is also one of our favorite camping spots. We spend a few nights here on every trip. Each site has an ocean view and a small palm tree. Other palms are scattered around. The beach in front of the RV spaces is treacherous, containing a huge pile of round boulders, which were chipped off the rocky point to the north by the action

of the water over the millennia. They are constantly rocking and rolling as waves bombard them, posing dangers to bare feet out for a casual stroll. A safer sand beach begins a few hundred yards south. There is ample parking on firm ground behind the sand beach suitable for tents and self-contained RVs. Hurricane Julliette caused extreme damage to facilities here, and some may still not be restored. Winter is the best time to come, as summer is hot. For things to do here, see the Pacific Coast Area, earlier in this chapter.

Campsites, facilities: There are 72 pull-through campsites with full hookups. Tent campers are welcome in a designated area on the beach with 18 *palapas.* Facilities include modest restrooms with flush toilets and hot showers, laundry facilities, a pool, a restaurant, a bar, and beachfront motel rooms. The water is safe to drink. For security, there is a gate and the owner lives on the premises. Obtain supplies in Todos Santos.

Reservations, fees: Reservations are accepted. Fees are high—$15 per night for a full-hookup site, $3 per person for no hookups, and $2 per day for parking. Long-term rates are $91 per week and $330 per month for sites with hookups.

Directions: From Todos Santos drive 4.5 miles south on Highway 19. A large sign marks the turnoff to the park. Follow the road two miles to the beach.

Contact: San Pedrito RV Park, Apartado Postal 15, Todos Santos, Baja California Sur, Mexico. There is no phone.

22 PLAYA LOS CERRITOS

South of Todos Santos
South Baja Sur map, page 147

Here it is—one of the most spectacular beaches in all of Baja. Of course, surfers have known this for years. There is ample space to park or pitch tents in front of the old RV park or to the north up against the rocky ridge. Winter is the best time to come, as summer is hot. For things to do here, see the Pacific Coast Area, earlier in this chapter.

Campsites, facilities: The beach is ideal for tent camping. There are no facilities or security. Obtain supplies in Todos Santos.

Reservations, fees: Camping is first come, first served. The fee is very low—$3 per night.

Directions: From Todos Santos drive 7.2 miles south on Highway 19. Take the marked turnoff for Los Cerritos RV Park and go two miles to the beach.

Contact: Drive in and park. Someone will come around to collect the fee.

23 VILLA SERENA RV PARK

East of Cabo San Lucas
South Baja Sur map, page 147

This is a new park, and the plants were small when we were there. Winter is the best time to come, as summer is hot. For things to do here, see the Cape Area, earlier in this chapter.

Campsites, facilities: There are 54 campsites with full hookups. Tiled restrooms with flush toilets and hot showers, laundry facilities, a covered patio with tables, and a pool are on the premises. Don't drink the water. A night watchman is on guard. Obtain supplies in Cabo San Lucas.

Reservations, fees: Reservations are accepted. Fees are high—$15 per night, $95 per week, $350 per month, and $1,800 per year.

Directions: From Cabo San Lucas drive 4.5 miles east on Highway 1. The park is on a hill with a distant view of the ocean.

Contact: Villa Serena RV Park, Km 7.5 Carretera Benito Juarez, Cabo San Lucas, Baja California Sur, Mexico, Mex. tel. 624/145-8165 or 143-1880, fax 624/143-0509. For reservations call U.S. tel. 800/932-5599, fax 408/778-1513.

24 EL ARCO RV PARK

East of Cabo San Lucas
South Baja Sur map, page 147

"Stunning" is just one word to describe the view of the harbor, El Arco (the Arch), and the rugged rocks of Land's End—and it's all yours when you set up camp here. There is a downside, though: the park is crowded and dedicated mainly to permanents, so it's rather unattractive for overnighters. Winter is the best time to come, as summer is hot. For things to do here, see the Cape Area, earlier in this chapter.

Campsites, facilities: There are 40 pull-through campsites, of which 24 have full hookups. Some come with concrete pads. Modest restrooms with flush toilets and hot showers, laundry facilities, a pool, and a restaurant are available. Don't drink the water. The park is secured with a chain and by the presence of numerous people. Tent campers are welcome. Obtain supplies in Cabo San Lucas.

Reservations, fees: Reservations are accepted. Fees are high—$15 per night for RVs with full hookups and $8 for tents. Long-term rates are $250 per month and $2,484 per year.

Directions: From Cabo San Lucas drive 3.3 miles east on Highway 1. The park is on a hill overlooking the ocean and Land's End.

Contact: El Arco RV Park, Apartado Postal 114, Cabo San Lucas, Baja California Sur, Mexico, Mex. tel. 624/143-1686.

25 BELLA VISTA RV PARK

East of Cabo San Lucas
South Baja Sur map, page 147

This park has a million-dollar view of the arches and the water. Dogs must be kept on a leash at all times. Winter is the best time to come, as summer is hot. For things to do here, see the Cape Area, earlier in this chapter.

Campsites, facilities: There are eight pull-through campsites and 16 others with full hookups, some with *palapas* and concrete pads. The park has trees, tiled restrooms with hot showers and flush toilets, a kitchen for group cooking, laundry facilities, a pool, boat parking, and a great view of Cabo's arches and the town from an elevated location. Don't drink the tap water; purified water is available. Security is provided by an electric gate in a perimeter fence and guards. Tent camping is not allowed. A bed-and-breakfast is available on-site for guests. Obtain supplies in Cabo San Lucas.

Reservations, fees: Reservations are accepted. Fees are high—$14 per night, $90 per week, $350 per month, and $3,500 per year.

Directions: From Cabo San Lucas drive 2.5 miles east on Highway 1. The park is on a hill overlooking the ocean and Land's End. Call ahead and they will escort you to the park the first time.

Contact: Bella Vista RV Park, Canacintra, 16 de Septiembre s/n, Morelos Y Leona Vicario, Col. Centro, Apartado Postal 658, Cabo San Lucas, Baja California Sur, Mexico, Mex. tel. 624/143-7381, fax 624/143-6682, email: cabo-cowboy@cabonet.net.mx.

26 CABO CIELO RV PARK

East of Cabo San Lucas
South Baja Sur map, page 147

Campers have a palm tree at each site and a view of Land's End. The park is situated in an open field, unfortunately not a very interesting place to camp. As the trees mature and improvements continue to be made, however, we trust it will become more attractive. Winter is the best time to come, as summer is hot. For things to do here, see the Cape Area, earlier in this chapter.

Campsites, facilities: There are 24 campsites with full hookups. A store and tiled restrooms with flush toilets and hot showers are on the property. Don't drink the water. The park is secured with a chain, and the manager lives on the premises. Tent campers are welcome. Obtain supplies in Cabo San Lucas.

Reservations, fees: All sites are first come, first served. Fees are moderate—$9 per night. Long-term rates are $210 per month.

Directions: From Cabo San Lucas head 2.3 miles east on Highway 1 to the park.

Contact: Drive in and talk to the manager.

27 CLUB CABO MOTEL AND CAMPGROUND RESORT

East of Cabo San Lucas
South Baja Sur map, page 147

This quiet, pleasant park is in a secluded setting away from town. Best of all, it offers beach access. The owners can tip you off to where the great surfing spots are, and they will even rent you a surfboard in case you didn't bring one along. Winter is the best time to come, as summer is hot. For things to do here, see the Cape Area, earlier in this chapter.

Campsites, facilities: There are 13 campsites, nine of which have full hookups. Facilities include restrooms with flush toilets and hot showers, *palapas,* trees, tables, barbecues, laundry facilities, a trampoline, a pool, a hot tub, and reasonable motel rooms. Don't drink the tap water; purified water is available on-site. The park is secured with a chain and motion-sensing floodlights, and the owner lives on the premises. Tent campers are welcome. Obtain supplies in Cabo San Lucas.

Reservations, fees: Reservations are encouraged, with a 10 percent discount. Fees are high—$15 per night per RV, $100 per week, and $400 per month; $14 per night for tent space, $100 per week, and $400 per month.

Directions: From the junction of Highway 1 and the Highway 19 bypass around Cabo San Lucas, drive south on the unmarked street in the big arroyo going toward Club Cascadas, following the signs to Club Cabo. Turn left on the sandy road to the east paralleling the beach and go past the back end of the Vagabundos del Mar RV Park (see next listing).

The park adjoins the Vagabundos park on its east side.

Contact: Club Cabo Motel and Campground Resort, Apartado Postal 463, Cabo San Lucas, Baja California Sur, Mexico, Mex. tel./fax 624/143-3348, email: clubcabo@cabonet.net.mx, website: cabobedandbreakfast.com.

28 VAGABUNDOS DEL MAR RV PARK

East of Cabo San Lucas
South Baja Sur map, page 147

This one's a winner—one of the most attractive and well-maintained parks in Baja. For landscaping there are lots of native mesquite trees and introduced palms. If you're boating or fishing, a bonus is that this is the closest park to the launch ramps in Cabo. Winter is the best time to come, as summer is hot. For more on things to do here, see the Cape Area, earlier in this chapter.

Campsites, facilities: There are 53 campsites (44 pull-through), all with full hookups, concrete pads, trees, and tables. Tent campers may use 44 of the sites. Facilities include clean, tiled restrooms with flush toilets and hot showers, a laundry facility, a pool, a restaurant/bar, and a meeting *palapa*. Don't drink the water. The park is secured with a gate and 24-hour guard service, and the manager lives on the premises. Obtain supplies in Cabo San Lucas.

Reservations, fees: Reservations are encouraged. Fees for both RVs and tents are high—$18 per night, $110 per week, $440 per month, and $3,250 per year for RVs or tents.

Directions: From Cabo San Lucas head one mile east on Highway 1 to the park on the south side of the highway.

Contact: Vagabundos del Mar RV Park, Apartado Postal 197, Cabo San Lucas, Baja California Sur, Mexico, U.S. tel. 800/474-BAJA (800/474-2252), fax 707/374-6843, Mex. tel. 624/143-0290, fax 624/143-0511.

29 EL FARO VIEJO RV PARK

In Cabo San Lucas
South Baja Sur map, page 147

The grounds of this recently spruced-up park with landscaped RV sites are very well maintained. Each site has trees and plants. This is not the ideal place for tent campers, being right in the city. It gets very crowded every night when the restaurant/bar patrons flock in. Winter is the preferred season, as summer is hot. For more on things to do here, see the Cape Area, earlier in this chapter.

Campsites, facilities: There are 24 large pull-through, full-hookup campsites for RVs and 12 sites for tents with concrete pads and trees. Clean tiled restrooms with flush toilets and hot showers, a store, and one of the best restaurants in Cabo San Lucas—known simply as the Trailer Park Restaurant—also are on the property. Don't drink the water. Security is good, as the park is inside a walled compound with a locked gate and a watchman. Obtain supplies in Cabo San Lucas.

Reservations, fees: Reservations are accepted. Fees are moderate—$12 per night for two people, plus $3 for each additional person.

Directions: The park is on the north end of town, one block west of Morelos (Highway 19) between Mijares and Felix Ortega.

Contact: El Faro Viejo RV Park, Apartado Postal 64, Cabo San Lucas, Baja California Sur, Mexico, Mex. tel. 624/143-1927.

30 BRISA DEL MAR RV RESORT

West of San José del Cabo
South Baja Sur map, page 147

This park is very popular with snowbirds who flock here for the winter. It is on a lovely beach close to San José del Cabo and, in fact, is the only RV park on a beach in the Los Cabos area. Winter is the best time to come, as summer is hot. For things to do here, see the Cape Area, earlier in this chapter.

Campsites, facilities: The resort offers 50 full-hookup campsites and 20 pull-throughs with tables. Facilities include tiled restrooms with flush toilets and hot showers, a dump station, a pool, a store, a bar and restaurant, Ping-Pong and pool tables, a volleyball court, and a horseshoe pit. Don't drink the water. Security is provided by a night watchman. Tent campers are welcome at all sites. Obtain supplies in San José del Cabo.

Reservations, fees: Camping is first come, first served. Fees are high—for RVs, $18.50 to $30 per night with full hookups; tents are $11 per night.

Directions: From San José del Cabo take Highway 1 west about two miles to Km 28. Brisa del Mar is on the beach.

Contact: Brisa del Mar RV Resort, Carretera Peninsular Km 28, San José del Cabo, Baja California Sur, Mexico, Mex. tel./fax 624/142-3999, email: mortimer@brisadelmar.com, website: www.brisadelmar.com/rvresort.

10 Best Beaches

① LOMA MARÍA TO TODOS SANTOS BEACHES

On the Pacific Ocean, south of the Bahía Magdalena complex and north of Todos Santos

South Baja Sur map, page 146

This is as straight as a coastline can get, with very few projections or points and no shelter for boats—just one long stretch of beach. The beaches here are generally not frequented by tourists. Punta Conejo is favored by surfers and windsurfers. Adventurers in four-wheel-drive vehicles might find the pristine beaches exciting to explore. Of course it's always wise for four-wheelers to travel in groups in remote areas in case of mechanical breakdown.

Directions: A rough dirt road approaches the coast from about 17 miles south of Santa Rita on Highway 1 (about 51 miles south of Ciudad Constitución), then runs south along the coast to Todos Santos. The beaches extend for some 110 miles. Punta Conejo can be reached more directly via a 12-mile, fair dirt road that exits Highway 1 at Km 80 (about 13 miles south of El Cien and 68 miles south of Ciudad Constitución). Other rough dirt roads leave Highway 1 for coastal ranches 29, 40, and 41 miles south of El Cien.

② SAN JUAN DE LA COSTA BEACHES

On the Sea of Cortéz, north of La Paz

South Baja Sur map, page 146

A number of sand, pebble, and mixed beaches are along the western shore of Bahía de La Paz. The dirt road north of San Juan de la Costa has soft, sandy stretches that can easily bog down larger vehicles, as is the case with side roads to the shore. Trailers are difficult to manage here. Pickups, vans, and four-wheel-drive vehicles will fare better. Fishing for roosterfish, grouper, snapper, pargo, sierra, and dorado improves the farther north you go.

Directions: Access is by the 24-mile paved road to San Juan de la Costa, which leaves Highway 1 at Km 17 about 10 miles north of La Paz, and the dirt road that continues another 35 miles to El Mechudo.

③ LA PAZ BEACHES

On the Sea of Cortéz, northeast and east of La Paz

South Baja Sur map, page 146

Long beaches such as Tecolote, Cachimba, La Sorpresa, and Arena de la Ventana are interspersed with sandy coves and rocky cliffs. This is a great area for exploring with groups of four-wheel-drive vehicles. The fishing can be exceptional as well. For types of fish found in the area and the names of companies leading sportfishing cruises out of La Paz, see the La Paz Area, earlier in this chapter.

Directions: These beaches extend from Playa Balandra and Playa Tecolote (see listings in this chapter), around Punta Coyote, and south to Bahía de los Muertos Beach. There are dirt roads east of Tecolote, and a network of rough, sandy four-wheel-drive roads fans out from the southeast edge of La Paz to the northern area. Other dirt roads that leave the pavement out of San Juan de Los Planes lead to the southern section. (For directions, see La Ventana and Punta Arena Beach listings in this chapter.)

④ PLAYA SAN PEDRO

On the Pacific Ocean, south of Todos Santos

South Baja Sur map, page 147

A popular surfing spot, this beautiful sand beach extends about 0.3 mile between two rocky points and is backed by a large palm grove. It is perfect for tent campers who can haul in their gear on motorcycles or ATVs.

Note: Many guidebooks and maps list this as Playa San Pedrito, though we quizzed locals who stoutly maintained it was Playa San

Pedro. Winter is the best time to come, as summer is hot. For things to do here, see the Pacific Coast Area, earlier in this chapter.

Directions: The turnoff from Highway 19 is 4.4 miles south of the southern outskirts of Todos Santos, just before the signs and entrance road to San Pedrito RV Park (see listing in this chapter). However, the road is currently closed to vehicular traffic, though motorcycles and ATVs can make it. After the turnoff, it's 1.5 miles to the beach.

5 PESCADERO BEACH

On the Pacific Ocean, south of Todos Santos
South Baja Sur map, page 147

We haven't found this one listed in other guidebooks or on maps. The wide beach is covered with a blanket of soft sand and is a favorite destination for surfers. Except for the northern reaches, it is remote, offering seclusion to those who make the effort to attain it. The beach slopes rather steeply, creating an undertow that can be dangerous to inexperienced swimmers. Winter is the best time to come, as summer is hot. For things to do here, see the Pacific Coast Area, earlier in this chapter.

Directions: The beach extends about four miles between Punta San Pedro south to Punta Pescadero. San Pedrito RV Park (see listing in this chapter) is at the north end. It's best to ask for directions in Pescadero on how to get through the fields.

6 PLAYA LOS CERRITOS

On the Pacific Ocean, south of Todos Santos
South Baja Sur map, page 147

This wide beach curves westward, exposing an unbroken five-mile sweep to clear view from Playa Los Cerritos (see listing in this chapter) at the north end. Walking on the soft white sand is pure joy.

Directions: The beach extends about five miles between Puntas Pescadero and Gaspareño.

7 EAST CAPE BEACHES

On the Sea of Cortéz, from north of Los Barriles to south of La Ribera
South Baja Sur map, page 147

These beaches form an almost continuous 25-mile strip. Blanketed with soft white sand, they become wider the farther south you go. Opportunities to find solitude abound, as many stretches between public access points are remote. The wide, sweeping beach at the southern end between Punta Colorada and Punta Arena invites long walks and is great for shelling. Private lands block many access points, but adventurous souls can find ways in. For information on the numerous fishing, diving, snorkeling, and windsurfing opportunities around here, see the East Cape Area, earlier in this chapter.

Directions: The beaches extend from four miles north of Los Barriles south to Punta Arena. The campgrounds from Quinta Maria to Correcaminos RV Park (see listings in this chapter) afford public access to this stretch of coastline. A sandy road parallels the coast in both directions from La Ribera, with numerous four-wheel-drive roads branching off it toward the beaches.

8 PUNTA ARENA TO SAN JOSÉ DEL CABO BEACHES

On the Sea of Cortéz, south of La Ribera and north of San José del Cabo
South Baja Sur map, page 147

Surfing is the main activity along this stretch of coast, and there are plenty of places to go. However, only small, maneuverable vehicles can make the drive safely. Choice campsites on this long string of magnificent beaches are inaccessible to larger highway vehicles because of dangerous road conditions. Side roads leading to beaches are packed wheel tracks in sand. A paved road on a new alignment is being built south of La Ribera. Ultimately it is supposed to go down the coast to San José del Cabo. Coming into La Ribera from Highway 1, this road veers south before town. Obviously, whatever realignment the new paved road takes will alter the log given below, but at least you will have something to go by as this remote coast opens up.

Directions: To get to La Ribera exit Highway 1 on a paved road that begins approximately 12 miles south of Los Barriles and drive about seven miles east. Los Frailes is about 22 miles south of La Ribera. The beaches extend for some 33 miles south of Los Frailes. Below is a log of accessible beaches, with mile marks starting from Los Frailes:

Mile 8: Rancho El Tule—Follow the wide arroyo to the beach. The people at the rancho seem somewhat hostile to travelers and have placed big speed bumps in front of the headquarters. They may not welcome campers, so be nice.

Mile 10.9: An access road leads to the beach.

Mile 14.4: Rancho San Luis is on the beach.

Mile 14.9: A short access road leads to the beach.

Mile 17.0: Rancho Boca de Las Palmas. A wide arroyo accesses the beach.

Mile 18.8: Rancho La Fortuna. A wide arroyo accesses the beach.

Mile 19.3: An access road leads to a big beach.

Mile 20.3: An access road leads to the beach.

Mile 20.8: Shipwreck Beach is a favorite of surfers. A good, short road accesses this big beach.

Mile 22.6: A big, sandy arroyo accesses the nearby beach.

Mile 23.9: An access road goes to Playa Tortuga.

Mile 24.6: An access road leads to the beach, between brush-covered dunes.

Mile 25.5-25.7: Several small parking areas are off the coast road, just above the beach.

Mile 32.0: A big beach is at the end of the access road.

Mile 33.4: Just outside San José del Cabo is an access road to the beach at La Playa.

⑨ BEACHES BETWEEN PUNTA GASPAREÑO AND LAND'S END

On the Pacific Ocean, south of Todos Santos and north of Cabo San Lucas

South Baja Sur map, page 147

The long, 33-mile stretch between Punta Gaspareño and Land's End is essentially one immense, unbroken beach. It's wide and backed by dunes, with soft white sand offering great opportunities for seclusion to those who are willing to hike. The slope is rather steep, and the surf pounds here, creating undertows that pose serious threat to inexperienced swimmers. Still, surfers like riding the waves off the points on this coastline.

Note: Development by private landowners along Highway 19 is forcing the closure of some access roads. There will probably always be some way in, though, since the Zona Federale (up to the high tide mark all around Mexico) is dedicated to the public.

Directions: Access the beaches from several four-wheel-drive roads off Highway 19. To reach Migriño Beach, drive 27 miles south of Todos Santos or 16 miles north of Cabo San Lucas on Highway 19 to Km 97, then follow the rough road in (suitable for small vehicles).

⑩ CAPE AREA DAY-USE BEACHES

Between San José del Cabo and Cabo San Lucas

South Baja Sur map, page 147

One of the best things about coming to the Cape is being able to loll about on these beaches soaking up the sun's rays and splashing around in the surf. People camping in this region find these day-use beaches delightful to visit, though they can become quite congested. Sadly, they are falling prey to development one by one, so you may find access to certain beaches restricted. Enjoy them while you can.

Directions: You can access several beaches off Highway 1. Routes are designated by road signs.

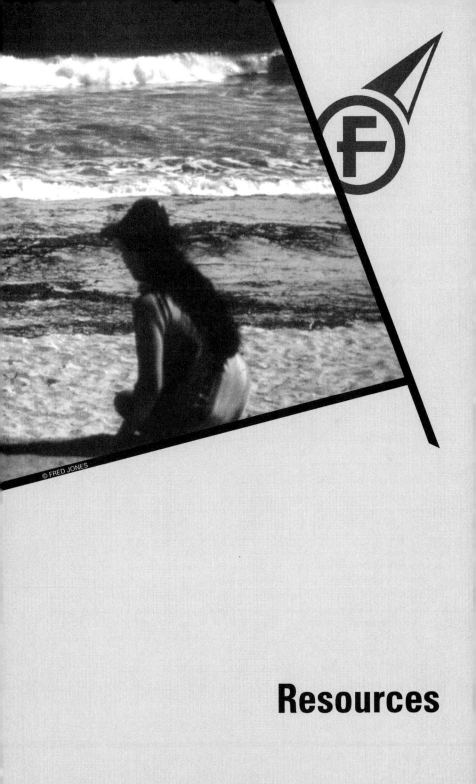

© FRED JONES

Resources

Spanish Phrasebook

Your Mexico adventure will be more fun if you use a little Spanish. Mexican folks, although they may smile at your funny accent, will appreciate your halting efforts to break the ice and transform yourself from a foreigner to a potential friend.

Spanish commonly uses 30 letters—the familiar English 26, plus four straightforward additions: ch, ll, ñ, and rr, which are explained in "Consonants," below.

Pronunciation

Once you learn them, Spanish pronunciation rules—in contrast to English—don't change. Spanish vowels generally sound softer than in English. (Note: The capitalized syllables below receive stronger accents.)

Vowels

a — like ah, as in "hah": *agua* AH-gooah (water), *pan* PAHN (bread), and *casa* CAH-sah (house)

e — like ay, as in "may:" *mesa* MAY-sah (table), *tela* TAY-lah (cloth), and *de* DAY (of, from)

i — like ee, as in "need": *diez* dee-AYZ (ten), *comida* ko-MEE-dah (meal), and *fin* FEEN (end)

o — like oh, as in "go": *peso* PAY-soh (weight), *ocho* OH-choh (eight), and *poco* POH-koh (a bit)

u — like oo, as in "cool": *uno* OO-noh (one), *cuarto* KOOAHR-toh (room), and *usted* oos-TAYD (you); when it follows a "q" the **u** is silent; when it follows an "h" or has an umlaut, it's pronounced like "w"

Consonants

b, d, f, k, l, m, n, p, q, s, t, v, w, x, y, z, and **ch** — pronounced almost as in English; **h** occurs, but is silent—not pronounced at all.

c — like k as in "keep": *cuarto* KOOAR-toh (room), Tepic tay-PEEK (capital of Nayarit state); when it precedes "e" or "i," pronounce **c** like s, as in "sit": *cerveza* sayr-VAY-sah (beer), *encima* ayn-SEE-mah (atop).

g — like g as in "gift" when it precedes "a," "o," "u," or a consonant: *gato* GAH-toh (cat), *hago* AH-goh (I do, make); otherwise, pronounce **g** like h as in "hat": *giro* HEE-roh (money order), *gente* HAYN-tay (people)

j — like h, as in "has": *Jueves* HOOAY-vays (Thursday), *mejor* may-HOR (better)

ll — like y, as in "yes": *toalla* toh-AH-yah (towel), *ellos* AY-yohs (they, them)

ñ — like ny, as in "canyon": *año* AH-nyo (year), *señor* SAY-nyor (Mr., sir)

r — is lightly trilled, with tongue at the roof of your mouth like a very light English d, as in "ready": *pero* PAY-doh (but), *tres* TDAYS (three), *cuatro* KOOAH-tdoh (four).

rr — like a Spanish r, but with much more emphasis and trill. Let your tongue flap. Practice with *burro* (donkey), *carretera* (highway), and Carrillo (proper name), then really let go with *ferrocarril* (railroad).

Note: The single small but common exception to all of the above is the pronunciation of Spanish y when it's being used as the Spanish word for "and," as in "Ron y Kathy." In such case, pronounce it like the English ee, as in "keep": Ron "ee" Kathy (Ron and Kathy).

Accent

The rule for accent, the relative stress given to syllables within a given word, is straightforward. If a word ends in a vowel, an n, or an s, accent the next-to-last syllable; if not, accent the last syllable.

Pronounce *gracias* GRAH-seeahs (thank you), *orden* OHR-dayn (order), and *carretera* kah-ray-TAY-rah (highway) with stress on the next-to-last syllable.

Otherwise, accent the last syllable: *venir* vay-NEER (to come), *ferrocarril* fay-roh-cah-REEL (railroad), and *edad* ay-DAHD (age).

Exceptions to the accent rule are always marked with an accent sign: (á, é, í, ó, or ú), such as *teléfono* tay-LAY-foh-noh (telephone), *jabón* hah-BON (soap), and *rápido* RAH-pee-doh (rapid).

Basic and Courteous Expressions

Most Spanish-speaking people consider formalities important. Whenever approaching anyone for information or some other reason, do not forget the appropriate salutation—good morning, good evening, etc. Standing alone, the greeting *hola* (hello) can sound brusque.

Hello. — *Hola.*
Good morning. — *Buenos días.*
Good afternoon. — *Buenas tardes.*
Good evening. — *Buenas noches.*
How are you? — *¿Cómo está usted?*
Very well, thank you. — *Muy bien, gracias.*
Okay; good. — *Bien.*
Not okay; bad. — *Mal* or *feo.*
So-so. — *Más o menos.*
And you? — *¿Y usted?*
Thank you. — *Gracias.*
Thank you very much. — *Muchas gracias.*
You're very kind. — *Muy amable.*
You're welcome. — *De nada.*
Goodbye. — *Adios.*
See you later. — *Hasta luego.*
please — *por favor*
yes — *sí*
no — *no*
I don't know. — *No sé.*
Just a moment, please. — *Momentito, por favor.*
Excuse me, please (when you're trying to get attention). — *Disculpe* or *Con permiso.*
Excuse me (when you've made a boo-boo). — *Lo siento.*
Pleased to meet you. — *Mucho gusto.*
How do you say . . . in Spanish? — *¿Cómo se dice . . . en español?*
What is your name? — *¿Cómo se llama usted?*
Do you speak English? — *¿Habla usted inglés?*
Is English spoken here? (Does anyone here speak English?) — *¿Se habla español?*
I don't speak Spanish well. — *No hablo bien el español.*
I don't understand. — *No entiendo.*
How do you say . . . in Spanish? — *¿Cómo se dice . . . en español?*
My name is . . . — *Me llamo . . .*
Would you like . . . — *¿Quisiera usted . . .*
Let's go to . . . — *Vamos a . . .*

Terms of Address

When in doubt, use the formal *usted* (you) as a form of address.

I — *yo*
you (formal) — *usted*
you (familiar) — *tu*
he/him — *él*
she/her — *ella*
we/us — *nosotros*
you (plural) — *ustedes*
they/them — *ellos* (all males or mixed gender); *ellas* (all females)
Mr., sir — *señor*
Mrs., madam — *señora*
miss, young lady — *señorita*
wife — *esposa*
husband — *esposo*
friend — *amigo* (male); *amiga* (female)
sweetheart — *novio* (male); *novia* (female)
son; daughter — *hijo; hija*
brother; sister — *hermano; hermana*
father; mother — *padre; madre*
grandfather; grandmother — *abuelo; abuela*

Transportation

Where is . . . ? — *¿Dónde está . . . ?*
How far is it to . . . ? — *¿A cuánto está . . . ?*
from . . . to . . . — *de . . . a . . .*
How many blocks? — *¿Cuántas cuadras?*
Where (Which) is the way to . . . ? — *¿Dónde está el camino a . . . ?*
the boat — *el barco*
the entrance — *la entrada*
the exit — *la salida*
the ticket office — *la oficina de boletos*
(very) near; far — *(muy) cerca; lejos*
to; toward — *a*
by; through — *por*
from — *de*
the right — *la derecha*
the left — *la izquierda*
straight ahead — *derecho; directo*
in front — *en frente*
beside — *al lado*
behind — *atrás*
the corner — *la esquina*
the stoplight — *la semáforo*
a turn — *una vuelta*

right here — *aquí*
somewhere around here — *por acá*
right there — *allí*
somewhere around there — *por allá*
street; boulevard — *calle; bulevar*
highway — *carretera*
bridge; toll — *puente; cuota*
address — *dirección*
north; south — *norte; sur*
east; west — *oriente (este); poniente (oeste)*

Accommodations

What is the rate? — *¿Cuál es el precio?*
Is that your best rate? — *¿Es su mejor precio?*
Is there something cheaper? — *¿Hay algo más económico?*
hot water — *agua caliente*
shower — *ducha*
towels — *toallas*
soap — *jabón*
toilet paper — *papel higiénico*
fan — *abanico; ventilador*
key — *llave*
manager — *gerente*

Food

I'm hungry — *Tengo hambre.*
I'm thirsty. — *Tengo sed.*
menu — *lista; menú*
order — *orden*
glass — *vaso*
fork — *tenedor*
knife — *cuchillo*
spoon — *cuchara*
napkin — *servilleta*
soft drink — *refresco*
coffee — *café*
tea — *té*
drinking water — *agua pura; agua potable*
bottled carbonated water — *agua mineral*
bottled uncarbonated water — *agua sin gas*
beer — *cerveza*
wine — *vino*
milk — *leche*
juice — *jugo*
cream — *crema*
sugar — *azúcar*

cheese — *queso*

snack — *antojo; botana*

breakfast — *desayuno*

lunch — *almuerzo*

daily lunch special — *comida corrida* (or *el menú del día* depending on region)

dinner — *comida* (often eaten in late afternoon); *cena* (a late-night snack)

the check — *la cuenta*

eggs — *huevos*

bread — *pan*

salad — *ensalada*

fruit — *fruta*

mango — *mango*

watermelon — *sandía*

papaya — *papaya*

banana — *plátano*

apple — *manzana*

orange — *naranja*

lime — *limón*

fish — *pescado*

shellfish — *mariscos*

shrimp — *camarones*

meat (without) — *(sin) carne*

chicken — *pollo*

pork — *puerco*

beef; steak — *res; bistec*

bacon; ham — *tocino; jamón*

fried — *frito*

roasted — *asada*

barbecue; barbecued — *barbacoa; al carbón*

Shopping

money — *dinero*

money-exchange bureau — *casa de cambio*

I would like to exchange traveler's checks. — *Quisiera cambiar cheques de viajero.*

What is the exchange rate? — *¿Cuál es el tipo de cambio?*

How much is the commission? — *¿Cuánto cuesta la comisión?*

Do you accept credit cards? — *¿Aceptan tarjetas de crédito?*

money order — *giro*

How much does it cost? — *¿Cuánto cuesta?*

What is your final price? — *¿Cuál es su último precio?*

expensive — *caro*

cheap — *barato; económico*

more — *más*

less — *menos*

a little — *un poco*

too much — *demasiado*

Health

Help me please. — *Ayúdeme por favor.*
I am ill. — *Estoy enfermo.*
Call a doctor. — *Llame un doctor.*
Take me to . . . — *Lléveme a . . .*
hospital — *hospital; sanatorio*
drugstore — *farmacia*
pain — *dolor*
fever — *fiebre*
headache — *dolor de cabeza*
stomach ache — *dolor de estómago*
burn — *quemadura*
cramp — *calambre*
nausea — *náusea*
vomiting — *vomitar*
medicine — *medicina*
antibiotic — *antibiótico*
pill; tablet — *pastilla*
aspirin — *aspirina*
ointment; cream — *pomada; crema*
bandage — *venda*
cotton — *algodón*
sanitary napkins — use brand name, e.g., Kotex
birth control pills — *pastillas anticonceptivas*
contraceptive foam — *espuma anticonceptiva*
condoms — *preservativos; condones*
toothbrush — *cepilla dental*
dental floss — *hilo dental*
toothpaste — *crema dental*
dentist — *dentista*
toothache — *dolor de muelas*

Post Office and Communications

long-distance telephone — *teléfono larga distancia*
I would like to call . . . — *Quisiera llamar a . . .*
collect — *por cobrar*
station to station — *a quien contesta*
person to person — *persona a persona*
credit card — *tarjeta de crédito*
post office — *correo*
general delivery — *lista de correo*
letter — *carta*
stamp — *estampilla, timbre*
postcard — *tarjeta*
aerogram — *aerograma*
air mail — *correo aereo*

registered — *registrado*
money order — *giro*
package; box — *paquete; caja*
string; tape — *cuerda; cinta*

At the Border

border — *frontera*
customs — *aduana*
immigration — *migración*
tourist card — *tarjeta de turista*
inspection — *inspección; revisión*
passport — *pasaporte*
profession — *profesión*
marital status — *estado civil*
single — *soltero*
married; divorced — *casado; divorciado*
widowed — *viudado*
insurance — *seguros*
title — *título*
driver's license — *licencia de manejar*

At the Gas Station

gas station — *gasolinera*
gasoline — *gasolina*
unleaded — *sin plomo*
full, please — *lleno, por favor*
tire — *llanta*
tire repair shop — *vulcanizadora*
air — *aire*
water — *agua*
oil (change) — *aceite (cambio)*
grease — *grasa*
My . . . doesn't work. — *Mi . . . no sirve.*
battery — *batería*
radiator — *radiador*
alternator — *alternador*
generator — *generador*
tow truck — *grúa*
repair shop — *taller mecánico*
tune-up — *afinación*
auto parts store — *refaccionería*

Verbs

Verbs are the key to getting along in Spanish. They employ mostly predictable forms and come in three classes, which end in *ar, er,* and *ir,* respectively:

to buy — *comprar*
I buy, you (he, she, it) buys — *compro, compra*
we buy, you (they) buy — *compramos, compran*

to eat — *comer*
I eat, you (he, she, it) eats — *como, come*
we eat, you (they) eat — *comemos, comen*

to climb — *subir*
I climb, you (he, she, it) climbs — *subo, sube*
we climb, you (they) climb — *subimos, suben*

Got the idea? Here are more (with irregularities marked in **bold**).

to do or make — *hacer*
I do or make, you (he she, it) does or makes — ***hago***, *hace*
we do or make, you (they) do or make — *hacemos, hacen*

to go — *ir*
I go, you (he, she, it) goes — ***voy, va***
we go, you (they) go — ***vamos, van***

to go (walk) — *andar*
to love — *amar*
to work — *trabajar*
to want — *desear, querer*
to need — *necesitar*
to read — *leer*
to write — *escribir*
to repair — *reparar*
to stop — *parar*
to get off (the bus) — *bajar*
to arrive — *llegar*
to stay (remain) — *quedar*
to stay (lodge) — *hospedar*
to leave — *salir* (regular except for ***salgo***, I leave)
to look at — *mirar*
to look for — *buscar*
to give — *dar* (regular except for ***doy***, I give)
to carry — *llevar*
to have — *tener* (irregular but important: ***tengo, tiene, tenemos, tienen***)
to come — *venir* (similarly irregular: ***vengo, viene***, *venimos,* ***vienen***)

Spanish has two forms of "to be." Use *estar* when speaking of location or a temporary state of being: "I am at home." *"**Estoy** en casa."* "I'm sick." *"**Estoy** enfermo."* Use *ser* for a permanent state of being: "I am a doctor." *"**Soy** doctora."*

Estar is regular except for *estoy,* I am. *Ser* is very irregular:
to be — *ser*
I am, you (he, she, it) is — *soy, es*
we are, you (they) are — *somos, son*

Numbers
zero — *cero*
one — *uno*
two — *dos*
three — *tres*
four — *cuatro*
five — *cinco*
six — *seis*
seven — *siete*
eight — *ocho*
nine — *nueve*
10 — *diez*
11 — *once*
12 — *doce*
13 — *trece*
14 — *catorce*
15 — *quince*
16 — *dieciseis*
17 — *diecisiete*
18 — *dieciocho*
19 — *diecinueve*
20 — *veinte*
21 — *veinte y uno* or *veintiuno*
30 — *treinta*
40 — *cuarenta*
50 — *cincuenta*
60 — *sesenta*
70 — *setenta*
80 — *ochenta*
90 — *noventa*
100 — *ciento*
101 — *ciento y uno* or *cientiuno*
200 — *doscientos*
500 — *quinientos*
1,000 — *mil*
10,000 — *diez mil*
100,000 — *cien mil*
1,000,000 — *millón*
one half — *medio*
one third — *un tercio*
one fourth — *un cuarto*

Time

What time is it? — *¿Qué hora es?*
It's one o'clock. — *Es la una.*
It's three in the afternoon. — *Son las tres de la tarde.*
It's 4 A.M. — *Son las cuatro de la mañana.*
six-thirty — *seis y media*
a quarter till eleven — *un cuarto para las once*
a quarter past five — *las cinco y cuarto*
an hour — *una hora*

Days and Months

Monday — *lunes*
Tuesday — *martes*
Wednesday — *miércoles*
Thursday — *jueves*
Friday — *viernes*
Saturday — *sábado*
Sunday — *domingo*
today — *hoy*
tomorrow — *mañana*
yesterday — *ayer*
January — *enero*
February — *febrero*
March — *marzo*
April — *abril*
May — *mayo*
June — *junio*
July — *julio*
August — *agosto*
September — *septiembre*
October — *octubre*
November — *noviembre*
December — *diciembre*
a week — *una semana*
a month — *un mes*
after — *después*
before — *antes*

Courtesy of Bruce Whipperman, author of *Moon Handbooks Pacific Mexico.*

Glossary

aduana — customs
agua purificada — purified water
bahía — bay or harbor
balneario — recreation area
basurera — town dump
caleta — cove
campo — camp
carnicería — meat shop
casita — little house
cuota — toll
ejido — a government-supported agricultural cooperative
farmacia — pharmacy
frutería — small fruit and vegetable store
garrafones — five-gallon bottles
gas butano — propane
hielo — ice
malecón — waterfront
palapa — an open-sided shade structure with a palm-frond thatched roof
panadería — bakery
panga — a tough, Mexican-designed fiberglass boat used by fishermen
playa — beach
punta — point
sol — sun
sombra — shade
vados — dips into stream channels

Information Sources

Mexican Tourism Board

United States
800/44-MEXICO (800/446-3942)

Canada
2 Bloor Street West, Suite 1801
Toronto, Ontario M4W 3E2
Can. tel. 416/925-0704, fax 416/925-6061
email: toronto@visitmexico.com
website: www.visitmexico.com

1 Place Villa Marie, Suite 1526
Montreal, Quebec H3B 2B5
Can. tel. 514/871-1052, fax 514/871-3825
email: montreal@visitmexico.com
website: www.visitmexico.com

Fishing

Mexican Fisheries Office
2550 Fifth Avenue, Suite 101
San Diego, CA 92103
U.S. tel. 619/233-6956, fax 619/233-0344

General Information

Vagabundos del Mar Boat and Travel Club
190 Main Street, Rio Vista, CA 94571
U.S. tel. 707/374-5511 or 800/474-BAJA (800/474-2252) fax 707/374-6843
email: info@vagabundos.com
website: www.vagabundos.com

Mexican Consulates

United States
Consular Representative
1201 F Avenue
Douglas, AZ 85607
U.S. tel. 520/364-3107, fax 520/364-1379
email: conmex@212.com

Consular Representative
480 North Grand Avenue
Nogales, AZ 85621

U.S. tel. 520/287-2521, fax 520/287-3175
email: consumex@dakotacom.net
website: www.nogalescity.com

Consular Representative
1990 West Camelback Road #110
Phoenix, AZ 85015
U.S. tel. 602/242-7398, fax 602/242-2957
email: consulado@consulmexphoenix.com

Consular Representative
553 South Stone Avenue
Tucson, AZ 85701
U.S. tel. 520/882-5595, fax 520/882-8959
email: contucmx@mindspring.com

Consulate
600 West 16th Street
Yuma, AZ 85364
U.S. tel. 928/344-0066, fax 928/344-0077
email: conyuma@sre.gob.mx

Consulate
331 West Second Street
Calexico, CA 92231
U.S. tel. 760/357-3863, fax 760/357-6284
email: consulmexcal@earthlink.net

Consulate
2409 Merced Street
Fresno, CA 93721
U.S. tel. 559/233-3065, fax 559/233-5638
email: consulado@consulmexfresno.net

Consulate
2401 West Sixth Street
Los Angeles, CA 90057
U.S. tel. 213/351-6800, fax 213/351-6844
email: lanmex01@worldnet.att.net
website: www.consulmex-la.com

Consulate
201 East Fourth Street #206-A
Oxnard, CA 93030
U.S. tel. 805/483-4684, fax 805/385-3527
email: consulmexoxnard@cs.com
website: www.sre.gob.mx/oxnard

Consulate
1010 Eighth Street
Sacramento, CA 95814
U.S. tel. 916/441-3287, fax 916/441-3176
email: consulsac1@quiknet.com
website: www.consulmexsacramento.com

Consular Representative
293 North D Street
San Bernardino, CA 92401
U.S. tel. 909/889-9837, fax 909/889-8285
email: conmex@gte.net

Consulate General
1549 India Street
San Diego, CA 92101
U.S. tel. 619/231-8414, fax 619/231-4802
email: mexconsd@electriciti.com
website: www.sre.gob.mx/sandiego

Consulate General
870 Market Street #528
San Francisco, CA 94102
U.S. tel. 415/392-5554, fax 415/392-3233
email: consulgral@consulmexsf.com
website: www.sre.gob.mx/sanfrancisco

Consulate
540 North First Street
San Jose, CA 95112
U.S. tel. 408/294-3414, fax 408/294-4506
email: consjose@sre.gob.mx

Consulate
828 North Broadway Street
Santa Ana, CA 92701
U.S. tel. 714/835-3069, fax 714/835-3472
email: stacon@pacbell.net

Consular Representative
48 Steele Street
Denver, CO 80206
U.S. tel. 303/331-1110, fax 303/830-2655
email: informacion@consulmex-denver.com
website: www.consulmex-denver.com

Consulate
2827 16th Street N.W.
Washington, DC 20009
U.S. tel. 202/736-1000, fax 202/797-8458
email: consulwas@aol.com

Consulate
1200 Northwest 78th Avenue #200
Miami, FL 33126
U.S. tel. 305/716-4977, fax 305/593-2758
email: conmxmia@bellsouth.net

Consulate
100 West Washington Street
Orlando, FL 32801
U.S. tel. 407/422-0514, fax 407/422-9633
email: conslmx@magicnet.net

Consulate
2600 Apple Valley Road
Atlanta, GA 30319
U.S. tel. 404/266-2233, fax 404/266-2309
email: abello@iainc.net
website: www.consulmexatlanta.org

Consulate
300 North Michigan Avenue, Second Floor
Chicago, IL 60630
U.S. tel. 312/855-1380, fax 312/855-9257
email: info@consulmexchicago.com
website: www.consulmexchicago.com

Consulate
39 West Jackson Place, Suite 130
Indianapolis, IN 46226
U.S. tel. 317/951-0005, fax 317/951-0006
email: consulmx@wcsonline.net

Consulate
1600 Baltimore, Suite 100
Kansas City, KS 61108
U.S. tel. 816/556-0800 to -03
email: conkansas@sre.gob.mx

Consulate
World Trade Center Building, 2 Canal Street #840
New Orleans, LA 70115
U.S. tel. 504/522-3596, fax 504/525-2332

Consulate
20 Park Plaza, Fifth Floor, Suite 506
Boston, MA 02116

U.S. tel. 617/426-4181, fax 617/695-1957
email: cmxboston@conversent.net

Consulate
645 Griswold Avenue, Suite 1700
Detroit, MI 48226
U.S. tel. 313/964-4515, fax 313/964-4522
email: cmexico653@aol.com

Consulate
1015 Locust Street #922
Saint Louis, MO 63101
U.S. tel. 314/436-3233, fax 314/436-2695

Consulate
3552 Dodge Street
Omaha, NE 68131
U.S. tel. 402/595-1841, fax 402/595-1845
email: consulmexomaha@qwest.net

Consulate
400 Gold Avenue Southwest #100
Albuquerque, NM 87102
U.S. tel. 505/247-2147, fax 505/842-9490
email: consulmexalb@qwest.net
website: www.users.qwest.net/~consulmexalb

Consulate
330 South Fourth Street
Las Vegas, NV 89101
U.S. tel. 702/383-0623, fax 702/383-0683
email: conlvegas@sre.gob.mx

Consulate
27 East 39th Street
New York, NY 10016
U.S. tel. 212/217-6400, fax 212/217-6493
email: webmaster@consulmxny.org
website: www.consulmxny.org

Consulate
P.O. Box 19627
Charlotte, NC 28219
U.S. tel. 704/394-2190

Consulate
336 East Six Forks Road
Raleigh, NC 27609
U.S. tel. 919/754-0046, fax 919/754-1726
email: conraleigh@sre.gob.mx

Consulate
1234 Southwest Morrison Street
Portland, OR 97205
U.S. tel. 503/274-1442, fax 503/274-1540
email: portland@sre.gob.mx
website: www.sre.gob.mx/portland

Consulate
111 South Independence Mall East, Suite 310
Philadelphia, PA 19106
U.S. tel. 215/922-4262, Fax 215/923-7281
email: deputyconsul@consulmexphila.com

Consulate
200 East 6th Street, Suite 200
Austin, TX 78701
U.S. tel. 512/478-2866, fax 512/478-8008
email: consulmx@onr.com
website: www.onr.com/consulmx

Consulate
724 East Elizabeth Street
Brownsville, TX 78520
U.S. tel. 210/542-4431, fax 210/542-7267
email: consulmexbro@aol.com
website: www.sre.gob.mx/brownsville

Consulate
800 North Shoreline Boulevard #410,
 North Tower
Corpus Christi, TX 78401
U.S. tel. 512/882-3375, fax 512/882-9324

Consulate
8855 North Stemmons Freeway
Dallas, TX 75247
U.S. tel. 214/630-7341, fax 214/630-3511
email: consuldall@aol.com
website: www.sre.gob.mx/dallas

Consulate
Edificio South Plaza Building 2398, Spur 239
Del Rio, TX 78840
U.S. tel. 830/775-2352, fax 830/774-6497
email: consulmexdel.titular@wcsonline.net

Consulate
140 North Adams Street
Eagle Pass, TX 78852
U.S. tel. 830/773-9255, fax 830/773-9397
email: consulmx@wcsonline.net

Consulate
910 East San Antonio Avenue
El Paso, TX 79901
U.S. tel. 915/533-3644, fax 915/532-7163
email: pressepa@elp.rr.com
website: www.sre.gob.mx/elpaso

Consulate
4507 San Jacinto Street
Houston, TX 77004
U.S. tel. 713/271-6800, fax 713/271-3201
email: cgdemex@pointecom.net
website: www.sre.gob.mx/houston

Consulate
1219 Matamoros Street
Laredo, TX 78040
U.S. tel. 956/723-6369, fax 956/723-1741
email: consul@srelaredo.org
website: www.sre.gob.mx/laredo

Consulate
600 South Broadway Street
McAllen, TX 78501
U.S. tel. 956/686-0243, fax 956/686-4901
email: consumexmc@aol.com

Consulate
511 West Ohio #121
Midland, TX 79701
U.S. tel. 915/687-2334, fax 915/687-3952

Consulate
Highway 67, Block 17, Kelly Building Addition 1

Presidio, TX 79845
U.S. tel. 915/229-2788, fax 915/229-2792
email: conmxpres@llnet.net

Consulate
127 Navarro Street
San Antonio, TX 78205
U.S. tel. 210/227-1085, fax 210/227-1817
email: cgmexsat@qwest.net
website: www.sre.gob.mx/sanantonio

Consular Representative
230 West 400 South, Second Floor
Salt Lake City, UT 84101
U.S. tel. 801/521-8502, fax 801/521-0534
email: conslc@burgoyne.com

Consular Representative
2132 Third Avenue
Seattle, WA 98121
U.S. tel. 206/448-3526, fax 206/448-4771
email: comexico1@qwest.net
website: www.sre.gob.mx/seattle

Canada
Consular Representative
710-1177 West Hastings Street
Vancouver, British Columbia V6E 2K3
Can. tel. 604/684-3547, fax 604/684-2485
email: mexico@consulmexvan.com
website: www.sre.gob.mx/vancouver

Consulate
199 Bay Street #4440, Commerce Court West
Toronto, Ontario M5L 1E9
Can. tel. 416/368-2875, fax 416/368-8342
email: cgmtoronto@consulmex.com
website: www.consulmex.com

Consulate
2055 Peel, Bureau 1000
Montreal, Quebec H3A 1A4
Can. tel. 514/288-2502, fax 514/288-8287
email: comexmt@consulmex.qc.ca
website: www.consulmex.qc.ca

Tourist Assistance, Embassies, and Consulates

There is a **Mexico-wide emergency number,** like 911 in the United States: 066.

Baja California Norte Tourist Assistance Offices

(if calling from the United States, dial 011-52 then the number; if calling from within Mexico, dial 01 then the number; if calling locally, dial the number without the area code)
Algodones: Mex. tel. 686/517-7635
Ensenada: Mex. tel. 646/172-3022
Loreto: Mex. tel. 613/135-0650
Mexicali: Mex. tel. 686/566-1277
Rosarito: Mex. tel. 661/612-0200
San Felipe: Mex. tel. 686/577-1155
Tecate: Mex. tel. 665/654-1095
Tijuana: Mex. tel. 666/688-0555

Baja California Sur Tourism Offices

Cabo San Lucas: Mex. tel. 624/142-1199
La Paz: Mex. tel. 612/124-0100, fax 612/124-0103

United States Embassy and Consulates

Embassy
Paseo de La Reforma 305
Colonia Cuauhtemoc, D.F., 06500, Mexico
Mex. tel. 55/5080-2000, fax 555/525-5040
email: cc@usembassy.net.mx

Consulate General
924 Avenida Lopez Mateos
Ciudad Juarez, Mexico
Mex. tel. 656/611-3000

Consulate General
Progreso 175
Colonia Americana Guadalajara
Jalisco, 44100, Mexico
Mex. tel. 333/825-2700

Consulate General
Avenida Constitución 411 Poniente
64000 Mexico
Mex. tel. 818/345-2120

Consulate General
Colonia Hipodrom,
Tijuana, Baja California, 22420 Mexico
Mex. tel. 664/622-7400, fax 664/681-8016
Emergency U.S. tel. 619/692-2154
Write to P.O. Box 439039, San Diego,
CA 92143

Consulate
Avenida Monterrey 141
Hermosillo, Sonora, Mexico
Mex. tel. 662/217-2375

Consulate
Avenida Primera 2002
Matamoros, Tamaulipas, Mexico
Mex. tel. 868/812-4402

Consulate
Paseo Montejo 453
Merida, Yucatan, Mexico
Mex. tel. 999/925-5011

Consulate
Calle San Jose
Nogales, Sonora, Mexico
Mex. tel. 631/313-4820

Consulate
Calle Allende 3330
Colonia Jardin, Nuevo Laredo, Nuevo Leon,
  Mexico
Mex. tel. 867/714-0512

Consular Agency
Boulevard Marina de Pedregal #1
Local #3, Zona Centro, Cabo San Lucas,
  Baja California Sur, Mexico
Mex. tel. 624/143-3566. Located behind Caliente
  Foreign Book next to Banamex. Monday–
  Friday 10 A.M.–1 P.M.

Consular Agency
Plaza Caracol #2, 3rd Level, #320-323,
  Boulevard Kukulcan, Km 8.5
Zona Hotelera, Cancun, Quintana Roo,
  Mexico
Mex. tel. 998/883-0272

Consular Agency
Plaza Villa Mar, El Centro, Local #8,
Avenida Juarez y 5th Avenue Norte

Cozumel, Quintana Roo, Mexico
Mex. tel. 987/872-4574. It is in the main square,
  second floor, right rear.

Consular Agency
Local 9, Plaza Ambiente
Ixtapa/Zihuatenejo, Guerrero, Mexico
Mex. tel. 755/553-2100

Consular Agency
Hotel Playa Mazatlan, Rodolfo T. Loaiza #202,
  Zona Dorada,
Mazatlan, Sinaloa, Mexico
Mex. tel. 669/916-5889

Consular Agency
Macedonia Alcala #407
Interior 20, Oaxaca, Mexico
Mex. tel. 951/514-3054 or 516-2853

Consular Agency
Edificio Vallarta, Plaza Zaragoza
  160-Piso 2 Int-18,
Puerto Vallarta, Jalisco, Mexico
Mex. tel. 322/222-0069

Consular Agency
Edificio Las Terrazas, Avenida Venustiano
  Carranza 2076-41
San Luis Potosi, Mexico
Mex. tel. 444/811-7802

Consular Agency
Dr. Hernandez Macias #72
San Miguel de Allende, Guanajuato,
  Mexico
Mex. tel. 415/152-2357 or -0068

Canadian Embassy and Consulates

Embassy
Calle Schiller #529
Colonia Bosque de Chapultepec,
Del. Miguel Hidalgo, D.F., 11580 Mexico
Mex. tel. 555/724-7900

Consulate
Centro Comercial Marbell, Local 23,
Esq. Prolongacion Farallon y Miguel Aleman
Acapulco, Guerrero, 39670 Mexico
Mex. tel. 744/484-1305

Consulate
Plaza Caracol II, 3er Piso, Local 330,
Boulevard Kukulkan Km 8.5, Zona Hotelera
Cancun, Quintana Roo, 77500 Mexico
Mex. tel. 998/883-3360

Consulate
Hotel Fiesta Americana, Local 31,
Aurelio Aceves 225, Sector Juarez
Guadalajara, Jalisco, Mexico
Mex. tel. 333/615-6215

Consulate
Hotel Playa Mazatlan, Zona Dorada,
Rodolfo Loaiza 202
Mazatlan, Sinaloa, 82110 Mexico
Mex. tel. 669/913-7320

Consulate
Edificio Kalos, Piso C-1, Local 108-A,
Zaragoza 1300 Sur y Constitución
Monterrey, Nuevo Leon, 06400 Mexico
Mex. tel. 818/344-2753

Consulate
Pino Suarez 700, Local 11-B, Multiplaza Brena
Colonia Centro, Oaxaca, 68000 Mexico
Mex. tel. 951/513-3777

Consulate
Calle Zaragoza #160, Interior 10,
Colonia Centro
Puerto Vallarta, Jalisco, 48300 Mexico
Mex. tel. 322/222-5398

Consulate
Plaza Jose Green, Local 9 (Banamex),
Boulevard Mijares s/n, Colonia Centro,
San Jose del Cabo, Baja California Sur, 23400
Mexico
Mex. tel. 624/142-4333, fax 624/142-4262
website: www.loscabos@canada.org.mx

Consulate
German Gedovious 10411-101,
Condominio del Parque, Zona Rio
Tijuana, Baja California, 22320 Mexico
Mex. tel. 664/684-0461, fax 664/684-0301

Road Signs

Encountering Mexican road signs for the first time can be confusing, especially if you don't speak Spanish. Since a few signs pertain to driving conditions that may be dangerous, it is wise to get acquainted with them before crossing the border:

SEDESOL
ACCESO A PLAYA
PLAYA MIGRIÑO

**ACCESO A PLAYA—
BEACH ACCESS**

PELIGRO

PELIGRO—DANGER

CURVA
PELIGROSA

**CURVA PELIGROSA—
DANGEROUS CURVE**

DESVIACIÓN

DESVIACIÓN—DETOUR

CONCIDA
CAMBIO DE LUCES

**CONCIDA CAMBIO DE LUCES—
DIM YOUR LIGHTS**

VADO—DIP

**PENDIENTE PELIGROSA—
DANGEROUS DOWNGRADE**

**ZONA DE DERRUMBES—
FALLING ROCK**

1 km

GASOLINERA—GAS STATION

INSPECCIÓN—INSPECTION

CONSERVE
SU DERECHA

**CONSERVE SU DERECHA—
KEEP TO THE RIGHT**

SOLO IZQ (IZQUIERDO)—
LEFT TURN ONLY

GANADO—LIVESTOCK

GRAVA SUELTA—
LOOSE GRAVEL

HOMBRES TRABAJANDO—
MEN WORKING

PUENTE ANGOSTO—
NARROW BRIDGE

NO TIRE BASURA—
NO LITTERING

NO ESTACIONARSE—
NO PARKING

NO REBASE—NO PASSING

ESTACIONAMIENTO—PARKING

PEATONES—PEDESTRIANS

PRECAUCIÓN—PRECAUTION

CRUCE FERROCARRIL—
RAILROAD CROSSING

RESTAURANTE—RESTAURANT

NO HAY PASO—ROAD CLOSED

ESCUELA—SCHOOL

DESPACIO—SLOW

TOPE—SPEED BUMP

**MAXIMA—SPEED LIMIT
IN KILOMETERS PER HOUR**

SEMAFORO—STOPLIGHT

ALTO—STOP

TELEPHONO—TELEPHONE

SANITARIOS—TOILETS

CIRCULACIÓN—TRAFFIC

**ESTACIONAMIENTO PARA
CASAS RODANTES—
TRAILER PARK**

**DOBLE CIRCULACIÓN—
TWO WAY**

**CAMINO SINUOSO—
WINDING ROAD**

CEDA EL PASO—YIELD

Special Days in Mexico

January 6
Día de Santos Reyes. This is the traditional day for giving Christmas gifts.

February 2
Día de la Candelaria. This is a Candlemas feast day commemorating the day the newborn Jesus was first presented at the temple in Jerusalem.

February 5
Día de la Constitución. This is an official holiday commemorating the Constitution of 1917, Mexico's present constitution.

Late February to early March, three days before Ash Wednesday
Carnaval. This is a carnival celebration during the week before Lent. Ensenada and La Paz are worth visiting at this time.

April, from Palm Sunday to Easter Sunday
Semana Santa. Holy Week.

May 5
Cinco de Mayo. Commemorating the defeat of the French in the battle of Puebla de Los Angeles in 1862.

September 16
Fiesta de la Independencia. Celebration of independence from Spain in 1821.

November 1–2
Día de los Muertos. On the Day of the Dead people visit cemeteries to pay respects to the deceased and bake special bread.

December 12
Día de la Virgen de Guadalupe. This is the feast day celebrating the Virgin of Guadalupe, Mexico's patron saint.

December 24–25
Día de la Navidad. Christmas Eve and Christmas.

December 31
Fin de Año. New Year's Eve.

Metric Conversions

Length

Kilometer	0.62 mile	multiply by 0.6 to find miles
Meter	39.37 inches	multiply by 1.1 to find yards
Centimeter	0.39 inch	multiply by 0.4 to find inches
Millimeter	0.039 inch	multiply by 0.04 to find inches

Area

Hectare	2.47 acres	multiply by 2.5 to find acres

Weight

Kilogram	2.2046 pounds	multiply by 2.2 to find pounds
Gram	0.035 ounce	multiply by 0.035 to find ounces

Capacity

Liter	1.057 quarts	multiply by 0.26 to find gallons

Speed

Kilometers per hour	0.6 miles per hour
Miles per hour	1.6 kilometers per hour

Temperature

Celsius temperature = Fahrenheit temperature -32° x 5/9

Fahrenheit temperature = 9/5 x Celsius temperature +32°

Index

*Page numbers in **bold**
indicate maps.*

AB

Abreojos Beaches: 120
Agua Verde (beaches): 144
Algodones: **76**
Alisitos Trailer Park: 55
Aquamarina RV Park:
   157–158
Arroyo Santa Agueda: **122**
backpacking: 20–22
Bahía Asuncion: **104**
Bahía Calamajue: 99
Bahía Concepción: **122**,
   125–126, 132–137
Bahía Concepción (beaches):
   142–143
Bahía de La Paz: **146**
Bahía de Los Angeles: **vi, 103**,
   107–108, 110–113, 119–120
Bahía de Los Angeles (beach-
   es): 119
Bahía de Los Angeles Junc-
   tion: **103**
Bahía de Santa Inéz: **122**
Bahía de Sebastian Vizcaíno:
   104, 120
Bahía Falsa Beach: 118
Bahía Magdalena: **123**
Bahía Magdalena (bay and
   barrier island beaches): 143
Bahía Magdalena complex:
   143, 168
Bahía San Juanico: **122**
Bahía Santa María (beaches):
   73, 97–98
Bahía Todos Santos (beach-
   es): 72
Bahía Tortugas: **104**
Baja Mar RV Sport Beach
   Club: 90
Baja Seasons Villas and RVs:
   56
Bella Vista RV Park: 164–165
bird-watching: 51 (San
   Quintín)

boat camping: 23
boating: 51 (San Quintín), 79
   (San Felipe and Puertoci-
   tos), 125 (Santa Rosalía-
   Mulegé), 126 (Bahía
   Concepción), 149 (La Paz)
Brisa del Mar RV Resort:
   166–167
Brisa Marina RV Park
   (ejido): 111
Buenaventura Resort Hotel,
   Restaurant, and RV Park:
   136
Buena Vista: **147**

C

Cabo Cielo RV Park: 165
Cabo Pulmo: **147**
Cabo San Lucas: **vi, 147**,
   164–166, 170
California Trailer Park and
   Motel: 58
Camacho RV Park: 129
Camalu: **45**, 66
Camp Archelon: 111
Campestre La Pila: 140–141
camping tips: 5–28
Campo García: 94
Campo Hacienda Beach: 83
Campo Jalisco: 83
Campo La Violeta: 95
Campo Los Amigos: 82
Campo Los Compadres: 85
Campo Los Delfines: **77**
Campo Mosqueda: 82
Campo Numero Uno: 86
Campo Playa Punta Arena:
   132
Campo Playa RV Park: 59
Campo Posada del Mar:
   88–89
Campo Punta Bufeo: **77**
Campo San Felipe: 89
Campo San Fernando: 92
Campo Sonora: 81–82
Campo Turistico Vallarta: 94
Canal de Cerralvo: **146**

Canal de San Lorenzo: **146**
Cantamar Dunes: 71
Cape Area: 152–154
Cape Area Day-Use Beaches:
   170
Cardonal: **147**
car travel: 33–39; *also see*
   driving safety
Casa Blanca RV Park: 156
Cataviña: **vi, 102**, 109–110
cave paintings: 106–107 (cen-
   tral peninsula)
Central Desert RV Park
   (ejido): 109
Chuy's Trailer Park: 54
Cielito Lindo Motel and RV
   Park: 67–68
Ciudad Constitución: **vi, 123**,
   140–141
Ciudad Insurgentes: **vi, 123**
Club Cabo Motel and Camp-
   ground Resort: 165–166
Club de Pesca RV Park: 91
Coco Loco Trailer Park: 53
Colonet: 65–66, 72
Colonia Elias Calles: **147**
Colonia Purisima: **123**
Colonia Vicente Guerrero:
   45, 66
communication: 40–41
Corona Beach Trailer Park: 60
Correcaminos RV Park:
   162–163
customs: 30–33

DEF

Daggett's Beach Camping:
   110–111
Diaz RV Park: 112
dining: 48–49 (Rosarito-La
   Misión), 50 (Ensenada), 80
   (San Felipe and Puertoci-
   tos), 125 (Santa Rosalía-
   Mulegé), 127 (Loreto), 150
   (La Paz), 151 (East Cape),
   152 (Todos Santos), 154
   (Cape Area)

diving and snorkeling: 125 (Santa Rosalía–Mulegé), 126 (Bahía Concepción and Loreto), 149 (La Paz), 150–151 (East Cape), 153 (Cape Area)
Don Vicente Motel and RV Park: 114
driving safety: 36–37
drugs: 33
East Cape Area: 150–151
East Cape Beaches: 169
East Cape Resort: 160–161
Ejido Campo No. 5: 63
Ejido Campo No. 7: 63
Ejido Campo No. 8: 63
El Arco: **103**
El Arco RV Park: 164
El Cachanilla RV Park: 85
El Cardonal Hide-a-Way: 159–160
El Cardón Trailer Park: 156
El Centenario: **146**
El Cien: **146**
El Coyote: **146**
El Dorado Ranch RV Park: 83–84
El Faro Beach Motel and Trailer Park: 60–61
El Faro RV Park: 92
El Faro Viejo RV Park: 166
El Litro Trailer Park: 163
El Moro RV Park: 138
El Pabellón RV Park: 68–69
El Padrino Motel, RV Park, and Restaurant: 116–117
El Palomar: 64
El Pescadero: **147**
El Progreso: **102**
El Rosario: **vi, 102,** 109
El Sauzal: **44,** 57–58
El Triunfo: **147**
Ensenada: **vi, 44,** 49–50, 56, 58–61, 65, 69–70, 72
Estero Beach Resort RV Park: 61–62
ferries: 39–40, 150 (La Paz)
firearms: 33
fishing: 49–50 (Ensenada), 50–51 (San Quintín), 79 (San Felipe and Puertocitos), 107 (Bahía de Los Angeles), 124 (Santa Rosalía–Mulegé), 125–126 (Bahía Concepción), 126 (Loreto), 127–128 (Bahía Magdalena and Puerto San Carlos), 148–149 (La Paz), 150 (East Cape), 151–152 (Punta Lobos), 152–153 (Cape Area)
food and drink: 6–12

GHI

Gecko Camp: 113
golf: 127 (Loreto), 154 (Cape Area)
Guadalupe: **44**
Guadalupe Canyon Hot Springs and Campground: 81
Guayaquil: **102**
Guerrero Negro: **vi, 104,** 113–115, 118–120
Guerrero Negro RV Park (*ejido*): 113
Guillermo's Hotel, RV Park, Restaurant, Bar, and Store: 112
Gypsys Beach Camp: 68
health: 23–28
history: 2–5
hunting: 51 (San Quintín)
insurance: 29–30
Isla Cerralvo: **146**
Isla Creciente: **123**
Isla Espiritu Santo: **146**
Isla Las Animas: **123**
Isla Magdalena: **123**
Isla Partida: **146**
Isla San José: **123**
Isla San Marcos: **122**

JKL

Jacaranda: 95
Joker Hotel, RV Park, and Restaurant: 59–60
Josefina's RV Park: 88
Juanito's Garden RV Park: 161
Juncalito Beach: 143–144
Juncalito Beach (campground): 138–139
Junta Santa María: **77**
Kadakaamán RV Park: 115
kayaking: 126 (Bahía Concepción)
King's Coronita Trailer Park: 58–59
La Capilla RV Park: 162
La Costilla: **77**
Laguna Hanson: **44**
Laguna Ojo de Liebre: 115
Laguna Ojo de Liebre Campground: 115
Laguna Percebu: **77**
Laguna Salada: **76**
Laguna San Ignacio: **104**
La Jolla Beach Camp: 62
La Jolla RV Park: 89
Lakeside RV Park: 116
La Misión: **44,** 47–49, 55–56, 71–72
Land's End: 170
La Paz: **vi,** 144, **146, 148**–150, 155–159, 168
La Paz (beaches): 168
La Paz RV Park: 157
La Playa Encantada: 84
La Poza Grande: **123**
La Puerta: **76**
La Purisima: **vi, 122**
La Ribera: **147,** 162–163, 169–170
La Rumorosa: **44**
Las Animas Camp: **103**
Las Cañadas Balneario: 64
Las Conchas RV Park: 93
Las Cruces: **146**
Las Cuevas: **147**
Las Palmas RV Park: 129
La Ventana: **146**
La Ventana Campground: 158
Lazaro Cardenas: **45**
legal aid: 30
licenses and permits: 28–29
Ligui (beaches): 144
Loma María (beaches): 168
Loreto: **vi, 123,** 126–127, 137–140, 143–144
Loreto Shores Villas and RV Park: 138
Los Barriles: **147,** 159–162, 169

Los Manzanos Campground: 70
Los Naranjos Beach: 132
Los Oasis RV Park: 155-156

M

Malarrimo Beach: 120
Malarrimo Motel, RV Park, Restaurant, and Bar: 114-115
Malibu Beach Sur RV Park: 65
Mal Paso Trailer Park: 55
Maneadero: **44,** 64
Manfred's RV Trailer Park: 140
Marco's RV Park: 87
Mario's Restaurant and RV Park: 113-114
Martin Quezada RV Park: 116
Martín Verdugo's RV Park and Motel: 161-162
Mexicali: **vi, 76,** 81-82
Mike and Bertha's RV Park—Palapa 206: 141
Miraflores: **147**
money: 40
mountaineering: 80 (San Felipe and Puertocitos)
Mulegé: **vi, 122,** 124-125, 130-132, 142-143

NOP

nightlife: 150 (La Paz), 154 (Cape Area)
Nuevo Leon: **76**
Ocean View RV Park: 62-63
Octavio's Campo Playa Escondida: 96, 98
off-roading: 51 (San Quintín), 79 (San Felipe and Puertocitos), 108 (Bahía de Los Angeles)
Old Mill RV Park: 67
Old Pier Motel and RV Park: 67
Orchard (Huerta Saucedo) RV Park: 131
Pancho's RV Park: 57
Parador Punta Prieta Trailer Park *(ejido)*: 110

Parque Nacional Constitución de 1857: **44,** 65, **76**
Parque Nacional Sierra San Pedro Mártir: **45,** 69-70, **76, 77**
Pescadero Beach: 169
Pete's Camp El Paraiso: 84
pets: 29
Pichilingue: **146**
Playa Armenta: 136-137
Playa Balandra: 155
Playa Blanca: 86
Playa Bonita RV Park: 87
Playa Bufeo: 98
Playa de Las Animas: 119
Playa de Laura RV Park: 89-90
Playa del Sol: 86
Playa de Tranquilo: 69
Playa El Burro: 134-135
Playa El Coyote: 135
Playa El Faro: 98-99
Playa El Marron: 118
Playa El Provenir: 97
Playa El Requesón: 136
Playa Encantada No. 2: 54
Playa Escondida: 134
Playa Grande: 82-83
Playa La Costilla: 98
Playa La Fonda: 71
Playa La Gringa: 110
Playa La Misión: 71-72
Playa La Perla: 136
Playa Las Almejas: 97
Playa Ligui: 139-140
Playa Los Cerritos: 163-164, 169
Playa Los Cocos: 134
Playa Mal Paso: 72
Playa María: 118
Playa Monalisa: 60
Playa Norte: 160
Playa Punta Banda: 72-73
Playa Punta Estrella: 97
Playa Rosarito: 71
Playa Saldamando: 56
Playa San Antonio del Mar: 73
Playa San Felipe: 97
Playa San Pedro: 168-169
Playa San Rafael: **103,** 119
Playa San Ramon: 73

Playa Santispac: 133
Playas San Francisquito: 119-120
Playa Tecolote: 155
Popotla Trailer Park: 54
Posada Concepción RV Park: 133-134
Posada Don Diego: 66-67
primitive camping: 16-19
Puertecitos: **vi, 77,** 78-80, 94-99
Puertecitos Campground: 96
Puerto Cancun: **123**
Puerto Chale: **123**
Puerto Escondido: 139
Puerto López Mateos: **123,** 142
Puerto Nuevo: **44**
Puerto San Carlos: **123**
Puerto San Ysidro: **44,** 65
Punta Abreojos: **104,** 120
Punta Arena: **147**
Punta Arena (beaches): 169-170
Punta Arena de la Ventana Beach: 158-159
Punta Baja: 94
Punta Banda: **44,** 62-63, 72
Punta Chivato: **122**
Punta Chivato (beaches): 130, 142
Punta Coyote: **146**
Punta Final: **77**
Punta Gaspareño (beaches): 170
Punta Pescadero: **147**
Punta Prieta: **103**
Punta San Fermin: 97-98
Punta San Fermin (beaches): 97-98
Punta San Jacinto Trailer Park: 66

QR

Quinta Maria: 160
Ramona Beach RV Park and Motel: 58
Rancho El Zimarrón: 94-95
Rancho Punta Estrella Beach: 93
Rancho Santa Ynéz: 109-110

Rancho Sordo Mudo RV
   Park: 57–58
Rancho Verde RV Park: 159
Rancho Vista Hermosa: 93
Rice and Beans Oasis RV
   Park: 115–116
Río Colorado: 76
Río Hardy: 76, 78
Río San Antonio: 45
Río San José: 147
Río San Rafael: 45
Río Santa María: 45
Río San Telmo: 45
Rivera del Mar Trailer RV
   Park: 137
Rosalillita Beaches: 118–119
Rosarito: 44, 47–49, 53–54, 71
Rosarito Cora RV Park: 53
Ruben's RV Park: 87–88
RV Park Nancy: 140

S
San Antonio: 53
San Antonio del Mar Beach:
   65–66
San Bartolo: 147, 159
San Bruno (beaches): 142
San Carlos: vi, 140
San Diego Beach: 85–86
San Evaristo: 123
San Evaristo (beaches): 144
San Felipe: vi, 77, 78–80,
   82–94, 97
San Felipe Marina Resort
   and RV Park: 91
San Francisquito: 103
San Ignacio: vi, 104, 115–117
San Isidro: 122
San Javier: 123
San José de Comondu: 122
San José del Cabo: 147,
   166–167, 169–170
San José del Cabo (beaches):
   169–170
San José de Magdalena: 122
San José Viejo: 147

San Juan de la Costa: 146
San Juan de la Costa (beach-
   es): 168
San Juan del Mar: 77
San Juan de Los Planes: 146
San Juanico: 122, 137
San Juanico Beach: 142
San Lucas Cove RV Park:
   129–130
San Pedrito RV Park: 163
San Pedro: 146
San Quintín: 50–52, 67–69, 72
Santa Anita: 147
Santa Rita: 123
Santa Rosa: 147
Santa Rosalía: vi, 122,
   124–125, 129–130, 142
Santa Rosalillita: 103
San Telmo: 45
San Telmo de Abajo: 45
Santiago: 147
Santo Domingo: 123
Santo Tomás: 44, 64
San Vicente: 44
Scorpion Bay: 137
Serenidad Hotel and RV
   Park: 131–132
shopping: 47–48 (Rosarito-
   La Misión), 50 (Ensena-
   da), 149 (La Paz), 154
   (Cape Area)
Sierra de Juárez: 78
sightseeing: 48 (Rosarito-La
   Misión), 50 (Ensenada),
   51–52 (San Quintín), 106
   (San Ignacio), 108 (Bahía
   de Los Angeles), 125
   (Santa Rosalía-Mulegé),
   127 (Loreto), 149–150 (La
   Paz), 151 (East Cape), 152
   (Todos Santos, Punta
   Lobos)
Sinai RV Park, Motel, and
   Restaurant: 109
snorkeling: see diving and
   snorkeling

Spa RV Park: 162
Speedy's Campo: 95–96
sporting events: 47 (Rosarito-
   La Misión)
surfing: 51 (San Quintín),
   152 (Todos Santos)

TUVWXYZ
Tecate: 44, 54–55
Tecate KOA on Rancho
   Ojai: 54–55
tennis: 127 (Loreto)
tidepooling: 80 (San Felipe
   and Puertocitos)
Tijuana: vi, 44, 46
Todos Santos: 147, 163–164,
   168–170
Todos Santos (beaches): 168
toll roads: 30
Tripui RV Park: 139
Vagabundos del Mar RV
   Park: 166
Valle de las Palmas: 44
Valle de San Quintín: vi, 45
Valle de Trinidad: 45
Victor's RV Park: 90
Villa de San Miguel: 57
Villa Ignacio Zaragoza: 123
Villa Jesús María: 103
Villa María RV Park: 131
Villa Marina RV Park: 92
Villa Morelos: 123
Villarino RV Park: 62
Villa Serena RV Park: 164
Villa Vitta Hotel, Restaurant,
   and RV Park: 112
Vista del Mar RV Park: 88
Vista Paradiso: 130
Vizcaíno: 104, 115
whale-watching: 12–13,
   106–107 (Central Peninsu-
   la), 127 (Loreto), 128
   (Bahía Magdalena)
wildlife: 12–16
windsurfing: 151 (East Cape)

About the Authors

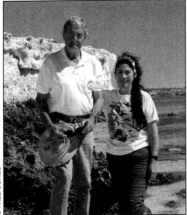

© FRED JONES

Fred and Gloria Jones have traveled extensively throughout Baja for many years. They have driven their camper from one end of the peninsula to the other innumerable times, explored off-highway in a four-wheel-drive truck, cruised both coasts in their boat, hiked and ridden horseback in remote mountain terrain, and scrutinized it all from the air. They have slept out in the open on the ground and in tents, truck campers, and boats. They have camped in the highest mountains and the deepest canyons, on beaches on Sea of Cortéz islands and along both coasts, and at campgrounds across the region.

Explorers, scuba divers, big-game fishermen, and naturalists, the couple has a deep and abiding interest in the history, archaeology, people, and culture of Baja California. Both have been active in the Commission of the Californias, a former coordinating body between the governments of California, Baja California Norte, and Baja California Sur, contributing their expertise on tourism and natural resources.

The Joneses currently manage a nonprofit travel club with 14,000-plus members that has specialized in Baja travel for nearly 40 years—Vagabundos del Mar. Fred is vice president and general manager, and Gloria is on the board of directors. Fred has had substantial experience managing campgrounds as director of the California Department of Parks and Recreation, which is responsible for the state park system. Gloria shared that experience as assistant to the director.

Between them, these award-winning freelance writers and photographers have coauthored two books besides this one, *A Climber's Guide to the High Sierra* and *The Desert Bighorn: Its Life History, Ecology and Management*; contributed to a compilation of hair-raising outdoor experiences called *No S—, There I Was* and the book *Best Places—Baja;* served as field editors for *Western Boatman* magazine and conservation editors for *Baja Explorer* magazine; authored numerous professional publications on wildlife, natural resources, parks, and recreation; and contributed many outdoor features and columns to newspapers and national and regional magazines. Fred is a member of the Outdoor Writers Association of California. Gloria is a member of both the Outdoor Writers Associations of America and California and is a past president of the latter organization.

Notes

Notes

Notes

Notes